# THE NFL ALL-PRO
# WORKOUT

# The NFL All-Pro Workout

A Complete Conditioning Program
for People of All Ages, Shapes, and Fitness Levels
From NFL Trainers, Coaches, and Players

**By Michael Creedman**

Illustrations by Dick Oden

St. Martin's Press/New York

Creative Director: David Boss
Editor-in-Chief: John Wiebusch
Senior Editor/Project Editor: Jim Natal
Designer: Cliff Wynne
Design Associate: Mea Fred

**Photography:** *Jim Cornfield*, front cover; *Bill Cummings*, 33; *Dallas Cowboys*, 63; *Jay Dickman*, 61; *Richard Mackson*, 48; *Al Messerschmidt*, 31 a, b; *Bill Mount*, 133; *John H.Reid III*, 117; *Richard W. Roeller* (The Buffalo News), 84; *Ron Ross*, 32; *M.V. Rubio*, 135;*Robert L. Smith*, 86; *Damian Strohmeyer*, 118; *Ben Threinin*, 134; *Greg Trott*, 103; *Michael Zagaris*, 101.

**The NFL All-Pro Workout**

ISBN 0-312-01071-0

Library of Congress Catalog Card Number: 87-42693

First Edition

10  9  8  7  6  5  4  3  2  1

Printed in the United States of America

*Readers are advised to consult a physician before beginning this, or any, exercise program. The author, editors, publisher, the National Football League, and NFL Properties, Inc. disclaim any liability, personal or otherwise, resulting from the use of the information in this book.*

# Acknowledgements

The author and editors extend their appreciation for the information and expertise shared by the coaches and trainers of the National Football League, in particular:

Jerry Attaway, San Francisco 49ers
Dean Bettenham, New England Patriots
Don Clemons, Detroit Lions
Otho Davis, Philadelphia Eagles
Clyde Emrich, Chicago Bears
Walt Evans, Pittsburgh Steelers
Garrett Giemont, Los Angeles Rams
C.T. Hewgley, Kansas City Chiefs
Rusty Jones, Buffalo Bills
Tim Jorgensen, Atlanta Falcons
Virgil Knight, Green Bay Packers

Bob Mischak, Los Angeles Raiders
Johnny Parker, New York Giants
Russ Paternostra, New Orleans Saints
Dave Redding, Cleveland Browns
Dan Riley, Washington Redskins
Phil Tyne, San Diego Chargers
Steve Watterson, Houston Oilers
Junior Wade, Miami Dolphins
Bob Ward, Dallas Cowboys
Jim Whitesel, Seattle Seahawks
Jim Williams, New York Jets
Kim Wood, Cincinnati Bengals

The efforts and cooperation of the following individuals, corporations, and institutions also are gratefully acknowledged:

Bill Anzelc, Anjon Systems
Marilyn Arai
Bill Barron
Kim Battles
Burt Birnbaum, Computer Instrument Corporation
Jaime Brenkus, Sound Body
Center Courts Fitness Center
Dr. Donald Chu, Ather Sports Injury Clinic
Kim Claycomb
Jan S. Ehrman, Gerontology Research Center, National
    Institute on Aging
Miguel Elliott
James Farrell
Chuck Garrity, Sr.
Dr. Andrew Goldberg
Ann Grandjean, Swanson Center for Nutrition
Barbara Hager
Stan James
Susan Johnson, The Aerobics Center
Scott Kabak
Jane Morrissey
Dr. Armand M. Nicholi, Jr.
Kathy Philpott
Eileen Sexton, American College of Sports Medicine
Starter Sportswear
Sheryl Strauss
Kevin Terrell
Rick Wadholm
Stan Wing

# Contents

# Preface

You don't need to be big, strong, and fast enough to play in the National Football League to benefit from the conditioning methods developed by NFL teams. The underlying principles used by the pros apply no matter your size, sex, age, or athletic ability. *The NFL All-Pro Workout* can work for you because it is designed for people who are determined to raise their level of fitness—and do it intelligently, progressively, and realistically.

What makes this book unique is that, for the first time, the experiences of NFL experts are condensed into one volume that covers the main areas of contemporary fitness and conditioning: strength training, cardiovascular conditioning, flexibility and agility training, diet and nutrition, mental training, and injury prevention.

*The NFL All-Pro Workout* is a flexible program that assumes no specific level of fitness. You can use it to begin training or to enhance the training regimen you already have. But no matter what your present fitness level is, following the suggested programs may require increased physical activity and exertion, and may entail a change in diet. It is best to consult a doctor before you start any new or different exercise and diet program. It's especially important to get a medical okay if you are over 35, more than 10 pounds overweight, or have a history of cardiovascular or medical problems in your family.

Used consistently, the information in this book will help bring out the best in anyone. But, while this is the latest word on the subject, it is not the last word. The area of human performance research is changing constantly. Ideas that seemed correct a few years ago now are considered archaic, even dangerous. For example, a decade ago, physiologists thought there were only two kinds of skeletal muscle fibers—fast twitch and slow twitch; we now are aware of at least four. Some coaches used to think anabolic steroids were safe to use; we know much better now. And aerobic exercise was wildly popular until all that bouncing created injuries; hence the current trend to low-impact aerobics.

So keep in mind that while this book represents the front line of current exercise physiology and thinking, our understanding of the human machine still is developing. By all means keep an open mind about new findings, but adopt them only if they make sense to you and don't represent any obvious dangers.

There is disagreement on some aspects of conditioning even among NFL strength and conditioning coaches. In fact, similar results have been achieved by coaches with extremely different training methods.

My job was to find and explain the common elements that are at the root of their success. In those instances where there was no clear consensus, we have presented all sides as fairly as possible to let the reader make his or her own choice.

*The NFL All-Pro Workout* includes a three-part conditioning approach based on the techniques professional football coaches apply to players at the beginning of training camp:

(1) Determine your current state of fitness.

(2) Decide what conditioning level to reach and maintain.

(3) Design an overall plan with specifics of training and diet to achieve your goals.

Again, let me stress that *The NFL All-Pro Workout* is a flexible program. Training should be specific to individuals and sports, needs and goals. No two athletes' conditioning programs will be alike.

I was impressed with the overall level of intelligence and sophistication of the players and coaches of the NFL. Many of the players who devote themselves to excellence in their sport have such healthy approaches, good work habits, and solid understanding of their fitness programs they would succeed in any profession. Indeed, as I discovered when I talked to several retired players, many players have gone on to very successful business and entertainment careers. They attribute their achievements later in life to the hard-won disciplines they learned in training rooms and on practice fields.

My personal experiences with the ideas in this book allow me to promise that almost anyone will find something in these pages that can help him realize more of his own potential.

—*Michael Creedman*

# 1 Muscling Up:

## *Strength Training*

"If conditioning were easy," says Junior Wade, the strength coach at Miami, "a lot more people would do it."

Maybe the only easy thing about conditioning is understanding its guiding principle: Muscles get stronger when they are used. The harder they are worked, the stronger they get.

NFL strength and conditioning coaches agree, however, that strength training alone won't do the job, and neither will just aerobics or good diet. Fitness is, and should be, a matter of balance. That's how it is approached in the NFL, and that's what NFL coaches and trainers recommend for anyone willing to make the effort—man or woman, young or old, athlete or armchair quarterback.

Rams linebacker Mel Owens says his success in the league stems from dedicating himself to a year-round conditioning program that includes weights, running, and diet.

"Discipline is the key," he says. "I got here by hard work and that's the only way I'm going to stay here."

Any personal fitness program starts with an evaluation, determining where you are physically, and where you want to be. You need to evaluate your current condition as objectively as the scouts who put college football players through performance drills before NFL draft day. Once you understand your strengths and weaknesses, you can set goals and plan how you'll achieve them.

"All men are created equal," says 49ers coordinator of physical development, Jerry Attaway, "but we are not all built the same."

Or, as former St. Louis Cardinals guard Conrad Dobler once quipped about his teammate, 6-foot 3-inch, 285-pound tackle Dan Dierdorf: "When they dig up Dan two hundred years from now, they're gonna wonder what he was."

Develop your fitness program based on your own body, its shape, quirks, needs, and abilities. And once you begin training, compare your progress with what you were able to do three weeks previously, not with a chart of "average performance" or with elite professional athletes. In other words, be realistic.

"The athletes who make it in the NFL," Attaway says, "are genetically different. I may work out with them, but I know I can't perform like them. My genes came from the bargain basement and theirs came from Jordache."

# The Pain Standard

With a 315-pound barbell resting on his chest, and his biceps pumped like a bodybuilder's, Rams tackle Jackie Slater provides his own point of view: "If it don't hurt, you're not working hard enough."

That may be true for world-class athletes like Slater and Owens who go to war every Sunday against others as strong and determined as themselves. For the average person, though, pain is not a good standard for determining how hard you're working.

"No pain, no gain" makes a handy slogan. It's short and it rhymes. But it doesn't really describe what Slater is saying and it is just plain wrong when applied to aerobics and stretching activities.

There is a line between working hard and working hurt that the average athlete shouldn't cross. Although self-discipline is needed to maintain consistency and intensity in a program, that doesn't mean you have to endure agony. Pain from overstretching warns of danger to fibers and tendons; severely aching feet after a grueling run can be a signal your lower extremities are taking a beating; cramps in the muscles may indicate you're lifting too much to be productive.

*discomfort is not pain*

To be sure, you will be sore after a tough workout. And the muscles will ache or burn on the last repetition during heavy lifts. But keep in mind that discomfort from intense muscle fatigue is quite different from the sharp pain that comes from a muscle tear or a ligament strain.

Obviously, pain that warns of possible injury is to be avoided. The discomfort of a totally fatigued muscle, however, actually is to be sought. Without working muscles so hard they sometimes come close to failing, substantial strength gains simply can't happen.

# Progression

If dedication is the key to success in weight training, progression is the combination to the vault. The idea is to build strength slowly by adding a little more stress at regular intervals.

*work slowly*

The idea of progression is ancient. Remember the classic fable of the Greek boy who decided he could lift a full-grown bull by starting out when the animal was but a calf and lifting it every day as it grew? Progression is founded on one of the soundest principles of exercise physiology: make changes slowly.

You build your body the way you build a brick wall: put down a solid foundation and add a little at a time until it's as big or strong as you want it. Build up stress on the muscles slowly, perhaps adding only a couple of pounds—never more than 10 percent—to your lift every third workout.

Body mechanisms are intricately interrelated. So changes in the strength of muscles have to be matched in the tendons that connect them to the bones, and in the ligaments that hold the joints together. Suddenly imposing stresses on any one part of the body causes stresses everywhere else as well. Too quick a start in any conditioning program is a good prescription for problems. Muscle tears, sore joints, and pulled tendons can delay your training unless progress is slow and controlled.

"Don't try lifting very heavy weights every time," says Virgil Knight, strength coach of the Packers. "Do something you can handle. If you want to get stronger, you don't have to go for the big numbers. Good hard reps and good technique in a steady progression is much more important."

## Tough Stuff: Pumping Iron

For most people, the hardest part of an all-round conditioning program is strength training.

*working to failure*

In strength training, the goal is to work the muscles until they almost won't work anymore. There's some controversy over whether the muscles should actually be worked to the point of failure, but everyone agrees that to get the most gains, you have to work the muscle fibers beyond the demands of previous activity.

Working even close to momentary muscle failure is uncomfortable. The muscles feel as if they're on fire. Normally that would be the signal to stop whatever you're doing. But in strength training, you keep pushing the muscle because that's the way to make the muscle develop.

Not many of us exercise that hard. Without a strong incentive to keep going, we'll usually take a breather when we get close to the point of exhaustion. It's a natural reaction that allows us to keep going longer. You have to short-circuit that natural reaction and continue if you want to make steady gains.

## A Muscle Mechanics Primer

You have approximately the same number of muscle fibers in your body now as when you were an infant. So does the average NFL player at 6 feet 2 inches and 220 pounds. In every body, of course, the fibers grow bigger and stronger as you change from child to adult. But research indicates that the total doesn't change much, if at all.

Each muscle is a bundle of anywhere from 200,000 to 500,000 individual fibers. Each fiber is an elongated cell. The fibers are divided into small bundles wrapped in a tough sheath material, and those little bundles are wrapped by another sheath that encloses the entire muscle mass. The sheath materials come together at the ends, where they become tendon and attach to bones.

Muscles contract when they receive an electrochemical signal through the nervous system. You move a limb by contracting a muscle on one side of the joint while relaxing the muscle on the other. The finely tuned interplay of contracting and relaxing muscles is what gives us such exquisite control of our bodies.

What may be surprising is that the mechanism that makes muscles move so smoothly is not in continuous operation. Individual fibers are either on or off. There is no half-throttle for fibers. So when you want to contract a muscle at, say, half speed, your nervous system signals only half of the muscle fibers to contract. Need to lift something extremely heavy? All the fibers are recruited to work.

Understanding something about muscle mechanics helps explain why you have to work your muscles to exhaustion when you're trying to build strength. Unless all of the available fibers in the muscle have been recruited, the entire muscle hasn't been worked. You must stress it with so much weight that even the extreme fibers that normally are neglected get called into action. Nobody knows for sure what percentage of the muscle fibers actually are available at any one time; the nervous system always holds back a portion in reserve.

*total effort*   When it comes to strength training, whether you are actually working 100 percent of the fibers or just using 100 percent of the ones available, it is true that anything less than total effort produces that much less in the way of results. There's also a threshold below which no benefits are recorded.

"To get any training effect," says Bears strength coach Clyde Emrich, "you have to be working against a resistance that's in excess of sixty percent of your maximum strength."

Most improvement in strength is a result of actual growth in the muscle fibers. Researchers say there also is a strength gain from the increased efficiency of the nervous system in mobilizing more of the fibers initially, and in calling on fresh fibers after the primary charge has been exhausted. It's also believed that training causes cellular structural changes that allow muscles to better tolerate build-ups of lactic acid and other by-products of the complex chemistry that produces human muscle power. *(See box in Chapter Four for an explanation of the muscle/nutrition interaction.)*

*work out*   The process of muscle growth is called hypertrophy. When muscles are not worked out, they begin to shrink. Atrophy occurs. And in fact, unless the muscles are exercised every three or four days, they begin to lose the gains made during the last workout. That's why it is important to maintain a regular workout schedule.

## WEIGHT TERMS

*Exercises* include the particular elements of lifting. That includes the stance, the grip, the muscles that should be performing the lift, and the weight that is to be lifted (barbell, machine, dumbbell, etc.). The exercise is defined by the starting, intermediate, and ending points.

*Repetitions,* or reps, are the number of times you repeat a particular exercise or lift during a set.

*Sets* are the sequence of continuous repetitions of an exercise. Frequently, a workout routine will call for two or more sets of an exercise. There is a brief rest period between sets to allow the muscles to recover.

*Intensity* is how much effort you put into each exercise in the workout, which usually is a function of how much weight you're lifting or how fast you're lifting it.

*Single and Compound Joint Movements* are defined by how many body joints and corresponding muscles are involved in the exercise. A barbell curl, for example, is a single joint movement (the elbow and biceps), while a bench press (elbow and shoulders; triceps, pectorals, deltoid) is a compound joint movement.

*Agonist/Antagonist* are the opposing muscles involved in any movement. Since muscles only can contract, there have to be muscles on both sides of any joint for full movement. When one muscle is contracting, it is the agonist, and the opposing muscle that relaxes to allow the movement is the antagonist.

*Concentric/Eccentric,* which is also called positive and negative movement, is not to be confused with agonist and antagonist. Concentric refers to the contracting phase of an exercise, such as when the biceps lift a weight through a curl. The eccentric, or negative, phase of the movement is when the muscle is lowering the weight. The muscle still is working to control the weight during this phase even though the fibers are lengthening, not contracting.

## At the Core

Most teams have training programs that include a core group of basic strength exercises that all players are expected to perform. The core program is designed to tone and strengthen the major muscle groups. The core group is a prerequisite to specific weight-training programs that improve strength, endurance, and speed, with modifications to work on the needs of each player position. A number of teams go even further. They have a computer-generated weight-training program for each player, keyed to his position, his state of conditioning, and the established standards he must meet.

*from general to specific*
Weekend athletes needn't buy a computer to plan an exercise program if they take *The NFL All-Pro Workout* approach, which features strength training as only one element of a set of basic activities (including aerobic, flexibility, and agility exercises) that condition the entire body, with specific routines added to help improve performance in specific sports.

Be sure to exercise all the muscle groups, because strength train-

*balance your workouts*

ing needs to be balanced. Overdevelopment of one group, such as quadriceps, without a corresponding improvement in the complementary group, the hamstrings, can increase the chances for injury. And be aware that most people have a natural tendency to work on the muscles that already are strong and neglect the weak ones that are less satisfying to exercise.

Exactly which exercises you do will depend on what equipment is available to you and what you hope to accomplish. A selection of exercises that work out the major muscle groups is described in Chapter Nine, including illustrations and instructions.

*full range of motion*

*use a spotter*

No matter what exercises you perform, there are a few other considerations to keep in mind. Be sure to go through the full range of motion in the exercise, all the way from fully stretched to fully contracted. Otherwise you won't retain flexibility in the joints and muscles that you're trying to build up. Also, when working out with free weights, try not to work alone, especially if you are planning to push yourself to the point of momentary failure. A spotter or coach can encourage, help with lifts, or add weight as needed, and help prevent injury if you lose control when reaching the point of muscle fatigue.

*negative movement*

When lifting, take your time. The idea is to stress the muscle, not to jerk the weight up as quickly as possible. And put down the weight slowly. Some coaches believe muscles develop more strength from the lowering motion, called "negative" movement, than from the contracting stage, the positive phase.

## Be Specific

If nothing else, strength training will get your body looking good because of the way it improves muscle tone. But to be really effective, weight training should be targeted specifically toward improving the activities and sports you pursue.

Weight training for specific sports means adding exercise routines that develop the muscles that are used in your sport, in a way that is similar to the way those muscles are used in the activity. "You don't train for an explosive sport like the shotput by running aerobics," says Rusty Jones, coordinator of conditioning for the Buffalo Bills.

Working on the specific muscle groups involved in their activities allows athletes to increase and balance the strength of different body parts. However, don't expect your weight training to take the place of actual skill training on the field.

The Bengals, for example, consider strength training as important as any other aspect of the game, including running practice plays or studying game films. Cincinnati is one of the few teams that requires every player to participate in the weight-training program. Nevertheless, strength coach Kim Wood warns against expecting weight training alone to make a difference in performance. "It's futile to measure a player by his ability to lift weights," he says. "What matters is how strong he is on the field. We're lifting weights so we can be better football players, not so we can lift more weight.

"Strength is a general phenomenon. Skills are very specific and they don't transfer directly. Skill has to be specifically trained in the way that it will be used. Using a heavy golf club in practice may help develop wrists and arms and shoulders, but it will screw up your golf swing. If you want to build up strength, do it in a weight-training program to develop the raw strength, but then go train by doing the skill itself."

Conditioning coach Tim Jorgensen says the specific workout program he brought to Atlanta is designed "to strengthen every joint and muscle to reduce the chances of injury to those joints. There are a lot of forces interacting out there on the field and our aim is to strengthen every group, but functionally. We don't want to overtrain and produce muscular bulk."

Walt Evans says the strength training work at Pittsburgh is designed to build up the skills that are most valuable during a game. They don't do tackling drills in the weight room, but they do their strength training in positions that relate to what they'll be doing on the field. "We want everyone to be able to do things in a low position," Evans says, "one in which you almost are in a sitting position on your feet. That way the players have strength developed that is available in the stance that's most used in the game."

Just as a tennis player would do different strength exercises than a wrestler, the Steelers have organized specific workouts to strengthen muscle groups most used by different positions. "The quarterback drill is pretty sophisticated," Evans says. "We've analyzed the throwing motion and developed exercises that give resistance to those muscles. With the quarterbacks, we also work on building up the muscles that would experience trauma when he gets hit."

Evans says that because weight training was once thought to mean simply adding bulk, "it was taboo for defensive backs and wide receivers to do weight training. Everyone figured that they would be slowed down. Now coaches recognize the advantages of good weight training in addition to the other routines."

# Hidden Strengths

*weight training builds endurance*

Strength training has benefits beyond the obvious. Stronger players have more endurance. That's because they use up a smaller percentage of their strength to do the same work as less well conditioned athletes. Because they have strength to spare, they don't have to put out maximum effort all the time. So they are more likely to have energy left during the last minutes of a close game.

Some players find that a hard workout actually eases sore muscles. "The recuperative abilities of lifting are tremendous," says Broncos center/guard Keith Bishop. "As long as I'm not injured so much that I can't lift a weight, doing lifting is a great way for me to feel better fast. We play a game on Sunday and then come in Monday feeling beat up and sore. But if I do some moderate weight reps, lifting weights is like a tonic or a medicine. It makes me feel good."

## The Most-Asked Questions

Newcomers in the weight room almost always ask the same questions. They want to know the essentials: What exercises should they do? How much, how often, and how hard should they lift? Most of the answers here either are unequivocal or represent a strong consensus of opinion among NFL coaches, but a few of the questions are subject to interpretation.

**Should I warm up and stretch?**

Yes, and in that order. Ride an exercise bike or do some rope skipping or light jogging. Ten minutes of warming up will get the muscles warm enough to begin stretching. For a heavy workout it is recommended that you stretch for about 10 minutes to gain full flexibility. You won't need much stretching for a light workout, but be sure to warm up beforehand.

*warm-up sets*   In handling heavier weights, most NFL teams recommend doing a warm-up set of the exercise with about half the weight you'll tackle during your target weight sets. Others work up to the heaviest set with lighter weights that gradually increase until they reach the full target weight exercise on the fourth or fifth set.

**How much weight?**

First answer this: "How much can you lift?" Since the idea of lifting weights is to work muscles right up to their maximum capacity, only you can tell how much to lift. Naturally, you'll be able to handle more weight in a squat exercise that uses the large, strong leg muscles than in a bench press that works out the smaller arm, chest, and shoulder muscles.

*one rep max*   If you are an experienced lifter, you can use the same guideline recommended by most NFL coaches: work with a percentage of the maximum weight you can lift one time, also known as the "one rep max," for each exercise. One rep max is calibrated in several ways. At Miami, every player does each basic exercise after he has thoroughly warmed up. "We put on a moderate weight and then keep adding ten or twenty pounds until we find his max," says strength coach Junior Wade.

When training to develop more strength, players lift very heavy weights, approaching 100 percent of one rep max, for as few as two or three reps per set. For improving muscular endurance, they will work with lighter weights, perhaps only 80 percent of max, but will perform 12 or more reps in each set and do as many as five sets.

However, if you are new to weight training, or just getting back after a long layoff, piling on the pounds until you can't lift any more is dangerous. Don't try to find your maximum immediately. Instead, use relatively light weights until you can do each exercise with good form.

After you have a rough idea of how much you can lift in each exercise, keep raising the poundage until you find that you have trouble doing the exercise properly at about the tenth repetition. Redskins strength and conditioning coach Dan Riley says the right weight for developing strength is when the player "reaches the point of muscular failure somewhere between the eighth and twelfth repetition." Muscular failure is defined as the point at which an athlete no longer can raise and lower the weight in good form through a full range of movement.

*don't overload*

Because the process of finding those maximum weights is based on trial and error, your first few weightlifting sessions should be devoted to calibrating yourself, determining how much you can lift. It's better to select a weight that's too light rather than too heavy, because overloading the body can cause injury. In fact, some strength coaches, such as Johnny Parker of the Giants, prefer to undertrain athletes, never giving them so much weight that they can't finish every rep they've been assigned. But keep in mind that an effective training weight still must be heavy enough to stimulate an increase in strength.

**How many reps?**

It depends on how much weight you are lifting and what you want to accomplish. At the start, you should keep the weight under your maximum and do at least 10 repetitions each set. After you have some lifting experience, follow this general rule from Wade:

"To add muscle and get stronger, use very heavy weights and few repetitions. To develop endurance and maintain strength, use lighter weights and multiple reps."

When they are trying to build up strength and muscle mass, bodybuilders and some players sometimes will lift so much weight they can do only a few repetitions per set. Riley agrees that very heavy weights do build strength, but "this also invites possible injury. Why take the chance?"

As for doing more repetitions with less weight, some people believe that an occasional set with a very high number of reps (up to 25) and low weights is useful in building up endurance and in stimulating large quantities of blood to flow through the muscle to flush out metabolic wastes and build up the vascular system. Riley points out that low weights don't involve enough muscle fibers to actually increase strength and therefore, in his opinion, high rep sets are mainly a waste of time that could be better used in other activities.

### How many sets?

The guiding principle is that during most workouts, the muscles being exercised should be worked to the point where as many fibers as possible have been used. Everyone agrees on that. But coaches who have demonstrated superb results take rather different avenues for arriving at that point.

Most coaches prefer the multiple set approach. They suggest that beginners start with two to three sets of 8 to 10 reps each, and then build up form and endurance before raising the amount of weight. The majority of teams and bodybuilders take the time to do multiple sets of each exercise in their routines.

However, Riley, Wood, and some others recommend doing just one set with intensity. Riley concedes that multiple sets can produce considerable gains, but he feels "the time spent is prolonged and unnecessary. How each exercise is performed is what stimulates strength gains," he says. "If a second set is done, it is obvious that the first set was not properly performed."

On the other hand, proponents of doing multiple sets argue that mental fatigue occurs before the actual physical fatigue sets in. When the going gets tough, our minds tend to signal that we can't do any more. So, the proponents claim, the idea of working to failure in just one set is more illusion than fact for most people. Thus, to insure that the muscles get fully worked, that every fiber possible is recruited, they urge performing more than one set with a predetermined number of reps in each. The number of reps you choose should be based on what amount of weight you know you can lift without strain for up to 12 times, a thirteenth being impossible due to fatigue.

*choose your own approach*

Where does that leave you? Pretty much free to go with whichever system seems right for your needs and psychological framework. The important consideration is that the set or sets succeed in tiring out the muscles being trained and recruiting the maximum number of muscle fibers. Also of great importance is change in your routine. Muscles adapt to the same routine over time and results fall off. Variety is a key.

### How long between sets?

Anywhere from 30 seconds to five minutes is the duration between sets in normal strength training sessions, where the objective is to improve strength or endurance. It takes a minimum of 60 seconds before muscles begin recovering after working to extreme fatigue; the heavier the weight, the longer the recovery period.

*muscle recovery*

"If you begin again too soon," Attaway says, "you don't have enough power to put into getting maximum effort from the sets." And you get minimum gains without maximum effort.

The reasoning behind these waits lies in the biology of the muscle fibers. When a muscle is worked to exhaustion, it no longer can use the anaerobic fuel in the muscle (powerful organic compounds known as ATP and CP). It takes several minutes to restore the ATP/CP balance enough to resume exercise. Even after a rest, there will be proportionately less energy available in a previously exhausted muscle. Instinct, as much as anything else, will tell you when you are ready to begin lifting again.

*circuit training*     In what's called circuit training, there is no rest between sets. In fact, some of the circuit training plans require aerobic-style exercises such as rope skipping or riding an exercise bike for 30 or 40 seconds between weightlifting exercises. The idea is to develop aerobic endurance at the same time you are working the anaerobic system in the muscles.

Some coaches feel circuit training simulates the kind of stress players are subject to during a game. Other coaches regard it as nonsense, pointing out that aerobic muscles don't begin taking over until individual muscles have been exercised for at least a minute. Since the circuit training never allows any one muscle to work that long, they contend, the heart is beating fast but the body is not really experiencing an aerobic workout. Better, they suggest, to do strength training for anaerobic performance, and do running or aerobic exercises separately.

**How long should a workout be?**

Bodybuilders put in two, three, or more hours a day to shape their muscles into competition form. Of course, not all of that time is spent lifting.

For football players, the commitment is a little less severe. Evans says the Steelers' workouts are an hour to an hour and fifteen minutes long during the offseason. "In season, we do twenty minutes of lifting two or three times a week," he says. "The main goal during the season is just to maintain condition. Building power and muscle is done during the offseason and at training camp."

For the average person just starting with weights, Evans recommends working out two or three times a week for half an hour.

Knight says, "If you want to really get stronger and get into better condition, then you have to be here every other day and work a minimum of thirty-five or forty-five minutes."

Dallas's Bob Ward offers a more formal guide to constructing an individualized program:

> **1-Warm-up:** 5-10 minutes
> **2-Flexibility/stretching:** 10-20 minutes
> **3-Leg and back strength:** 10-20 minutes
> **4-Arm and shoulder pushing strength:** 7-15 minutes
> **5-Arm and shoulder pulling strength:** 7-15 minutes
> **6-Trunk and abdominal strength:** 5-8 minutes
> **7-Warmdown and stretch:** 5-10 minutes

"Including warm-up, stretching, exercise, cooldown, and a shower, an ideal workout should take at least an hour," says San Diego Chargers' director of strength and conditioning, Phil Tyne. "But anything beyond twenty minutes of actual workout time is better than nothing."

**How should exercise be sequenced?**

*work big to small*

In general, the order in which exercises are performed begins with the large muscle groups and eventually works around to the individual muscles.

Some coaches recommend doing the lower body first, because those are larger muscle groups than the upper body. Whenever you start, be sure that you work out major groups before moving to the individual muscles.

For example, you would not want to do triceps extensions with dumbbells before doing a bench press exercise. The extensions work out the triceps. The bench press works out the arms, shoulders, and chest. But if you have worn out the smaller triceps muscles with the extensions, you won't be able to fully perform the press.

It's a case of exercising the chains before working out the individual links. *(See Chapter Nine for a detailed discussion of how to sequence exercises for maximum benefits.)*

**Why stretch afterward?**

After your workout, take the time to stretch. This helps the body cool down slowly. Because the muscles are more flexible after the body has warmed up, stretching after a workout can be more efficient. You will be able to flex into positions that extend the range of normal motion. There's also much less danger of pulling muscles during flexibility exercises when the muscles are warm.

**How often should I work out?**

*allow recovery time*

If muscles have been exercised to the point of extreme fatigue, they need at least 48 hours to recover. That means no muscle group should be heavily worked two days in a row. Rest is an important part of the strength training routine, so be sure to leave at least a day between hard workouts. You can, however, stretch or walk or do other mild exercise every day or interspersed between anaerobic workouts.

The best gains come from doing full body workouts three times a week, or upper body workouts on three days and lower body exercises on three other days. Many players do a running/aerobics day alternated with a strength training day.

Rest, but try not to let more than three days go by without getting back to training. The muscles begin to atrophy when not used.

Bodybuilder Bill Pearl provides a good general rule for beginners in his book on weight training, *Getting Stronger*. "You can maintain a reasonable amount of fitness working out once a week; twice a week will make a definite improvement; three times a week you will see noticeable improvement."

Pearl works out six days a week, starting promptly each morning at 4:30. He splits his routines to work out different groups of muscles on alternate days so each grouping has a day of rest to recover from the previous workout. That kind of training routine is appropriate for bodybuilders and powerlifters, but probably not for anyone else.

Athletes who are lifting weights to improve their general condition, or to gain better strength to compete in other sports, shouldn't spend that much time in the weight room. Three days a week working out with weights and three days doing aerobics or skill exercises is a good schedule for those who are seriously building toward athletic competition.

*rest well*     Getting enough rest is one of the most neglected elements in the conditioning equation. But it should be right up there with the other important elements of fitness training, says Dr. Donald Chu, director of the Ather Sports Injury Clinic, Castro Valley, California.

"Giving the body time to recover is important, especially for the recreational athlete," Dr. Chu says. "You stress the body to a point of failure and then let it recover. But if you overstress it, something *will* fail. The key is to stress your body almost to failure and then let it recover," he says. "Then you'll be able to stress it even more because that is the way the body adapts."

According to Dr. Chu, there are just three main rules to assure productive strength training:

**(1)** Do exercises that will translate to the sport for which you are training.

**(2)** Do your training in a good progression, starting slowly and building strength and endurance gradually.

**(3)** Allow time to recover from the training.

**Free weights or machines?**

"Just look at the films after a game and try to tell which team is the free-weight team and which team uses Nautilus," Cincinnati's Kim Wood says. "You can't!"

Free weights and machines both have a place in an all-around fitness program, though either can be sufficient alone.

Exercise machines were invented to overcome some of the problems with free weights. The most obvious is the sheer clutter of different size barbells and weights to accommodate different people and different exercises. That led to machines such as the Universal Gym, which put the weights in an adjustable stack connected to pulleys and cables that are hitched to various handles and levers that are pulled or pushed or lifted to provide the resistance.

By putting the weights in a stack and connecting it to cables and chains, the force of gravity was no longer a limiting factor. You don't have to put 200 pounds on your shoulders and squat to build up your thighs. You can lean against a backrest in a machine and push against 200 pounds of resistance. It puts the same load on the leg muscles, but it doesn't put pressure on the spine. By using handles on the ends of cables that pull on the weight stacks, baseball pitchers and football quarterbacks can build up arms and shoulders using exercises similar to the throwing motion. They don't have to lie on their backs and do pullovers with free weights.

Nautilus-type machines go a step further. They also put the weights in an adjustable stack, but they add a cam to change the resistance during the exercise. The idea is to deliver the maximum resistance a muscle can handle through its full range of motion. In any free-weight exercise, as the weight increases, there is a place in the motion where the lifter no longer can move the weight. He may be able to start the lift and to finish it, but he reaches a "sticking point" in the middle. That often is because of physics, not his strength.

*the sticking point*

In doing a barbell curl, for example, the bar is held at thigh level and the forearms are raised to the chest using the biceps. It is much easier to move the weight when it is close to the body than when it is out in front. That's where the sticking point occurs in a curl. What that means is that you can't lift beyond a certain angle; the weight has to be reduced enough to get through the sticking point and complete the movement. The problem is that the muscle is not fully taxed, then, during the early and later stages of the movement.

The cams of Nautilus-type machines overcome that problem by increasing force required during the beginning and end of the motion. There are a number of different Nautilus machines, each designed to work out and isolate particular muscles or groups in a way that provides constant stress through the full range of motion. (The "sticking" problem also is resolved with free weights by experienced lifters who alternate the angles of their lifts.)

Sometimes the problem of a sticking point is not the physics of gravity and leverage but a weakness in the muscle group itself. Particularly after injury, a player may be able to develop only half of his maximum strength at some point in the range of motion of some joint. With free weights and Nautilus he would be limited to working through only a fraction of the range of an exercise or would have to use much lower weight.

Neither of those alternatives is very good. Restricting the range won't exercise the weak part of the muscles that need it most. Reducing the weight will mean that the rest of the muscle group will tend to weaken until it reaches the strength of the weakest part.

Another kind of exercise machine has been developed recently that works on an entirely different basis. It limits the speed with which an exercise can be accomplished. If the machine is set, say, to permit one cycle every three seconds, that's how much it will allow, no matter how much force you apply. These so-called *isokinetic* machines take all the force you put in and resist just enough to do the cycle in the selected time.

The athlete puts in as much effort as he can for a 30- or 40-second interval. If he has a weakness at any point in the range, the machine will accommodate it, but it also will provide total resistance in those places where he is strong. Clearly, these machines are extremely useful in rehabilitation.

"The fundamentals of weight training are universal," says Bob Mischak of the Raiders. "All of it is progressive weight training using different tools. When it comes to machines versus free weights, I think it's only the style that's in dispute. You know, everybody wears a jacket, but the color and the cut are a little different."

"Our team is made up of players from a lot of different programs," Mischak explains, "so we provide a complete facility with flexibility and choice so a player can continue using whatever he is comfortable with."

"For someone just starting out," says Green Bay's Knight, "I would set him up with some free-weight exercises and some machines. They are just tools, and some are better suited to certain things. A bench press with free weights gives you balance and the knowledge that it is all yours to handle. A Nautilus bench machine will give you a little better range of motion, but it doesn't give a sense of balance and rhythm. So I believe in using them both."

Denver quarterback John Elway prefers free weights. "I feel I get more out of them," he says. "I think you can get the same amount of flexibility from using free weights as you can from machines, as long as you're careful to simulate the same range of motion."

Strength coach Don Clemons favors free weights for his Detroit players because they provide such complete freedom of movement. He does, however, have machines for certain lifts and situations.

"With a machine, you don't have to control the side-to-side movements of a free weight with fine motions," he explains. "For athletes, that fine control requirement is a plus. For injured athletes, older people, novices, and women, I would recommend machines."

Although a few coaches are adamant about using free weights almost exclusively, most NFL conditioning coordinators agree with Mischak, who says "the muscles don't see the technique you are using. The quality of what you do is what counts, not the way that you do it."

# Lift Safely

Lifting more than 100 pounds of iron is not something one does casually. Losing your grip with a barbell poised over your head is dangerous. That safety factor is one reason experts urge free-weight users to work out with a partner or coach.

*wear belt and gloves*

During heavy lifts, some trainers suggest wearing a wide leather support belt to reduce the chances of a back injury should you over-stress a supporting muscle. Another useful item is a pair of lifting gloves to prevent the bar from slipping out of sweaty fingers. The gloves, which sometimes are padded, also keep you from building up calluses on the palms.

With Nautilus, Universal, and other machines, the dangers are a little less obvious. You can lose control of the handles on a Nautilus or Universal machine. The consequences may be less radical than a barbell falling on your chest, but people can get hurt by out-of-control handles or be thrown or twisted out of the seat. That's why most machines now have seat belts. As in cars, buckle up.

In the NFL, some coaches run a very tight training room, with a minimum of chatter and all the time devoted to the workouts. Others feel the atmosphere needs to be friendly and warm, the clubby kind of place where players enjoy being. After all, given the hard work involved in a strength workout, the idea is to make the weight room as attractive as possible.`

*horseplay can hurt*

Every strength coach in the league insists on strict safety rules. No one throws anything and the joking is strictly limited to words. Pushing or bumping each other could lead to tipping a weight stack, dropping a barbell, or worse. "With the players we have and their importance to the team, the last thing you would ever want is to have somebody injured in the weight room," the Rams' Garrett Giemont says.

Any time you feel pain, stop. If it continues, see a doctor. If you haven't been working out regularly, be sure you get a medical okay before starting any strenuous conditioning program.

## Form Counts

Using proper form increases efficiency. It doesn't make the exercise any easier, but it makes your muscles work to the maximum on each repetition you do. That makes progress faster and reduces the chance of training injury. If you are cheating to lift a greater weight, you may be getting less benefit than if you used proper form with less weight.

The Bears' Emrich feels that a major responsibility of the strength coach is to assure that athletes learn the proper form when they start lifting. "If you do a dead lift there is exposure to back injury if you don't do it right," he says. "Go to a gym and have someone properly instruct you. Sure, sooner or later you would pick it up on your own, but in the meantime you risk injury and waste a lot of time working out inefficiently."

Miami's Wade agrees that good form prevents injuries in the weight room. "It's when you're herky-jerky that you're subject to injuries," he says. "If you don't do it right, you don't get the benefits. If you cheat, you come up short. Sure, by using improper form you can do an extra twenty pounds, but what do you gain? You're not getting any stronger."

## Daily Variety

Keeping boredom out of the weight room is important to maintaining interest over the long haul. "You've always got to have something a little different than what you've been doing the last few weeks," Knight says. "It gets to be drudgery if you do the same thing three days a week. So the more variety you can put in there, the better."

The Giants' Parker is a fanatic about variety. He spends weeks during the preseason planning the workouts his team will do. "The higher the level of skill of the athlete, the more important it is to have variety," he says. "The higher his skill, the quicker he adapts, and once the body adapts, it shuts down growth. So to keep our players constantly growing and making improvements, we have to have a variety in loading."

*individual targets*

At the Giants' elaborate weight-training center, the order of exercises, the exercises themselves, the weights used, and the sequence are changed every day. To make that complexity manageable, all players do the same routines in the same order. "The only difference is that defensive end Leonard Marshall will lift heavier weights than quarterback Phil Simms," Parker says. "Each player gets a target weight that he is expected to be lifting at the end of each ten-week cycle, and he bases all his lifts on specified percentages of that number."

At Cleveland, Dave Redding gives Browns players six different ways to do bench presses and lets them take their pick. "They can use dumbbells, or barbells, or machines," Redding says, "just so they can keep it going."

Perhaps the champion of weight-room innovation is the Bengals' Wood. "We'll use progressive resistance exercise in all forms. Our players use Nautilus and thick-handled barbells and dumbbells. One of the keys to a good program is variety, so sometimes we'll lift a sledgehammer or a shotput or we'll curl anvils. The thing is you can get into a groove with a barbell or a machine, but with an anvil, you can't get a groove. It forces you to use additional muscles."

Wood says that "having off-beat gizmos in the weight room adds interest" to an otherwise static workout program. But he emphasizes that the unusual touches "are always used within the basic program structure."

## Where to Work Out

The ideal workout situation is what the professional teams provide for their players: clean, well-ventilated training rooms with a complete range of equipment and competent coaches on hand to help and provide advice.

Commercial gyms and some health spas also can deliver those in-

gredients, at least in the area of physical amenities and equipment.
A commercial gym will more likely have a no-nonsense approach
and be a little more heavily oriented toward free weights. They may
not have a full set of Nautilus equipment or amenities such as whirl-
pools and steam rooms. They probably will have instructors well
suited to helping with bodybuilding and weightlifting.

A health club or Nautilus facility usually is a more sociable atmosphere than a commercial gym, appealing more to men and women
interested in maintaining body tone and appearance than to those
whose strength training is linked to sports performance. The
equipment at these establishments ranges from complete to inadequate. A spa that is primarily an aerobics studio won't have the
weights and machines you'll want for a varied program. And some
Nautilus facilities are strictly set up for using machines and don't
offer the flexibility of free weights and static apparatus.

An increasing number of health clubs and Nautilus facilities do
provide not only the basics, but such amenities as handball and racquetball courts, professional massage, steam rooms, and a pleasant
atmosphere.

Schools and colleges also are good places to work out. Even if you
don't attend the school, you may be able to enroll in adult courses
that make the gym equipment available to the public. And don't
forget other public facilities such as YMCAs and city park and rec-
reation departments.

An increasing number of companies have installed exercise
equipment on their premises because they discovered that well-
conditioned employees are more productive workers. Some of
these company gyms have the space, equipment, and staff to compare with a well-equipped commercial gym. At worst, they're still
probably as complete as most home gyms.

Finally, you can work out at home using inexpensive free weights
and exercise benches. There are plenty of rowing machines, Universal exercise stations, and other gear available that will make the
home gym more complete. Some people cooperate in setting up a
neighborhood gym in someone's garage, contributing cash, equipment, and/or facilities. The advantage of having other people involved is that you are more likely to have a training partner to
encourage you and spot lifts during your workouts. Obviously, any
coaching will be limited to the participants, unless you find a fitness
coach who will make house calls or you drop in to a gym every so
often for a tune-up.

*selecting
a trainer*

Getting good supervision while developing a workout program
can keep you from wasting time or getting hurt. A trainer will show
you the right form for using weights and machines.

At a commercial gym, be sure the trainer you select has experience in strength training for the kinds of sports and other activities
you want to pursue. If his or her orientation is strictly toward body-

building and weightlifting, you may find the routines he recommends don't really support your priorities.

Health clubs do have some excellent trainers on staff. But talk with members first and ask questions before signing up because some of those coaches are really salesmen, dedicated to signing up new members, not improving their workouts.

At a school or YMCA-type of gym, try to find a coach or trainer who understands the modern theory and practice of weight training. Be grateful for a good coach or a helpful trainer, but be wary. Don't accept any strength coach's direction unless you really understand how it fits in with your program and corroborates what you've learned from outside sources.

# Wonder Women

"When it comes to fitness, women basically are not that much different from men," says the Chargers' Tyne.

"We see women now getting stronger and more muscular and see them doing well in marathons. There are, of course, some physiological differences, but as far as conditioning, they can work hard, they can sweat, they can do resistance work. I usually recommend that they stay with lighter weights, but only because most women are not trying to build a muscular mass. They're trying to tone the muscles and firm the muscles."

Because women have less experience with weight training and have less total strength, most coaches recommend they emphasize the use of machines in their strength training programs. As for aerobics and flexibility, no one recommends anything different from what they would suggest for men.

The differences in exercise for men and women, though minor, should be considered. First, although women can become quite strong, they generally can't build the bulging muscles that men develop. That's because they don't have much testosterone, the male hormone, in their bodies. Combined with heavy lifting, testosterone is what makes a man's muscles get big.

Women have proportionately wider pelvic bones than men. That increases the angle between the thigh and calf and puts more stress on those joints. Women should consider using less weight in exercises such as squats that put pressure on the knee joints.

Body fat is higher in women than in men, also a result of hormonal gender differences. Aerobics, weight training, and good nutrition will bring the fat level down, but reducing it below about 10 percent may lead to irregular menstruation and other biochemical complications.

*workouts and pregnancy*  Working out while pregnant is easier for women who already have developed a high level of fitness. However, starting an ambitious bodybuilding program after conception is not recommended.

By the time she is pregnant, a woman is coping with the stresses and nutritional needs of building another body inside her. For the woman who already is in condition, maintaining fitness with workouts that are modified as the pregnancy progresses is a good idea, but only after consultation with a doctor.

If you are considering having a child, get in shape now. Being in condition not only can help in delivery, it will make returning to form after pregnancy that much easier.

# Kids' Stuff

Most kids are natural competitors. With their energy and enthusiasm they're conditioned to learn new skills and look for challenges. That's the essence of youth.

*avoid heavy lifting*

The Browns' Dave Redding suggests that "kids at puberty want to do what the older guys do but they shouldn't try. At that age you shouldn't be too intense. I would have them do lots of machine apparatus first to build a certain level of strength and then let them go onto free weights."

Young athletes who want to improve should be especially attentive to Redding's advice about cheating in the weight room by using dangerously bad form to lift more.

"There is not much danger for a person older than fifteen, depending on their growth, and even younger if they already are in circuit-type training," the Rams' Giemont says. "But when a newcomer starts doing heavy weights is when problems can develop. I'd recommend that kids just learn the concepts of lifting when they are teenagers, and for them to avoid heavy weights until then. You want to be sure kids' joints have matured before having them work out really hard. I'd be more interested in motivating them to realize that only they can develop themselves; that at their age they can do anything they want if they'll only work for it."

# *Jacoby and Morris: Two Extraordinary Joes*

Redskins tackle Joe Jacoby stands 6 feet 7 inches, weighs 315 pounds, and has arms like tree limbs. Giants running back Joe Morris is a foot shorter and more than a hundred pounds lighter, but is proportionately powerful.

In fact, a reporter once said to Giants coach Bill Parcells that Morris was, "for his size," one of the strongest players he ever had seen. "He's strong for *any* size," Parcells replied.

Similarly, prior to a game with the Redskins, an opposing superstar defensive end privately rated Washington's offensive line. Casually ticking off the weaknesses he would exploit in each man, the player stopped at Jacoby's name. "That's the only guy in this league I can't handle," he said. "He's too strong."

Jacoby and Morris differ on what methods and what equipment will best increase their strength; Jacoby works out mostly on Nautilus equipment while Morris avoids machines, using free weights almost exclusively.

What they share is an absolute dedication to a rigorous program of diet, running, and, above all, weight training.

"Jacoby came in here as an unknown free agent at two hundred seventy-five pounds and built himself up to three hundred fifteen and an all-pro," says Redskins strength coach Dan Riley.

During the offseason Jacoby trains on a five-day-a-week schedule. He works at strength training on Nautilus machines for about an hour on Monday, Wednesday, and Friday. Tuesday and Thursday he stretches, does neck exercises and sit-ups, and pushes his cardiovascular system by raising his heart rate to 85 percent of maximum for 20 minutes of running (at least two miles) on a treadmill.

Jacoby begins each of the three weightlifting days with a series of neck exercises. He does a

*Tackle Joe Jacoby*          *Running back Joe Morris*

dozen of each: back to front, side to side, rotary, and shrugs.

Then the heavy work starts. "We go right for the legs. I'll do twelve reps each of leg presses, squats, leg extensions, and leg curls," Jacoby says.

"We put on enough weight so that I'm really straining by the time I get to the last four reps. And as we get toward the season, we build up gradually each week and put more weight on. It's hard work. And when it starts getting easier, we add weight."

Athletes tend to get stale doing the same exercises with the same weights all the time. "To prevent that," Jacoby says, "Dan [Riley] adds different variations to break up the monotony. The routine changes every day."

For example, instead of working the press machine with both legs, Jacoby sometimes will stack weight that is reasonably difficult for both legs and then push out. But on the return stroke, the negative or eccentric motion in which the muscles can handle a greater load, he will control the weight using just one leg at a time.

When that gets dull, he'll put on a little less weight but do the push and return with one leg while holding the other leg straight out in the air.

On leg curls or extensions, Jacoby sometimes

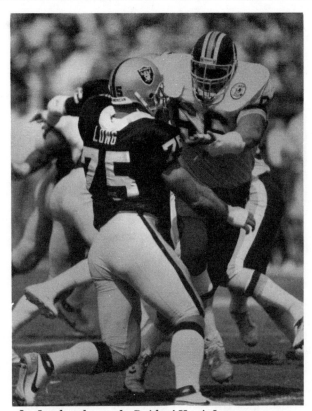

*Joe Jacoby takes on the Raiders' Howie Long.*

changes his routine by moving through the exercise two or three times slower than normal, thereby changing the effort for his muscles.

"The idea is that it gives us different things to do every day," he says. "With this system, there are different ways to do it and still get the same effect."

When his lower body work is finished, Jacoby takes a "breather" with sit-ups, leg lifts, work on the abductor-adductor machine, and lower back exercises.

Jacoby doesn't know what his workout will be until he comes in and takes a card that Riley has prepared for him. It contains the order of exercises, the weights, number of reps, and particular method of doing each routine.

"Usually he works the chest more one day," Jacoby says. "The next time the work is more on shoulders, arms, and back. But there's always something different and it's always hard."

It gets *really* hard every couple of weeks when Jacoby is asked to squeeze all the exercises that normally take 45 minutes into just 20 minutes. This 20-minute compressed workout is intended to build endurance.

"You're exhausted after you're done," Jacoby says. "It's a little like circuit training except you use the same weights you worked up to over two months at normal speed."

Jacoby shows up religiously in the weight room every day he's scheduled. Partially, it is because he recognizes how weight training has helped give him an edge on the field. But with the encouragement and variety Riley provides, Jacoby claims he genuinely enjoys the workouts, tough as they are.

Occasionally, to get yet another different way to strengthen specific exercise muscle groups, Jacoby will use free weights for dumbbell flies and incline bench presses. He lifted free weights in college but never felt comfortable with explosive movements that now are popular with some coaches. "We get plenty of explosive training in actual practice on the field," he says.

Because he already is so strong, Jacoby has to lift enormous weights to get the training effect he needs. That's one of the reasons he prefers machines, where the weights are safely stacked inside the mechanism. "In college," he says, "I was always afraid of the weight falling on me. I wasn't skilled at doing some of the fast movement lifts. And with the heavy loads I have to carry, I would be reluctant to do free weights if they changed the program here. I certainly wouldn't do power cleans or heavy squats. I think they're dangerous."

Power cleans and squats, however, are the core of Morris's training program.

Morris, who plays at about 198 pounds, can bench press more than twice his weight—415 pounds at a recent testing. Like Jacoby, he works hard to develop his body to its limit.

During the offseason, Morris takes it relatively easy. He runs every day, does push-ups and sit-ups, and just tries to maintain his mus-

*Joe Morris is quick through the line, deceptively strong, and has exceptional cutting ability.*

cle tone. He even lets up on his low-fat diet and indulges in an occasional ice cream cone or sausage pizza after the playoffs.

But as winter ends, he begins the serious work of building strength for the season to come. His conditioning program is structured around a strict four-days-a-week of weightlifting designed by New York's strength coach, Johnny Parker. "Monday and Tuesday are tough on me," Morris says. "Wednesday is a day off from lifting, and Thursday is light. But Friday is a killer, too."

He awakens about 8 A.M. and immediately begins a series of sit-ups. Not just ordinary sit-ups, but a total of 160 movements that require flexibility and agility as well as muscle strength. The easiest is a series of 20 with his legs bent and held in the air as he sits up to touch his chin to his knees. The rest are harder, involving stretching and contracting the abdominal muscles more thoroughly than the usual sit-ups kids are taught in gym classes.

Morris then arrives at Giants Stadium about mid-morning and begins with some slow stretching that readies his muscles for the heavy workout to come.

"I just stretch real slowly—I don't bounce," he says. "I stretch muscle groups I'll be using. I'm not a big stretching guy—it takes about seven minutes. Then I go in and figure out what my weights will be for that day."

Parker's program is designed to make everyone on the team stronger, but at different levels. The exercise routine for the day is the same for all players; the individual simply plugs in his own numbers. Every lift is calibrated as a percentage of each player's maximum lifting strength. The maximum is not how much they can lift when they start, but the poundage they are expected to be able to lift at the end of each ten-week program cycle.

No matter what the exercise, the first set is done as a warm-up, with weights only 40 percent of maximum. And the first exercise is always the power clean.

That controversial exercise starts like a dead lift with the bar pulled off the floor mainly with leg power. As the bar rises above the knee, two carefully coordinated movements have to occur simultaneously to accelerate it even more; the shoulders, arms, and back add their power and the lifter raises up on his toes. The idea is to get the heavy bar rising in a ballistic motion that will keep it moving while the next movement takes place. At the peak height, the wrists are flipped backward and the elbows are thrust under the bar into a bench-press position. The lifter actually has to drop his body down under the bar and use his legs to push up into the ending position with the bar resting on his shoulders under his chin.

The lift involves as much athletic coordination as strength. Done wrong, it can be dangerous. That's why Jacoby and many coaches won't use the power clean. But the majority of teams in the NFL do include the maneuver in their weight-training program. Morris explains why: "The power clean is the most natural exercise a football player can do. If you look at football in terms of what motions you are using on the field, then you can see that when you power clean it is actually the same exercise as pass blocking where you try to get your hands under a guy and then lift him up. Just like what happens on the field, the power clean needs speed and strength, not just one or the other."

Morris warms up by doing two sets of six power cleans, each at 40 percent of his maximum weight. Then he will do five more sets with weights ranging from 50 to 70 percent of maximum. The number of reps declines as the weight increases.

The Giants' program is based on a 10-week cycle, with weight increasing each week until the players hit 100 percent of their predicted maximum by the last week. Parker plans the weights for each man so they ideally never miss a lift. "I always want them to be slightly undertrained," he says. "I want them never to miss a rep."

For the Giants and Parker, the couple of hours in the weight room four days a week and the interval training sessions on the track are all that are needed to get Morris in top shape for training camp and the season. But Morris has other ideas.

"After I do what they want, I get to do things for myself," he says. The elaborate sit-ups every morning are only one example of his drive to deliver more than is asked of him. He loves to run. So several afternoons a week during the preseason he goes to a neighborhood park to do sprints and agility drills, and run hills.

"The only thing I have to remember," he says, "is that doing too much will leave me burned out."

To Morris, the heavy schedule and the heavy weights make good sense:

"Sure, all that work is hard on me," he says, "but I've seen the results. I know if I put out extra when training, I'm gonna have more to give when we really need it in a game."

# 2 Breathing Easy:

## *Aerobic/ Cardiovascular Fitness*

Louie Kelcher, the 6-foot 5-inch, 282-pound former San Diego Chargers defensive tackle, once summed up his feelings about aerobic training. "If I have to run forty yards to catch somebody," he said, "I ain't gonna catch him nohow."

Attitudes have changed. Professional football players now know they require aerobic training to achieve peak performance. Aerobic exercise is what conditions the cardiovascular system, which is, after all, at the heart of all athletic endeavors. Most NFL conditioning coaches strongly advise their players to do some running and other aerobic conditioning to complement their strength programs during the offseason. Yet when players do follow through on aerobic exercise, it's because they need it, not because they like it. When it comes to physical activity, they'd still rather do something else.

Oddly enough, the type of exercise that NFL players like least is the kind that most people do. The weekend athlete generally works out by choice with some form of aerobic conditioning such as running, swimming, or cycling. Rarely does the non-professional do the extensive weightlifting that NFL players must endure. But in athletic conditioning, weightlifting alone is not enough. Neither is running nor any other aerobic activity practiced to the exclusion of everything else. For maximum output, there must be a balance between strength training and aerobic training.

## Miracle Fibers

Football primarily requires strength, skill, and speed, not aerobic endurance. Athletes in the pro ranks have explosive strength. Their bodies tend to be dense in what are called "fast" muscle fi-

## *Aerobic and Anaerobic: Who's On First?*

Aerobic means "in the presence of air." Aerobic exercise is the training that benefits the cardiovascular system, which includes the heart, lungs, and blood vessels. To understand why conditioned athletes need to have both aerobic and anaerobic (without oxygen) systems operating at top efficiency, consider the way our bodies turn food into energy.

The starting point is a body chemical with the jawbreaking name, adenosinetriphosphate (shortened to ATP). It is ATP, triggered by a nerve stimulus, which causes a muscle to contract. ATP is powerful stuff, but it needs constant replenishing. Without a high level of ATP available, muscles can't work.

There are three ways to get the ATP recharged. One is easy and automatic and is the body's first reaction to a stimulus. It involves another body chemical called creatine phosphate (CP), which already is stored in the muscle cells and is broken down chemically to produce energy and more ATP.

ATP and CP, as elements of the muscle cells themselves, are ready to provide instant muscle action. It's stored ATP and CP that power the shotput, the 40-yard dash, and a lineman's explosion when the ball is snapped.

But for muscular effort of anything longer than about 15 seconds, the muscles need another source of power. This second source is glycogen, which is produced when carbohydrates are digested. Glycogen also is stored as fuel in the muscles as well as in the liver. When the muscles have used up that initial surge of power from stored ATP and CP, glycogen maintained in columns alongside the muscle fibers is brought into action. Glycogen releases energy by breaking down in an anaerobic process that forms more ATP.

After about two minutes of intense exercise, the anaerobic glycogen system needs recharging, too. The problem is not that there's no glycogen left, but that the waste products formed when it was broken down to form ATP, particularly lactic acid, obstruct further glycogen processing.

On comes the third energy system, the aerobic, which needs oxygen to function. It can run on any or all of the body's fuel sources: carbohydrates, fats, or proteins. The aerobic system can't fuel the same intensity of exercise as the anaerobic systems, but it can keep working for a much longer time.

When the aerobic system cuts in and oxygenated blood starts flowing into the muscles, the build-up of lactic acid is retarded. Athletes can't perform with muscles full of lactic acid. That's why your heart speeds up when you exercise: To deliver more oxygenated blood to relieve lactic acid build-up. When a muscle can't get enough oxygenated blood and lactic acid levels rise, the muscle has overdrawn its energy supplies. The muscle begins to feel as if it is burning. If the stress isn't relieved, the muscle just gives up. It fails.

In aerobic exercise, the build-up of lactic acid is called the oxygen deficit, or debt. Oxygen debt begins to mount when exercise intensity gets high enough to raise the heart rate over about 70 to 80 percent of maximum capacity. Highly trained athletes often don't begin building an oxygen debt until they're running at 90 percent of maximum. Once the debt point is reached, as signaled by a rapidly beating heart and gasping for breath, even the best athletes have to stop. How long they have to stop is a function of their aerobic conditioning.

bers; they have relatively few of the "slow" muscle fibers of, say, a marathon runner.

*fast and slow muscle fibers*

Fast muscle fibers deliver tremendous power for less than 30 or 40 seconds. They contract quickly without the use of oxygen, hence they are termed *anaerobic*. The slow endurance muscle fibers, which contract more slowly, are *aerobic*, which means they work with oxygen. Endurance fibers that work with the aerobic system gradually begin picking up the load only after about a minute of strenuous activity. They then can keep going for hours.

## The Heart of the Matter

The overriding consideration for every athlete, whether he favors fast muscle fibers or endurance muscle fibers, is to train the cardiac muscle, the heart. Your heart beats from 40 to 220 times a minute every day of your life. A well-trained athlete may pump as many as 42 liters of blood a minute through his body. A gasoline pump running at that rate could fill a small car's gas tank in a matter of seconds. The cardiac muscle never rests, except between beats.

Making the heart muscle stronger requires an entirely different kind of exercise than weight training, for example. Weight workouts entail high-intensity exercise for short periods with rests between sets. Weight training also works out muscles individually or in tightly isolated groups. What is required to benefit the heart and cardiovascular system is aerobic exercise, where the idea is to work a large number of muscles at lower intensity for a longer, more continuous period.

A 40-yard dash that is over in five seconds involves tremendous exertion that leaves the heart pounding. Ten repetitions lifting a 200-pound barbell probably will result in an outpouring of sweat. But neither the dash nor the lift will do much to increase the heart's capacity.

## Playing the Percentages

Improving the aerobic system requires the same kind of dedication and consistency that goes into speed or weight training. There's a minimum effort required to make any gain, but that varies with the

*aerobic fitness*

individual. Perhaps the most respected advice on aerobic activity comes from The Institute for Aerobics Research, at the Aerobics Center in Dallas, founded by Dr. Kenneth Cooper. Cooper, who popularized the concept of aerobics, believes that at least 20 minutes of rhythmic exercising, three times a week, is essential to achieve aerobic fitness.

Exactly how hard must you work aerobically? Depending on your age, condition, and how much you want to improve, aerobic exercise has to have enough intensity to boost the heart rate to between 60 and 85 percent of the heart's maximum.

The American College of Sports Medicine reports that exercising at a pace below 60 percent of maximum heart rate yields little improvement in aerobic capacity. At under 60 percent, the heart isn't pumping enough blood to force open small blood vessels in the cardiovascular system to make it more efficient.

Pushing above 90 percent of the maximum pulse rate is not recommended either. "At a rate much higher than eighty-five or ninety percent of maximum, the heart no longer is as efficient," Redskins conditioning coach Dan Riley says. "It doesn't have time to completely refill itself at those rates and is pumping out less blood with each beat."

A simple formula to estimate your maximum heart rate has been developed by the Aerobics Institute. If you are male, just subtract half your age from 205. For example, a twenty-year-old man would have a maximum of 195 and a 60-year-old a top rate of 175. Women can find their maximum estimated heart rate by subtracting their age from 220.

## *Aerobic Heart Rate Targets*

| MEN | AGE IN YEARS | | | | | | | WOMEN | AGE IN YEARS | | | | | | |
|---|---|---|---|---|---|---|---|---|---|---|---|---|---|---|---|
| % Max. | 20 | 25 | 30 | 35 | 40 | 50 | 60 | % Max. | 20 | 25 | 30 | 35 | 40 | 50 | 60 |
| 60% | 117 | 115 | 114 | 112 | 111 | 108 | 105 | 60% | 120 | 117 | 114 | 111 | 108 | 102 | 96 |
| 70% | 136 | 134 | 133 | 131 | 129 | 126 | 122 | 70% | 140 | 136 | 133 | 129 | 126 | 119 | 112 |
| 75% | 146 | 144 | 142 | 140 | 138 | 135 | 131 | 75% | 150 | 146 | 142 | 138 | 135 | 127 | 120 |
| 80% | 156 | 154 | 152 | 150 | 148 | 144 | 140 | 80% | 160 | 156 | 152 | 148 | 144 | 136 | 128 |
| 85% | 165 | 163 | 161 | 159 | 157 | 153 | 148 | 85% | 170 | 165 | 161 | 157 | 153 | 144 | 136 |
| 90% | 175 | 173 | 171 | 168 | 166 | 162 | 157 | 90% | 180 | 175 | 171 | 166 | 162 | 153 | 144 |

## Perpetual Motion Machines

The basis for aerobic conditioning is continuous exercise. Short bursts of intense activity with long rests between are anaerobic. They don't get the lungs and heart stressed for a long enough period to establish a training effect.

*training effect*    The term "training effect" actually refers to two separate but related phenomena. The long-term training effect is the result of adaptations the cardiovascular system makes over time to the stress of aerobic training. The benefits include: a reduction in the resting heart rate; an increase in the ability to burn oxygen during exercise; a decrease in the risk for contracting cardiovascular disease; and an all-around boost in energy levels and endurance.

The short-term training effect is an increase in the body's metabolic rate that continues, several recent studies report, even after aerobic exercise stops. According to the Aerobics Center's Susan Johnson, "The range of results would indicate that for an average person, the metabolic rate rises fifteen to eighteen percent after aerobic exercise and stays in that range for six to eight hours afterward, and, in some cases, longer."

Most authorities agree the aerobic system doesn't work at full capacity until after the equivalent of 12 minutes of fast running or about 20 minutes of easy jogging. According to Dr. Cooper, unless aerobic exercise is regular, it may be wise to forget it entirely. He states in his book, *The New Aerobics*, that "now-and-then exercise will not help . . . strengthen the heart so that it can stand a really tough workout."

Steelers strength and conditioning coach Walt Evans says, "You need an aerobic base to recover quickly from anaerobic exercise."

Running and jogging are among the most efficient aerobic workout components, but there are many other effective exercises as well, including swimming, bicycling, climbing stairs, rowing, cross-country skiing (not downhill skiing, which is mainly anaerobic), jumping rope, and sports that call for constant movement such as soccer or handball.

*aerobic exercise burns fat*

Aerobic conditioning provides an added bonus for people who are overweight. Aerobic workouts are by far the best way to lose extra pounds. That's because the body burns only glycogen during anaerobic exercise, but burns up fat once the system turns aerobic.

A less tangible benefit of aerobic exercise is the discipline it creates, says Evans. "Distance running has something to do with mental toughness. Players look at distance running as torture and we tell them to just get through it, even if they have to walk in some places. Once they do complete their two, or three, or four miles without stopping, they develop more self-discipline and confidence in other areas as well."

## Building Aerobic Endurance

The key to building aerobic endurance is to get the heart rate up to the training level and then to keep going, rhythmically working out the major muscles for the duration of the session.

Sprinters, weightlifters, and other short-burst, strength-oriented athletes often have trouble with the endurance side of conditioning because they work too hard at it. A natural tendency of sprinters is to run fast. It feels uncomfortable for some of them to simply jog at a fraction of their normal pace. Weightlifters also tend to over-exert themselves when pulling oars, for example, on a rowing machine. The problem for these athletes is to hold back at first so they'll be able to get through the discomfort while the body switches over from the anaerobic to the aerobic system. That switch usually is completed in one to five minutes. Many joggers find the first mile the hardest because their aerobic system has not yet kicked in to provide the energy for extended exercise.

Research indicates that for the average athlete, it's much better to schedule longer, less intense aerobic sessions than to attempt to do a hard twenty or thirty minutes. Most NFL teams have their players run only two or three miles at most, especially during the early pre-season when they are building an aerobic base.

Like strength training, heavy aerobic sessions should be separated by at least a day for rest, but there shouldn't be an interval of more than three days between workouts. Taking a day off after a long, hard run doesn't mean you can't go for a short jog or engage in other activity. It's just good practice to give the cardiovascular system and the specific muscles involved in the workout enough time to recover and repair themselves.

*cooling down and stretching*

After a workout, cool-down and flexibility stretching is important to good aerobic conditioning. It also may be a vital safety consideration. The action of the leg muscles during running, for example, helps to force blood back up toward the heart. When the runner stops moving, the blood tends to pool in the lower limbs, putting additional pressure on the heart to pump harder just when it is beginning to recover from the workout.

Don't sprint to the end of a run and stop. Walk or jog slowly for at least five minutes afterward. And be sure to stretch. Post-workout stretching, when the muscles are most pliable, will reduce soreness and help you stay limber for the next session. Extensive stretching before an aerobic workout is not recommended; the muscles are cold and are more vulnerable to over-stretching that could cause muscle tears. *(See Chapter Three for specific flexibility suggestions.)*

## Aerobic Ideas

Besides running and jogging, jumping rope is a good rhythmic aerobic exercise. But it takes time to learn the skills and to build enough endurance to go 15 to 20 minutes non-stop at a rate that is at least 80 turns a minute.

Bicycling also is an excellent aerobic activity, either on the road or with a stationary exercise machine. Again, to qualify as an aerobic exercise, the heart rate and the duration of exercise are what count. To maintain elevated heart rates during long downhill segments, instead of coasting, some cyclists apply the brakes enough so they have to continue pedaling.

Rowing is an aerobic exercise that has the advantage of working a large number of upper and lower body muscles. If you have access to water and a boat, it is a great way to get an outdoor workout. However, a rowboat doesn't have the sliding seat that uses the leg muscles that you'll find in a racing-type scull, which is simulated on an indoor rowing machine. To maintain aerobic endurance in a rowboat means working the arm and back muscles more than most beginners can handle.

Swimming is another water-related exercise that rates high in aerobic value. It uses a wide array of muscles, has the advantage of being cooling on hot days, and is fairly convenient. Your goal should be to swim continuously for at least 20 minutes with your heart rate in the target training range.

Cross country skiing is an increasingly popular endurance exercise. A number of Cleveland Browns players have begun taking to trails on a golf course near their training facility. Cleveland strength and conditioning coach Dave Redding says, "I've turned on eight or ten guys to cross country skiing. It's great aerobic training and it puts no stress on the big guys."

The exercise is rated at the top of aerobic workouts because, with the action of poling and kicking, cross country skiing brings all of the major muscles and the cardiovascular system into play. It also gives players in a northern climate a chance to get outside at a time when many other outdoor activities are impossible to pursue. With the advent of roller skis, which are like a combination of roller skates and skis, and machines such as the NordicTrack and Fitness Master, cross country-type training is possible in the middle of summer.

Other exercises that provide a good aerobic workout are hiking and walking (if done with continuity). And several players, including Patriots linebacker Andre Tippett and Dallas defensive tackle Randy White, study martial arts. Rams linebacker Mel Owens says his karate exercises not only provide an aerobic workout when they are done continuously, but they also enhance balance and hand quickness.

## Gauging Training Efficiency

For beginners, older people, or those who haven't exercised for a while, the first aerobic workout should be a trip to your doctor's office. Be sure there isn't any medical reason to restrict activity. Once you get approval, start out with a 15- or 20-minute walk at a pace slow enough that you're not gasping, but fast enough to leave you perspiring lightly.

*monitoring heart rate*

From then on, whether you jog, bicycle, swim, jump rope, or do any of the other aerobic exercises, pay attention to your heart rate. Doing so helps keep the sprinters and lifters from putting out so much energy at the start of exercise that they have nothing left for the finish. It also will assure that experienced runners don't stride along at a well-practiced pace that isn't fast enough to provide much of a training effect.

A rule of thumb that works fairly well for joggers and hikers who exercise with a partner is called the "conversation constant." Because the rate of breathing is tied directly to heart rate, it's obvious that heavy breathing means a racing heart. Never run or walk so fast that you can't maintain a conversation. Conversely, if you can quote passages from Shakespeare, the pace probably is too slow.

## Fancy Footwear

The concept of training specificity carries over to the shoes you wear while you work out. Running shoes are running shoes for good reasons; they provide cushioning for your feet, act as shock absorbers for your knees, and help alleviate excessive pronation or supination (outward or inward twisting of the feet) as you run. But running shoes are no good for tennis; they don't provide enough lateral support and aren't built to take the quick starts and stops that tennis demands. Likewise, tennis shoes are inadequate for basketball. There seemingly are special shoes for every athletic pursuit, from aerobic dancing to volleyball. This is not a conspiracy by athletic shoe manufacturers. It's just a fact of life; no one exercise can prepare you for playing all sports, and no one shoe can work well for all activities. However, a few shoe companies are introducing dual-purpose "cross training" shoes into their lines for people who ride their bikes to the tennis courts or the gym, for example, and don't want to have to change shoes to play or work out.

*taking your pulse*

A more accurate way to measure your aerobic level is to take your pulse. Stop at intervals and check your heart rate. You can measure the pulse on any artery where you can feel a strong throb of blood being forced through when the heart contracts. Probably the best and safest spot is on the radial artery inside the wrist, just below the thumb. A good measure is to count the pulse for 10 seconds and multiply by six. Measuring for 30 seconds probably won't be accurate because if you are in any sort of condition your heart rate begins returning to normal after 10 or 15 seconds. If your heartbeat is in the target range, keep going at the same pace. If not, adjust your speed to get into the target range.

Featherweight heartbeat monitors now are available that automatically take the pulse and signal when the athlete is outside his or her target range.

"This is going to revolutionize the weekend warrior," says the Oilers' Steve Watterson. "Pulse meters allow the athlete to work in the area of his heart capacity and not have to worry about the intensity. It tells when to speed up or slow down and even times the run and tells him when to stop. The advantage is that you can think about anything you want. You challenge yourself more and your mind is free to make such techniques as positive imaging work."

Professional athletes find that the best feature of an automatic heartbeat monitor is that it keeps them working within the training range even as skill and endurance improve. For example, at the start of an aerobic running program, a jogger may reach his target heart rate by running at only five or six miles per hour. As he gains strength and improves form, running six or even seven miles per hour may no longer boost his heart into the training range. The automatic monitor measures heart beat and not speed, so can help solve that problem. To use most automatic monitors, the athlete first sets the upper and lower target rates he wants to maintain. Then he attaches the unit and takes off. The monitor beeps until his heart rate gets above the training threshold and then quiets down. If he slows down, it squawks again. Over the limit, it signals to slow the pace. Monitors are like having a coach in your pocket, because they can record your heart rate and elapsed time at various points along the course so you can review performance precisely and adjust training accordingly.

Heartbeat monitors are useful in any serious training program and fun to use. But at prices that range from $100 to more than $300, they are an expensive accessory.

Checking heart rate, whether by high-tech equipment or with just a stopwatch and your fingers, is valuable in determining how fast you recover from workouts. If your heartbeat doesn't return to normal within 10 minutes of ending a session, you may be pushing yourself too hard.

*pushing too hard*

A related mistake is failing to give yourself enough rest in between workouts. Dr. Donald Chu, director of the Ather Sports Injury Clinic in Castro Valley, California, suggests measuring your heart rate every morning when you wake up. "If you find the rate is ten or twelve beats higher than normal," he says, "it's an obvious sign that the body has not yet had enough recovery time and that you should take it easy for another day."

## Speed Work vs. Distance

Though distance running helps develop good aerobic capacity and positive mental attitude, few sports require marathon-style training. The sports to which aerobic conditioning is directly transferable include soccer, cross country skiing, perhaps singles tennis and basketball, and, of course, the long distance track events.

Most sports, including football, require brief bursts of high intensity. Because conditioning for sports should be as specific to the activity as possible, NFL coaches like their players to spend most of their training time doing short sprints and strength training when they're not actually practicing specific skills. Given this kind of a program, and the aerobic fitness requirement, how is a balance reached?

First, training for aerobic fitness doesn't necessarily mean you have to run long distances. When the Green Bay Packers arrive at the team's training facility after the offseason, they start out with only one lap around a quarter-mile track.

"For big guys, that is distance," says Packers strength coach Virgil Knight. "I'm not in favor of having 280-pound linemen running long distances because with their bulk, the pounding can lead to injuries. But I am in favor of them being in condition."

The Browns' Redding says his players spend much of the off-season doing long, slow distance work, either running or working out on a rowing machine, bike, or Stairmaster (a self-powered treadmill that is like walking up the down escalator). "They give me twenty to thirty minutes three days a week in the first few weeks," he explains. "We want to build up endurance and get body fat down."

*anaerobic running*

NFL teams switch into anaerobic running as the playing season gets closer. They feel that once an aerobic base has been established, the players need to work on specific running skills that will be used in game situations. Such skills are honed in drills that include shuttle runs and intervals. Shuttle runs require players to run 6 to 10 dashes in succession for 20 to 110 yards, with only the time it takes to walk back to the starting line for recovery. Intervals are similar, generally done on a track, with sprints of one lap or less followed by the same distance or less of walking or jogging until another anaerobic sprint begins. The interval distances become shorter but more intense, and the rest periods briefer as training proceeds.

The jog and stride is an adaptation of a Scandinavian training program called *fartlek*, or speed play, which combines the aerobic workout of distance running with the anaerobic conditioning of intervals. In fartlek, the athlete starts out on a distance run of at least three miles at a slow pace, which serves as a warm-up. He then selects a distance to sprint. It can be as informal as deciding to sprint to the next road sign or to run hard in the shade and jog in the sunny patches. Or the session can be more structured, like jog and stride, with a set distance for sprinting and another period for recovery while running more slowly. In any case, the idea is to make building sprint strength and raising aerobic capacity seem like play.

# Team Running Programs

Aerobic workout plans of NFL teams are as different as their uniforms. But they all serve the same purpose: to condition players for the aerobic endurance they'll need to play at maximum effort for all 60 minutes of every game for an entire season. Following are three examples of NFL aerobic programs.

### Kansas City Chiefs

At Kansas City, the aerobics program lasts a minimum of four weeks. It includes two to three miles of jogging for three or four days a week. The pace is just fast enough to keep the pulse of a young player at 140 to 160 beats per minute for about 25 minutes, no matter his size. That translates to about eight to twelve minutes per mile, depending on the distance being run.

Experienced runners may find that pace and distance rather

modest. But football players tend to burn out after short distances because their quick muscle fibers are more developed. On the other hand, when the team's running program switches to more anaerobic workouts with repeated sprints, very few distance runners would be able to keep up the pace.

As soon as the Chiefs have their distance training finished, they are asked to include some "striding" in their distance runs. They jog 200 yards and then run 200 yards before jogging another 200 yards and so on until the run is completed.

"The important thing is that there is no rest period over the entire distance," says C.T. Hewgley, the Chiefs' conditioning coach. coach. "The jog and stride sequence prepares the body for intense efforts after short recovery periods. The athlete begins to train through the pain threshold and develop mental toughness."

In the third stage of the Chiefs' endurance program, players run full speed at distances of 110 to 220 yards with short rests between sprints. "The rest should be at least thirty seconds so the heart can completely recover and fill with blood," Hewgley says, "but ninety seconds is too much because it allows the heart rate to drop below a level which allows any endurance gain."

### Pittsburgh Steelers

Pittsburgh has an entirely different philosophy about running. Conditioning and training coach Evans says his players spend six to eight weeks early in the year developing their aerobic endurance.

*distance incentives*

They run three or four days a week, taking up to 30 minutes to do a circuit of as long as four miles. How does Evans get players who don't like distance running to follow through?

"We don't run them on a track," he says. "We run them through the city. We have different courses mapped out so that running becomes the kind of challenge each player needs."

From Three Rivers Stadium, just across the river from downtown Pittsburgh, the Steelers have access to bridges, narrow old streets, waterfront paths, and parks within a few minutes run from the locker room. "By going through the city and over bridges the players see things that are interesting and they see people," Evans explains. "That way it isn't such drudgery. We also can program in a certain amount of resistance by having them go up and down hills."

### Washington Redskins

Washington doesn't do its aerobic conditioning on city streets or on a track. Redskins players run mainly on treadmills in the team's air-conditioned training facility. According to conditioning coach Riley, the treadmill is simply a convenience for the coaching staff so they can continuously monitor the players' heart rates during the 20-minute workouts.

"Big guys find that if they tune into their heart rates, they don't have to run as fast as they thought to stimulate the training of the cardiovascular system," Riley says. As do most other coaches, Riley urges his players to work at the upper end of their capabilities during training, a full 85 percent of maximum heart rate. "Aerobics is like any other form of exercise," he adds. "If you want to increase the fitness level you have to increase the intensity."

## Playing Hot and Cold

Playing football in the NFL is a little like learning meteorology the hard way. From torrid Tampa Bay in August to the frozen turf of Green Bay in December, the weather extremes tax a team's adaptability. There's no choice on game day if the weather is bad except to go out and play. But during practice, teams have developed some common sense rules for dealing with heat and cold that apply to any athlete.

Never work out in rubber or plastic suits that don't allow air to circulate. Some of these "sauna" suits are promoted as quick weight reducers, which they are. The body overheats because it can't cool normally through perspiration. So the body perspires even more. The result is a severe loss of body fluids that shows up as a big weight reduction. A pint of water weighs about a pound, and a big man could easily lose two to five pounds in one sweating session. However, the weight all pours back on as soon as he drinks fluids. The body is dehydrated and stressed by such forced heating. And such suits not only are dangerous, they don't help burn off any more fat. In fact, because the heat stress interferes with natural cooling, the aerobic effect of any workout that's being done in a non-breathable suit actually is reduced.

*drink enough water*

During workouts in hot weather, as much water as possible should be taken in to prevent dehydration. The body's perspiration mechanism is its chief cooling system. If there is not enough fluid in the body, sweating will be reduced and overheating and heat exhaustion may result. Stop exercising if you start to hyperventilate or feel dizzy, especially in humid weather when the natural cooling process of sweating is less efficient. Keep the head covered in the sun and wear loose fitting clothes such as fishnet jerseys, or tie shirts up to expose more skin for better cooling. During football games, players make ample use of cold towels when on the bench and take helmets off on the sidelines.

*dress in layers*

Cold weather brings its own set of problems, primarily frostbite, hypothermia, and stiffness. Wear thin layers of clothing and be sure they aren't so tight they cut circulation. Keep your head, groin, and armpits warm; they tend to lose heat most quickly. Because cold muscles are more prone to injury, it is even more important than usual to warm up and stretch completely during cold weather workouts. Cold air in the lungs may be painful in extreme weather, but it isn't harmful. Frostbite, however, can be a more serious problem. Mentally monitor your extremities to be sure they still have feeling.

The Oilers play home games in the constant temperature of the Astrodome. But they have a strategy for playing outdoors in the cold that helps them adapt. "Warm up inside and get the body really working before you go out into the cold," Houston's Watterson advises. "You may never get warm if you run outside because the blood is used to protect vital parts from the cold and never gets fully into the muscles."

# *Broncs on Bikes*

*Denver quarterback John Elway drops back behind the protection of guard Keith Bishop (54) and the offensive line.*

Quarterback John Elway is working hard, deftly avoiding collisions and outrunning a hulking lineman, showing off the kind of mobility and quickness that helped him lead the Denver Broncos to Super Bowl XXI.

But Elway and the lineman, his own teammate guard-center Keith Bishop, are not on a football field. It's springtime in the Rockies and they're pedaling mountain bikes up a rugged ski trail, dodging potholes and rocks.

They are having fun, though the main reason for the ride is to improve aerobic conditioning. "I can't stand to run," says the 265-pound Bishop, "but I enjoy riding the bike." So, during the offseason before training camp begins, Bishop and Elway take their families and their equipment to Vail, Colorado, to work out amidst the mountain scenery.

"Mountain biking always is an adventure when you're with Keith," says Elway. "It's a heck of a good time, and it's better on the body than some other exercise. There's no pounding on the joints. You get a good workout and it's more fun than running."

At 8,000 feet, the air is thin and any exertion makes the cardiovascular system strain. Pumping up a dirt road that gains 3,000 vertical feet in only three miles is a tough morning's exercise. Trying to make that climb in an hour, with the added ballast of a 28-pound mountain bike, requires enormous stamina.

Bishop is only two-thirds of the way up the trail by the time Elway reaches the 11,000-foot level, ready to stretch and enjoy the view.

"At my weight, that ride up the mountain is really hard," Bishop says. "It's a constant climb with no flat spots. But I just keep going, even if I have to slow down." As he passes the 10,000-foot elevation, the thin air and constant exertion make his lungs ache. "But the benefits are tremendous," says Bishop. "You get much more development because of the altitude factor. That's why I think more and more guys on the team will be doing this to get into offseason aerobic condition."

More than a dozen Broncos became mountain bikers after Bishop began using his heavy-duty, 18-speed machine. "When I bought it, they all looked at me because it was so expensive," Bishop says. "But pretty soon there were guys doing their aerobics on bikes instead of jogging."

Though jogging for at least 30 minutes several times a week is a good way to maintain cardiovascular fitness, many NFL coaches feel running distances puts too much stress on the feet and lower legs of big men. The latter was the case for Bishop, especially after his knee was injured in a scrimmage pile-up several years ago.

Broncos offensive lineman Mark Cooper was one of the team members impressed by Bishop's bike. "I bought one because I'd just had knee surgery and I couldn't run or do squats," Cooper says. "I was afraid that by the time training camp opened I'd be so far behind I wouldn't be able to keep up. So I rode the bike a lot and by the time I was able to run again, I found my aerobic condition was good enough to just move right in at my old position."

Other non-impact aerobic conditioning methods, such as swimming, exercise bicycles, and rowing machines often are substituted for running, particularly by players such as Bishop and Cooper who must rehabilitate or protect injured knees and ankles. But many athletes find those activities boring or inconvenient.

"I always liked the idea, but I could never find a bike strong enough to hold up under me," says Bishop. Ordinary ten-speed bikes with their skinny tires and lightweight frames don't work well for big men who are accustomed to running over obstacles, not going around them.

Mountain bikes, however, are designed specifically to withstand shocks, rocks, stumps, and bumps. The straight handlebars are designed and positioned for maximum control; the rider sits up straight, not hunched over in the traditional racer's stance. The seats quickly can be raised to provide more powerful leg action uphill, or lowered to allow better balance for riding downhill. They've got brakes engineered to hold on long, steep hills. And, most important for the Broncos, mountain bikes are made with reinforced alloy frames, sturdy wheels, and fat, knobby tires that can hold up under the pounding of an off-road trail as well as the poundage of an offensive tackle.

Even so, the bikes are not totally immune to NFL-style punishment. Bishop remembers that the last time he pedaled the 52-mile round trip from his home in suburban Englewood to the Broncos' training facility in Denver, "I had three flat tires." That's when he began questioning the wisdom of bicycle-commuting.

But it wasn't the flat tires, or even the danger from dodging downtown traffic, that finally convinced Bishop to confine his aerobic bicycling to parks and mountainsides. The reason he stopped commuting was that all his aerobic exercise was burning off so many calories that he was getting too slim to provide pass protection for his mountain biking buddy Elway.

# 3 A Flexible Approach:

## *Warm-Ups, Stretching, and Agility*

New York Jets' wide receiver Al Toon was involved in a play last season that graphically illustrates why it is so crucial to be flexible and resilient. Coming over the middle on an obvious passing down, he leaped two feet in the air, reached backwards, and somehow managed to twist his wrists enough to get both hands on the ball. Just as the ball touched Toon's fingers, he was hit by two defenders coming from opposite directions. He was knocked upward and sideways at the same time, his feet flopping in one direction while his head was pushed the other. Remarkably, Toon held on to the ball, even after he slammed into the turf with yet another defender applying a hit to his ribs in an effort to dislodge the ball. Jets fans held their breath, fearing their deep receiving threat might be badly hurt. But as the officials cleared the pileup, Toon bounced up and trotted back to the huddle.

What makes for that kind of resilience? Strength, training, conditioning, experience, and, most of all, flexibility. Like other NFL athletes, Toon has coordinated his strength program with one geared to improving and maintaining flexibility. He lifts weights to develop strength and stretches to keep muscles loose. In addition, he runs agility drills that toughen the ligaments that hold joints together. As a result, every joint in his body glides through its full range of motion protected by tough and pliable muscles, tendons, and ligaments.

Non-professionals, especially younger athletes, consider the limbering-up process to be so obvious that they never learn how to do it properly. They stretch too little, too much, or at the wrong time. In fact, many coaches maintain that more people are hurt by stretching wrong than by not stretching enough.

# Stretching for Results

The objective of pre-exercise stretching is to keep muscles elastic, prepare for rapid movement, and smooth the transition into all-out effort.

*stretching specificity*

Your conditioning program should include flexibility routines that are compatible with your overall goals. If you are a bodybuilder, stretch out muscles shortened by high intensity lifts. A skier will do more stretching of the lower body muscle groups that get a workout on the hill; a tennis player should develop flexibility in the shoulders, and in the oblique and abdominal muscles that are involved in twisting motions.

It is essential to stretch if you're involved in burst activities such as football, baseball, soccer, running, skiing, racket sports, or cycling. These sports with their brief periods of strenuous exertion often leave the muscles tight and painfully stiff. Anyone who has failed to stretch after the winter's first day of skiing or the season's first touch-football game may recall waking up the next morning feeling stiff and sore.

But stretching is more than just a way to reduce soreness. It helps players to perform better.

"Players have to be flexible to do what we ask them to do," says Walt Evans, strength and conditioning coach of the Pittsburgh Steelers. "If you can't get low in your stance and jam the opponent, there is no way you can play this game."

The need for a limber body also is vital for skill players who aren't involved in much heavy blocking and tackling. "Wide receivers with good shoulder flexibility are quicker to get their hands up where they should be," Evans says. "And if quarterbacks are not flexible they get rotator-cuff problems or back injuries. On the other hand, if players are flexible, their bodies have resilience and they get fewer muscle strains."

Flexibility is so important that many teams are making it a factor that is judged, measured like speed in the 40-yard dash or weight capacity on bench presses.

While recognizing that different bodies have different flexibility parameters, Pittsburgh nevertheless has established some standards for hamstring, shoulder, and back flexibility that all players are expected to achieve.

"We have a sit-and-reach box that shows the flexibility of their hamstrings," Evans says. "Players sit on the floor with a box up against the soles of their shoes. A yardstick fastened to the top of the box measures how far the player can reach beyond his toes. An inch or two is average, three to four inches is considered good, and five inches or more is excellent.

"This test correlates very well with hamstring problems that can show up later in the season. If players don't hit the norms for flexibility in this test, we don't let them run sprints until they do."

As a result of the flexibility tests and an increased emphasis on stretching, the Steelers have suffered fewer injuries. "In 1984, when we started the program," Evans says, "we didn't have one hamstring problem and the few we have had since, we think, are a result of artificial turf."

---

## What Stretching Does

Chargers' strength and conditioning coach Phil Tyne, who co-authored the book *Total Stretching*, lists these reasons why stretching aids performance:

- It makes tendons and ligaments more elastic.
- It reduces the thickness of muscle fluids (the same way warming up the oil in a car's engine works).
- It mobilizes the blood in the muscles and generates heat.
- It begins bringing lubricants into the joints to prepare for rapid movements.
- It starts a gradual increase in cardiovascular activity so the system won't be shocked when exercise begins.

---

# Warming Up by the Rules

The same principles of gaining and maintaining flexibility that guide NFL players apply to all of us. They're summarized in the following three basic rules.

**Rule 1: Warm up before you stretch.** NFL players jog and toss the ball around before they begin actual stretching. San Diego's Tyne says about 10 minutes of light exercise will raise body temperature enough to make muscle fibers pliable.

*stretching too soon*

Over-eager runners sometimes make the mistake of stretching too soon. They drive to a track or park, get out of the car, stretch hard for five minutes, and then take off at full speed. Hard stretching without warming up first actually may do more harm than good because it can tear muscle fibers instead of stretching them. Muscle is a little like taffy candy in the way it reacts to temperature changes. When cold, it is stiff. Warmed up, the muscle, like the taffy, is much more easily stretched. To minimize the odds of getting hurt, runners should jog slowly for a half mile or so to warm up before stretching.

Slow joggers don't have to warm up first. They just need to start gradually, then pick up the pace after five or ten minutes. Because jogging puts less stress on the joints, some experts feel stretching is necessary only after a workout.

For athletes involved in explosive movements, stretching is strongly recommended before a workout or competition. After a warm-up and a complete stretching session, get right into the workout. Don't let your body cool down again by talking or waiting around for a machine or a barbell to become available.

Look on the sidelines during any football game and watch the kickers. Although they may not have to go in for some time, they always are warming up, stretching and staying prepared for the sudden call to perform. At a track meet, sprinters, shot putters, and high jumpers spend more time in warm-ups and stretching than in their actual events.

**Rule 2: Stretch *after* the exercise as well.** This may be more important than pre-workout stretching because stretching promotes blood flow. A 10-minute session after a workout helps to remove metabolic residue that can cause soreness and stiffness. Because muscles are more pliable after exercise, you can make more progress in extending the range of motion of normally tight joints.

Unless muscles are lengthened after a hard workout has contracted them, the fibers will be shorter the next day, thus limiting range of motion. That's one of the reasons bodybuilders developed a reputation for being "muscle-bound." Without a good post-workout stretch, the next session of any exercise will be slowed by having to work through tight muscles.

**Rule 3: Don't force anything.** Don't bounce or try to stretch so far it hurts. It's okay to feel a little tightness, but if you feel pain in a muscle or joint, you're trying too hard or there's something wrong. "It should not be a personal contest to see how far you can stretch," warns Bob Anderson in his book, *Stretching*. NFL coaches agree that stretching should be tailored to each athlete's muscular structure, flexibility, and varying tension levels. "The object," writes Anderson, "is to reduce muscular tension . . . not to concentrate on attaining extreme flexibility, which often leads to over-stretching and injury."

# Static, Dynamic, and PNF Stretching

There are four recognized types of stretching, all designed to lengthen muscles and loosen joints: ballistic, static, dynamic, and PNF (for "proprioceptive neuromuscular facilitation").

*stretch, don't bounce*

Researchers rule out anyone using the ballistic stretch. Ballistic stretching is the bouncy toe touching that some kids were taught in high school, the object being to lunge as far as possible to get a more extreme stretch. It isn't recommended for anyone because bouncing beyond the normal range of motion is dangerous.

Ballistic stretching actually causes muscles to tighten up. Muscle fibers have sensors that warn the brain whenever they are in danger of over-stretching. These muscle sensors are called "spindles." They sense when a muscle has stretched too far or too fast and send a signal to stop. The signal takes the form of pain and an involuntary contraction.

*static stretching*

Static stretching is done very slowly and gently so as not to cause a contraction of the muscle being stretched. To do it properly, stretch the muscle until tension is felt and then stop. Don't stretch so far that you feel pain. By easing off the stretch before feeling pain, the spindles don't signal for contraction. Your muscle relaxes and it lengthens. The muscle has stretched when you are in the same position but the tension has eased, which generally happens in about 30 to 60 seconds. Stretch again until you feel tension, then relax once more.

*dynamic stretching*

Dynamic stretching is a combined warm-up and stretch. It starts out with very gentle swinging motions of the limbs and gets more vigorous as the muscles get limber. It is favored by track and field athletes and by dancers. Dynamic stretching simultaneously warms, loosens, and rehearses movements by specific muscle groups. As with static stretching, the idea is to increase the range of motion gradually so the spindles are not activated.

*PNF stretching*

PNF stretching tricks the spindles into relaxing by contracting the muscle for a few seconds in the *opposite* direction of the desired stretch. The concept is tricky to understand without an actual demonstration. But, in essence, it works by circumventing the spindles by doing their job for them—you voluntarily resist a stretch by pushing against a force trying to stretch the muscle.

Most PNF exercises require stretching partners to apply the force you must resist. For example, while lying on your back on the floor, instead of pulling your leg toward your head for a hamstring stretch, you would have your partner hold the leg in the stretched position while you resist him. By trying to push your leg out of the stretched position, you are contracting the muscle you want to stretch. Sensing the voluntary contraction, the spindles are inactivated. But after resisting for a few seconds, you relax and the stretch occurs almost automatically.

"PNF stretching allows joints to achieve a greater range of motion than other methods," Tyne says. "And tricking the spindles doesn't cause any damage, because they signal for an involuntary contraction long before the muscles actually are in any danger of tearing."

*breathe while stretching*

In all stretching exercises, it is important to breathe slowly and easily. That helps keep the body relaxed, which is a necessary condition for complete stretching.

And remember to stay within the limits of your own body. "There have been loose-jointed athletes and tight-jointed athletes, and both have been successful," says Clyde Emrich, Chicago's strength and conditioning coach. "It's a matter of style and adaptation. Don't try to stretch as much as the loose-jointed athlete, if you are not, just because he can do it easily. If you over-stretch, you can injure yourself. You've got to go with what nature gives you and not try to be something you are not."

Almost all NFL conditioning coaches agree that no matter

whether you are loose- or tight-jointed, some kind of stretching is important. As for which is best—dynamic, static, or PNF—most NFL coaches use them all depending on what works best in a particular situation.

Redskins strength and conditioning coach Dan Riley takes a philosophical approach. "Like everything else, there is no one, magic stretch," he says. "The main thing is to organize a series of exercises that stretch all the major muscle groups: Achilles, hamstrings, back, groin, hip flexors, and quads."

*make your own program*

How you program your stretches is up to you. Many NFL teams believe that having variety in stretching helps players stay interested longer. Don Clemons, the strength coach at Detroit, holds a different opinion. "We do the same stretches each time," says Clemons. "We start at the top and work our way down the body. That way, the team has done the routine so many times that when each player goes home and works out in the offseason, he will remember what to do and continue getting the benefits that stretching provides."

# Another Angle on Stretching

In Cincinnati, strength coach Kim Wood doesn't have a formal stretching program. But he does agree that the body must be limber and warm prior to any workouts or competition. Wood believes the critical need is to combine strength and flexibility, not to concentrate strictly on flexibility. "What we want to do is increase the structural integrity of the major joints," he says.

Wood's players stretch by doing warm-ups that rehearse the workouts they're about to begin. The warm-ups and accompanying calisthenics involve exercising all the joints and muscles in the same way they will be used in the workout or game.

Bengals players are free to do additional stretches, but Wood insists that they participate in the team warm-ups that precede weight training, drills, and games. And he is unswerving in enforcing attendance in the weight room and at running workouts. "The important idea is to get each player prepared in whatever way you can," says Wood. "Football training really is more art than science."

Without a formal flexibility program, how has Cincinnati's injury rate compared with the rest of the NFL? The Bengals' record over the years ranks among the best, right along with some teams that do extensive stretching. But that should not be surprising because Wood's approach assures his players have good flexibility and full strength before they exercise.

Even a maverick such as Wood, who dislikes what he considers faddishness about flexibility, concedes there is a place for formal stretching programs. "It would be wise," he says, "for older athletes, weekend players, or those who are recovering from injury to have a

## The DOMS Syndrome

Every athlete has experienced soreness after exercise. But have you noticed that many times it takes more than 24 hours for the soreness to set in? You may feel great after a hard workout, even the first one following a long lay-off from exercise. Then, whammo, two days later you barely can walk. That latent muscular pain is called the "DOMS" syndrome (for delayed-onset muscle soreness).

There have been three physiological theories advanced to explain what causes DOMS. The first of these, lactic acid build-up, has lost favor because lactic acid levels in muscles don't stay high enough long enough to cause such pain. Another theory, ischemia (inadequate blood flow) caused by muscle spasms has been discarded because research results can't be duplicated. That leaves the last theory, microscopic tears in muscle tissue, and resultant inflammation and fluid accumulation, which result from performing unaccustomed exercise. This is the theory currently in vogue among exercise physiologists.

Interestingly, studies have shown that movements that lengthen muscles ("eccentric contractions") cause more DOMS than those that shorten muscles ("concentric contractions").

Is there anything you can do to prevent or alleviate DOMS? Not much, it seems. Stretching can help prior to exercise. So can aspirin and massage afterward. Some experts say working out temporarily relieves the pain. But if you're like most people, that will be the last thing you want to do.

checklist they follow to be sure that everything gets stretched out before they do any exercise."

## The Injury Correlation

Dr. Donald Chu, director of the Ather Sports Injury Clinic in Castro Valley, California, uses a battery of strength and flexibility tests to predict how athletes will perform in competitive situations. His tests help evaluate athletes for college and professional teams, including the Detroit Lions.

Chu has strong views on how flexibility influences a player's ability to perform. "Unless an athlete has a full range of normal motion in the major joints," he says, "he is much more likely to suffer a disabling injury."

*stretch for safety* According to Chu, the normal range of motion for the neck means being able to turn fully enough to touch each shoulder with the chin. A player who can turn his head only halfway around toward his shoulder is at greater risk of injury than someone who can touch his chin on his shoulder. The reason, Dr. Chu explains, is that if the player with good flexibility and normal range of motion has his head twisted around to his shoulder during a play, his muscles will not be over-stretched. But the same play could cause a player with a stiffer, less flexible neck a problem. If the twisting force is strong enough, his head will be pushed beyond the neck muscle's limit. Three results are possible, all of them bad: the muscle will tear to accommodate the movement; a ligament or tendon will tear or weaken; or a bone could chip or break.

# Agility Ability

To most people, agility means deft, quick, and easy movements. To football players, agility has a more specific definition. Houston's co-ordinator of strength and rehabilitation, Steve Watterson, says "football agility involves rapid movement, change of direction, acceleration, stopping, falling, balance, and body control."

The Oilers' agility drills are designed to condition players in those game skills. Linemen shuffle sideways as fast as they can, reversing direction every five yards or on command. Running backs practice 10-yard explosive sprints. Quarterbacks rehearse agility skills specific to their position, such as drops. They repeat the techniques of the three-, five-, and seven-step drop over and over, taking a snap, running backwards for the precise number of steps, and stretching to a throwing stance. The agility inherent in that maneuver has to be practiced to the point of being automatic because in a game situation the quarterback must unerringly adjust to divots in the grass, seams in the artificial turf, and blitzing linebackers in the backfield while he is looking downfield for an open receiver.

Football-specific drills such as drops and shuffles don't provide much benefit to athletes who surf, ski, or play racquetball. However, there are agility drills used in the NFL that contribute to development of speed, flexibility, and the ability to accelerate and change direction. To the extent they augment overall conditioning, they are useful in any sport.

*spring ahead, fall back*

An increasingly popular agility drill in the NFL involves a recent addition to the exercise repertoire called *plyometrics*. Plyometrics work out the muscles and nerve pathways involved in bounding and jumping. These exercises use the stretch reflex to increase leaping ability. The basic idea is to hit the ground and jump back instantly, almost as if the muscles were made of springs. The theory is that when a muscle is stretched quickly by landing, the spindles signal for a contraction to protect the muscle from over-stretching. By exploiting that reflex, more muscle fibers can be recruited for a rebound leap, and more power is generated. In football, plyometrics are used to improve a running back's ability to hurdle linemen or a receiver's ability to leap for a pass. The same conditioning theory works for basketball players, skiers, high jumpers, or any athlete who needs the agility to spring and explode into action.

Cincinnati's Wood doubts the value of plyometrics and fears it may cause injury to large, heavy athletes. San Diego's Tyne agrees that not everyone should try plyometrics. But when he helped train the U.S. Olympic Volleyball team, Tyne says, "We achieved tremendous increases in vertical jumping—sometimes as much as four inches. But you want to do it very carefully and not at every workout. You also want to be sure that it is done on padded surfaces, and with lots of rest between sets."

Atlanta's strength and conditioning coordinator, Tim Jorgensen, says NFL teams spend practice time on agility drills because they improve game performance. "The ultimate objective," he says, "is to improve the quickness and reaction time of each particular player. We do that by working on body control and coordination. They work on combative-type movements against each other and they practice reacting fast. To help speed their reaction times, we run drills where they run or jump one way or another depending on a sight or a sound."

Having superior agility often can overcome the advantage of greater strength or weight. "That's why two-hundred-twenty-pound linebackers can stuff two-hundred-fifty-pound linemen," says Jorgensen. "The more agile player gets in a mechanical advantage position. An agile guy can beat a stronger guy because he can use better technique."

The Steelers' Evans thinks agility drills help linemen develop quick hands to get inside an opponent's shoulders where they need to be in order to control him. To practice agility, the Steelers sometimes become stealers. "We'll go down to the Pirates' locker room and get out some baseballs and have our guys field grounders," says Evans. "We put out ten or fifteen balls and have guys field them. It gets them low and develops eye-hand coordination. We also have basketball and softball teams during offseason, and some guys study martial arts."

*dance steps*

Teams such as the Steelers and Rams also have enrolled players in aerobic dance classes, or have held them at team facilities. "Most of the players like it," Evans says. "They have a good time and it loosens up their bodies."

A few players have tried ballet dancing. Wide receiver Lynn Swann of the Steelers made the idea acceptable to macho football players years ago and now Jets wide receiver Toon is continuing that tradition. Ballet is a demanding activity that requires extreme strength, flexibility, agility, body control, and balance. For a world-class dancer, just accomplishing a tremendous leap on stage isn't enough, it has to look as though he isn't even trying.

# Do It Yourself

*work to your goals*

In designing your own agility drills, it's important to develop programs that fit specifically into your conditioning goals. For example, a baseball player might include eye-hand agility drills in his conditioning package, while a soccer player would be more interested in coordinating movements of the feet, legs, and head.

A boxing speed-bag is a good way to develop coordination and build endurance in the upper body. Most NFL teams have punching bags in their training rooms because they promote the kind of rhythmic and repeated movements that increase agility, especially for linemen.

*jumping rope*    One of the best all-around agility exercises is jumping rope. Skipping for 15 minutes is a tremendous aerobic workout and helps develop "quick and light" feet. According to Detroit's Clemons, jumping rope "is especially useful for the bigger athlete who needs to develop quickness." He recommends concentrating on landing softly and bounding up off the toes. Crashing down flat-footed doesn't promote a quick bound and a light step and therefore can be just as likely to cause leg injuries as long-distance running.

To make the rope-jumping exercise more agility-intensive, add crossovers of the hands, double jumps, backward steps, and one-leg skips to your routine. Clemons notes that heavy jumping can be an extremely tiring activity, so he suggests beginners do three sets of five minutes and then extend the time as endurance builds.

A favorite college football drill is running through a horizontal rope ladder strung a foot above the grass. It is excellent for improving foot dexterity and eye-foot coordination. Lacking a rope maze or a series of rubber tires to run through, foot agility can be improved by running down a line and crossing feet over, landing the right foot on the left side of the line and the left foot on the right.

Cross-country running is a good agility builder as well, particularly if there are obstacles such as rocks, tree roots, and logs along the trail. Athletes who are (quite rightly) concerned with potential accidents from trail running and rock-hopping, can get the same kind of workout on a grassy field with much less risk.

*designing agility*  Plastic cones make good course markers for agility exercises.
*drills*    They don't cause injuries or get broken when accidentally hit during drills, and they are inexpensive and easily available. Depending on your sport, they can be arranged to improve the skills that will be needed. For skiing, line up cones in a straight line and run through them, alternating sides. Put them closer together to simulate slalom runs or offset them to get more of a downhill course.

Put four cones in a box shape, with perhaps five to seven yards on a side, and sprint from one to the other in a predetermined pattern, pivoting around some, touching and reversing direction at others, and simply rounding inside or outside of others. Start with 30-second routines and work up to a minute at full speed.

The patterns of drills that can be designed with cones or other equipment is limited only by your imagination. But, like any other conditioning exercise, agility drills are productive only to the extent that they are performed at full intensity.

# *Bill Bates: One Tough Cowboy*

Dallas conditioning coach Bob Ward calls Cowboy Center "probably the best facility in the world for training sportsmen."

The center contains a quarter of an acre of outdoor weight training equipment, a posh locker room, a giant whirlpool spa, and a half-mile running track.

What sets the track apart are the options, among them: an up-and-down section to work muscles that don't get exercised on a standard flat surface, eight Universal exercise machine stations spotted around the periphery, and a 50-foot sand pit that helps strengthen calves and ankles.

The Cowboys and Ward have been in the vanguard of new football training concepts for a long time, particularly in the areas of agility, flexibility, and speed.

"Cowboy Center is like a salad bar," Ward says. "We have so many workout modalities that if someone comes here and says he is bored, then he'd have a real problem with *any* conditioning program."

Bill Bates, the Cowboys' hard-hitting safety and special teams captain, is an example of development through training.

"Bates came to us running a 4.7 forty," Ward says. "After devoting himself to the conditioning program, he runs a 4.5."

Ward attributes much of Bates's improvement to a couple of gadgets that are designed to improve speed and running strength. One is a Sprint Master machine that tows players on a rope so they can run faster than normal. The other, which holds them back, also on the end of a rope, is called a Power Cam.

Bates came to Dallas in 1983 as a free-agent from Tennessee. He immediately impressed the coaches with his hustle and his hitting. He's still impressing them, still hustling and trying to get better every season. Bates works out all year long, Monday through Saturday, starting

*Bill Bates's hard work pays off on the field.*

every day at 8:30 A.M. He does this because he's a professional athlete; his job depends on his being in top physical condition. Most non-pros would find Bates's regimen too rigorous and intensive.

Like most pro athletes, Bates starts his training sessions with a warm-up—a half-mile jog around the Cowboys' track. Then he starts a full 20-minute stretching routine that he also does on game days.

"I'll reach over and touch my toes and hold that for a count of ten," Bates says. "Then I'll cross my feet and touch my toes again to isolate the stretch on each leg."

After the toe touching, he performs backwards roll-overs, which involve lying on his back with his legs so far back over his head that he can touch his feet on the grass behind him.

Then he sits with his legs straight out in front of him and grabs his feet, trying each time to extend his stretch and hold for a count of 10. Bates stretches far enough to feel a strain, but not so much that there is pain.

He then spreads his legs wide and reaches out for more toe touching. In this position, the hamstring muscles of each leg can be stretched individually. That done, he brings his feet in toward his crotch and gently, but firmly, pushes his knees to the floor. This series works out the groin area, a vulnerable muscle group often neglected in flexibility drills.

Next Bates does a back roll that lands him in a semi-split. After holding that position for a count of 10, he'll duck walk forward and backward on his heels to complete the groin stretch and the session.

"Then I'm ready for my workout," Bates says.

His workout pattern is three days of weight training a week and alternating days of running and agility drills. He prepares a written set of goals for each day's exercises. "My idea is that I'll make it challenging and do the routines with everything I've got," he says. "If my body gives out before I finish all the reps, I'll just quit rather than do the rest of them halfway."

When Bates works on quickness, he concentrates mainly on running exercises that improve flexibility, strength, and neuromuscular control. Bates credits some of the improvement in his speed to a videotaped running analysis that revealed some minor flaws in his form. The rest of his speed improvement came from increased flexibility and working out with the Power Cam and Sprint Loading machines about which coach Ward is so enthusiastic.

Fast runners have flexible legs that allow them a long, powerful stride. To assure that his legs stay flexible, Bates does a series of agility drills.

He starts with 50-yard runs at moderate speed. He does four sets of four runs. Each set exaggerates a specific running motion: straight

bounding, butt kicks, outside leg bounding, and across-the-body bounding. The bounding exercises make Bates look like a kangaroo on the track; he accentuates the push-off by actually leaping into the air on each step. The objective is to help lengthen the stride and develop strength in the push-off motion.

The "butt kick" runs are designed to limber up the quadriceps with backward leg swings so extreme they kick the buttocks on each stride.

After those 16 loosening-up dashes, he is ready for a running-form drill. It consists of 10 all-out sprints of 100 yards, each time trying to concentrate on a particular technique. The techniques are full backswing, lifting knees, pulling through on the power stroke with the leg extended, and bounding.

"You work on one technique each sprint," Bates says. "Run a hundred yards, then walk fifty yards to recover, and then sprint another hundred yards." He takes a five-minute breather and then heads for the last exercise.

"I do the speed work first, before I'm tired out, so I can concentrate on good form," he says. "Then I'll go to the Power Cam to finish so I'm totally exhausted at the end."

With the Power Cam, Bates straps on a wide belt attached to a rope. The rope is wound around a drum that has a variable braking action. He sets the brake for heavy resistance on the first set and then sprints away for 50 yards, pulling against the rope and running as fast as he can, and with the best form. The rope pulls loose from the drum at the end. Then he walks back, rewinds the rope, and does it again, usually reducing the load each time so he can maintain good form even as his muscles become fatigued.

On alternate days, Bates hooks himself to the SprintMaster for overspeed training. This time the rope will pull him forward much faster than he can normally run. That overspeed exercise, similar to running full-tilt down a gentle hill, trains the neuromuscular system so it can coordinate the muscles that have been strength-

*Cowboy Center is one of the best equipped, most up-to-date training complexes in the world.*

ened by the Power Cam exercises.

What's the payoff for all that effort? "There have been situations where I'll keep up with the fastest receivers and make interceptions where I know that I couldn't have made the same play a couple of years ago," Bates says. "I wasn't as fast or flexible."

Although he sees tangible results, such as his improvement from 4.7 speed to 4.5, Bates claims that his gains are equally psychological. "I know I'm prepared," he says. "I didn't always have the speed or confidence to cover a guy like Willie Gault [Bears wide receiver], but now I feel that I do. I know I have the physical ability to do the job because I worked out so hard on my skills before the game and even before the season."

Some of the Cowboys train in the martial arts, including esoteric kick boxing, stick fighting, and other Asian fighting skills that aid in building concentration and coordination. Bates attends those classes during the preseason, but doesn't keep it up during the year. He skips the aerobics classes altogether. However, he does find it useful to continue with one of the other agility drills taught by Ward. "I'll get out three five-pound sand bags and do some juggling to keep my coordination going," Bates says.

Bates also keeps up with skill games that sharpen eye/hand coordination. After his intense workouts, he almost always goes looking for a game of handball, racquetball, or tennis—just some friendly competition to finish off the morning.

# 4 Body Fuel:

## *Diet and Nutrition*

Diet is the keystone to fitness. Strength, endurance, as well as such seemingly unrelated things as the ability to relax, all depend on the right nutrients being available in the body at the right time.

The choice is very clear: Eat right and you'll be able to gain strength and endurance. Eat wrong and you'll watch fat accumulate as endurance ebbs away.

But even the best-designed diet alone can't make you muscular. Chewing doesn't substitute for lifting, running, and stretching. Carrots, codfish, and whole-grain cereals can't do the hard work for you.

"There is no magic food that makes a workout any easier," says Jerry Attaway, director of physical conditioning for the San Francisco 49ers. "You still have to strain in the weight room and sweat on the track. It's just that unless you're eating right, you may not make maximum gains."

## How Much Is Enough?

The first step on the road to eating right is tailoring calorie intake to your body's actual needs. As in all tailoring, you must begin by taking good measurements. In losing or gaining weight the critical measurement is finding just how much food you need. The answer depends on your size, age, sex, genes, your level of daily exercise, and a number of other factors, some of which still are not completely understood. Any calorie guide is just an estimate, subject to revision as you evaluate progress.

One of the best quick calorie-estimating guides comes from Ann Grandjean, associate director of the Swanson Centre for Nutrition in Omaha, and chief nutrition consultant to the U.S. Olympic Committee. It's summarized in the box on page 68.

## Calculating Calories the Easy Way

In the chart below, find the activity category that fits you best. Grandjean's levels are Active, Moderate, and Sedentary. The active category is for someone whose job involves regular manual labor or who works out more than an hour a day. Moderate applies to anyone exercising more than half an hour a day or working at a job that requires light physical labor, such as a waitress. You qualify for sedentary if you have a desk job and do less than 20 minutes a day of steady walking, running, or other exertion. Then match your weight and sex with the appropriate activity level to find the approximate number of calories per day you need to maintain current weight.

| Body Weight MEN | 100 Lbs. | 125 Lbs. | 150 Lbs. | 200 Lbs. |
|---|---|---|---|---|
| Sedentary | 1550 | 1938 | 2325 | 3100 |
| Moderate | 1900 | 2375 | 2850 | 3800 |
| Active | 2200 | 2750 | 3300 | 4400 |

| WOMEN | 100 Lbs. | 125 Lbs. | 150 Lbs. | 200 Lbs. |
|---|---|---|---|---|
| Sedentary | 1350 | 1688 | 2025 | 2700 |
| Moderate | 1600 | 2000 | 2400 | 3200 |
| Active | 1800 | 2250 | 2700 | 3600 |

Calorie estimates are calibrated for people with an average amount of body fat. Those with more body fat need fewer calories per pound of total body weight, and lean bodies need more than average, so you may have to adjust total suggested calories three or four percent. For a closer approximation of caloric needs, use the figures in the following chart and multiply by pounds of body weight:

| | WOMEN | MEN |
|---|---|---|
| Sedentary | 13.5 | 15.5 |
| Moderate | 16.0 | 19.0 |
| Active | 18.0 | 22.0 |

# The Home Training Table

Eating right means more than just getting enough calories to fuel the body's engine. A balance of fats, proteins, and carbohydrates must be consumed. An athlete must drink enough water to keep the internal cellular structure sound. There also needs to be a daily supply of vitamins and minerals that keep subtle biochemical and hormonal reactions on track. Without all these elements, energy levels drop, mental and physical health can deteriorate, and long-term health problems may arise.

So what kind of diet is recommended by NFL experts? A well-balanced diet with less fat, less protein, and a lot more complex carbohydrates than the average American eats.

"It's so simple and basic that it's embarrassing," says Dan Riley, conditioning coach for the Redskins. "We want players to eat well-rounded diets with at least sixty percent of the calories coming from carbohydrates, increase the amount of water they drink, and shy away from fats and sugar."

*complex carbohydrates*

The carbohydrates Riley and other NFL coaches are touting are called complex carbohydrates, which include whole-grain bread, cereals, pasta, and fresh vegetables and fruits. They don't recommend loading up on simple carbohydrates such as the sugars found in candies and soft drinks. Simple carbohydrates should be a small portion of the total because they're digested very quickly and can confuse the body's blood sugar system.

A high-carbohydrate diet can be a treat for people who love to eat. Because complex carbohydrates contain only about half the calories of the same quantity of fats, even dieters (provided they exercise regularly) can eat the same quantity of food on which they previously gained weight, but take in a lot fewer—and better—calories.

Someone like former Baltimore Colts guard Art Donovan would have loved it. "I'm a light eater," he once said. "I start eating as soon as it's light."

*diet ratio*

Just about all NFL diet experts agree that carbohydrates should contribute almost two-thirds of the total calories eaten every day. Some favor as much as 70 percent from complex carbohydrates, especially for players trying to lose weight. There's a little less agreement on the ratio of fat to protein. Most experts would like fat trimmed to below 20 percent of total intake; a few recommend the fat level be cut as low as 10 percent. But no one thinks fats should be allowed to get as high as the whopping 40 percent of total caloric intake that today constitutes the average American's diet.

To match the NFL guidelines, your diet should contain from 60 to 65 percent carbohydrates with another 15 to 20 percent each from fat and protein. The league's conditioning coaches agree that the old habit of feeding athletes massive slabs of red meat to build muscle is as dated as the Single-Wing formation.

"We need less than a gram of protein a day for each kilogram of body weight," explains Washington's Riley. "That means a six-ounce piece of chicken gives a big man enough protein for the entire day."

## Making the Cuts

It may be hard to accept that ordinary people should be eating the same kind of diet as the one recommended for heavy-duty athletes such as NFL players. Obviously, there's a great deal of difference between the nutritional needs of a 160-pound lawyer who rides a bike on weekends and a 245-pound linebacker who is training so hard he can lose weight on 5,000 calories a day.

But the body chemistry of the lawyer and linebacker work in the same way and are subject to the same biological laws. Adjusted for body size and activity, the high-carbohydrate diet applies whether you're playing tackle for the New York Giants or working for a giant corporation.

*eat what you need*

Most diet suggestions simply are ideas for matching what you eat to what you really need. "I put it back on the players," says Tim Jorgensen, the strength and conditioning coordinator for the Falcons. "We encourage them to eat more complex carbohydrates because they'll run out of gas faster eating just salad and steak than if they've been putting away pasta and beans."

Players can feel the difference in performance when they're eating right. Buffalo linebacker Jim Haslett started eating breakfast, cutting fat, and boosting carbohydrate consumption because he was having trouble maintaining weight during the offseason. As a result of his new approach to eating, Haslett, who ended the 1985 season at 230 pounds, showed up at training camp five months later weighing 245. What's more, he reduced body fat from 15 percent to 8 percent. "You feel better when you eat right," Haslett says. "I have more energy, even in the fourth quarter, and I'm stronger."

As part of its research for developing a computer diet program now used by several NFL teams, Anjon Sports Conditioning Systems, of South Bend, Indiana, evaluated the diets of thousands of active men and women. "We found the fat content of their diets to average about forty-five percent," reports Bill Anzelc, Anjon's president. An NFL-style diet would include fats equal to less than half that amount.

*reduce fat by half*

Cutting half the fat out of your diet may be more difficult than it sounds. It means sharp cutbacks in fried foods, pepperoni pizza, milk shakes, ice cream, butter, cheese, and gravies. It also means eating red meat and pork only occasionally.

Getting off the fat eating habit will involve some changes in lifestyle. But the benefits are overwhelming. High-fat diets can cause chronic exhaustion, irritability, restlessness, and decreases of muscle tissue plus an increased susceptibility to degenerative diseases such as heart disease, cancer, diabetes, and gout. The old health-food slogan that "you are what you eat" may be at least partly true. There's increasing evidence that eating fat puts fat on the body faster, calorie for calorie, than other foods.

Without a lot of fat cluttering the diet, there's room for better things. For instance, complex carbohydrates boost energy storage in muscles, prolong endurance, and promote repair and growth of muscle tissue. Giving up some of those fatty foods doesn't seem such a sacrifice when you consider some of the recommended carbohydrate alternatives: whole-grain breads and rolls, cereals, pancakes, waffles, French toast, pasta, brown rice, vegetables, fruit, juices, and even some jams and jellies.

Stepping up the intake of fresh produce has the added benefit of providing excellent sources of natural fiber, vitamins, and minerals *drink plenty of water*

as well as contributing to the body's supply of water. More than incidentally, water intake for athletes, especially on high-carbohydrate diets, should be at least six to eight glasses a day. Without plenty of water, players suffer from fatigue, more muscle pulls, a higher body temperature, and experience a deterioration in performance.

*limit sweets and alcohol*

Finally, an NFL-style diet limits sweets and alcohol. Cakes, cookies, candy, soft drinks, and other sweets are made with refined sugar. Many sweets, such as candy bars and cookies, deliver a double dose of trouble because they are high in fat as well as refined sugar.

An occasional beer, glass of wine, or shot of hard liquor won't hurt, especially in an athlete burning off 6,000 or more calories a day. But two or three 150-calorie beers could sack the careful diet plan of a weekend athlete. For both the professional athlete and the average guy, more than moderate use of alcohol hinders reaction time, hand-eye coordination, accuracy, and balance. Beer, wine, and hard liquor also can impair body temperature regulation, decrease strength, speed, and endurance, and slow muscle growth.

While all coaches agree on diet goals, not all teams are willing to dictate what players should eat. "I provide them with the nutrition information that they need," explains Green Bay Packers strength-conditioning coach Virgil Knight, "but I'm not going to spoon feed them." Some other coaches agree that with the tremendous pressures to learn new plays, perfect difficult skills, and perform during games and workouts, piling new diet rules on athletes is just too much.

"We take an educational approach," says Steve Watterson, the Oilers' strength and rehabilitation coordinator. "We use a computer system that displays what each player has been eating and lets the player see for himself which of those things is high in fat and which is high in carbohydrates." The idea is to let each player choose which of his favorite foods will fit the nutritional program he needs, within reason. For example, a player who won't give up steak could still trim fat intake by switching from filet mignon to flank steak, which has about half as much fat per ounce.

Getting professional football players to eat right might seem to be an easy assignment, that they would approach it as just a part of their job. But players are human. Even athletes whose livelihoods depend on being in top shape get bored eating the same things

*stay committed*

week after week. A diet will work only if the dieter sticks with it. Some people can't stay on a diet, no matter what the incentive.

Cincinnati Bengals strength coach Kim Wood remembers a team that had an outstanding lineman who weighed more than 300 pounds and always was having problems making the weights his coach prescribed. "The coach had written into the contract a clause that penalized the player $15,000 if he didn't make weight on a certain day," Wood says. "The night before one weighing, all the player had to do was lose three pounds. He could have done that just by going without breakfast." Instead, the player went out that night and stuffed himself. It turned out to be a very expensive meal.

"If someone wants to lose weight," Wood says, "the motivation has to come from inside him."

It's not always the players who are at fault. Coaches have been known to be foolish about weight, too.

"In judging performance, there is a lot of playing around with numbers," Wood says. "What counts isn't the numbers, it is the art of knowing your personnel." He tells the story of a running back who was, at the time, among the best in the league. He weighed 195 pounds at the end of the season and the coach told him that he'd better not weigh any more when he showed up at training camp.

"The coach had been impressed with some studies that showed that guys the runner's size were best at that weight," says Wood. "So that's what he wanted the guy to be." The player didn't have an eating problem, and in fact had a body-fat percentage of under five percent, extremely low even for championship-level athletes.

Several months later, when the back checked in at training camp, he weighed 210 pounds and the coach threatened him with being cut if the weight didn't come off quickly. "But there wasn't any fat on him," Wood remembers. "He'd been doing strength training and sprints during the offseason and the extra weight was all in lean muscle." But the coach insisted and the player had to go on an extreme diet. Since there was no fat to lose, the weight came off of the muscle mass. "By the time he finished, the guy got down to 195 pounds. But he wasn't as fast at the lighter weight as he was at 210. He never got back to his old form."

For most people, and most football players, diet difficulties revolve around eating too much, too often. Wood remembers still another experience when his head coach asked him to find an overly hefty player during the offseason and take him to an expensive weight-reduction center. "I spent four days in Arkansas trying to find him," Wood says. "When I finally did, the guy agreed to come along to the fat farm. If he didn't, he was going to risk losing a big contract the next season."

At the health center, the player was put on a severely restricted diet that would guarantee substantial reduction in fat. "It was like a cup of rice and a glass of lemon water for breakfast and not much more for lunch and dinner," Wood chuckles. But when the player was weighed after a week on the regimen, he curiously hadn't lost any weight at all.

Several weeks later, Wood drove down to visit the player and talk about the weight-training program that was simultaneous with the diet. The weightlifting was progressing well, but the player had gained five pounds on the restricted diet.

When Wood said he was going to go out for lunch, the player suggested a hamburger restaurant across the street, and offered to walk over and join him. "We walked in there and all the guys from the kitchen came out to greet him. 'Hey, Buddy. You gonna have the usual?' is what they said," Wood recalls. "And the guy just sort of blushed and mumbled 'Nah, just a little cottage cheese.' "

Eventually, that player, like many others whose craving for food overcame their sense of professional responsibility, ate himself out of the league.

The new computerized diet programs may end all that. Because such programs allow players to select their own menus and still stay within calorie and fat intake guidelines, many players may be better able to keep their weight under control.

# Programmed Nutrition

The Houston Oilers use the computerized nutrition program from Anjon Systems. It was co-developed by Rusty Jones before he became conditioning coach of the Buffalo Bills, another team that uses the program. The Anjon program makes it easy to check what each player is eating, show him what he should be eating, and then give him options that appeal to his personal tastes. What makes it work is that it offers so many choices; its data base is so complete it lists the calories and nutrients in things from the most popular brands of breakfast cereals to light beers. Besides the Bills and Oilers, the program also guides diet decisions for players on the 49ers, Browns, and Giants (all three, interestingly, were playoff teams in 1985 and 1986).

*pregame meals*

Elsewhere in the league, players also are switching to high carbohydrate/low fat/low protein diets. The new attitude is perhaps most evident at the pregame meal, which by union contract contains a variety and quantity of foods that one coach describes as "having caloric possibilities that are awesome."

While the pregame meal doesn't add much to a player's performance (he's actually playing on the energy from meals eaten during the previous two days), it can bog him down if it causes upset, draws blood away from muscles due to digestive processes, or in any way affects his psychological state.

Traditionally, football players at high school, college, and professional levels have been offered pregame meals heavy in steak, eggs, and sausage. That's changing.

Jim Williams, the Jets' conditioning and fitness coach, says, "When I came here four years ago, we asked players to be more aware of what they ate. We've been pretty successful. In 1984, there would be fifty steaks prepared for the pregame meal. Now we're down to twenty-five...and most of those are eaten by the coaches."

Nose tackle Jim Burt of the Super Bowl XXI champion Giants was a traditional pregame steak eater. But a couple of years ago he took his coach's advice and began eating spaghetti instead. The result, according to Burt: "I felt lighter and I played better."

Although developing a diet plan is made easier by having data in a computer, it doesn't change the basic goal: to meet your daily calorie budget with foods that contain more than 60 percent complex carbohydrates, and 15 to 20 percent each of fat and protein.

*avoid a rigid approach*

A diet should be flexible enough to allow for an occasional hot fudge sundae. It should let you trade off the fats and calories from other meals as long as the daily balance comes out right. Without a computer, you can figure out what to eat by totaling up the calories and fat-content information from calorie counters and nutrition sheets available in most bookstores and health-food shops.

A simpler system is to be guided by the proven and reliable approach based on the four food groups. Using this approach, a good

## *Byte-Size Bites*

Programs such as the one developed by Anjon for professional teams now are available for home computers. It is possible to do all the calculations by hand, of course, but having it in the computer lets you instantly see how any food choice will affect calorie counts, and allows dieters to play "what if" to match preferences with diet goals.

Computer diets are most useful for analyzing home-prepared meals where contents can be controlled. The difference in even a tablespoon more or less of an ingredient automatically can be factored into a calorie total. Here's the breakfast diet of one NFL player whose goal was 4,000 calories a day:

|  | Cal. | Carb. gms. | Fat gms. | Prot. gms. |
|---|---|---|---|---|
| 4 buttermilk pancakes | 656 | 96 | 20 | 20 |
| 3 tbs. maple syrup | 150 | 39 | 0 | 0 |
| 2 tsp. butter | 68 | 0 | 8 | 0 |
| 16 oz. orange juice | 224 | 52 | 2 | 4 |
| 1 banana | 101 | 26 | 0 | 1 |
| 1 apple | 96 | 24 | 1 | 0 |
| 1 cup skim milk | 88 | 13 | 0 | 9 |
| 1 cup water | 0 | 0 | 0 | 0 |
| Totals | 1383 | 250 | 31 | 34 |

This player's breakfast could be modified for a moderately active "civilian" with a 3,000-calorie goal by cutting back to two pancakes, two tablespoons of syrup, one teaspoon of butter, and eight ounces of orange juice, retaining everything else. The totals then would read: 857 calories, 162 grams of carbohydrate, 17 grams of fat, and 21 grams of protein. Or, substitute the following breakfast:

|  | Cal. | Carb. gms. | Fat gms. | Prot. gms. |
|---|---|---|---|---|
| 2 whole-grain pancakes (6″ diameter) | 328 | 47 | 11 | 11 |
| 2 tbs. maple syrup | 100 | 26 | 0 | 0 |
| 1 scrambled egg | 98 | 1 | 7 | 6 |
| 8 oz. tomato juice | 46 | 10 | 0 | 2 |
| 1 cup skim milk | 86 | 12 | 1 | 8 |
| 1 med. banana | 101 | 26 | 0 | 1 |
| 2 slices whole-wheat toast | 112 | 22 | 1 | 5 |
| 1 tbs. jam | 54 | 14 | 0 | 0 |
| Totals | 925 | 158 | 20 | 33 |

Packaged foods generally list their nutritional make-up in terms of grams per ounce or per serving. To determine how many calories you are getting from the fat content of a product, figure that there are a little more than eight calories in every gram of fat.

*the four food groups*   daily diet would include about 12 servings of food from the major food groups: four servings every day of cereals and grains; four servings of fruits and vegetables (fresh if possible); two servings of dairy products (including such items as skim milk, low-fat yogurt and cheese, and ice milk); and two servings a day of fish, poultry, or low-fat meat.

Above all, try to ensure that reasonable calories and proportions are maintained. The body needs a full range of nutrients to enhance long-term health and short-term performance. Some fad diets and pop weight-reduction plans promise quick weight loss by restricting foods to an unbalanced diet of one or two narrow groups. These have proved to be non-productive in the long run and even can be dangerous.

# Diet and Weight Control

Is there a way to get your body weight where you want it?

Yes!

Is it going to be easy?

Maybe not.

Losing weight could be especially difficult if you're simply looking for a quick fix. But if you're willing to adjust exercise and eating patterns, an NFL-style diet will help you to feel good, look great, and perform up to your potential.

Despite the current interest in nutrition and how it affects us, there still are a number of areas that are controversial—such as whether certain vitamins can ward off disease and increase vigor. In fact, even with all the very convincing scientific research on the subject, there may be more wacko theories advanced about nutrition than about any other human activity. There certainly is no shortage of diet gurus ready to offer nutritional advice. Weight-training magazines and broadcast talk shows are overflowing with diet book authors and food faddists hawking exotic formulas, supplements, and eating programs. In addition, food processing companies spend about $13 billion a year to convince us that their particular product is tasty and/or good for us. With a total U.S. food budget of more than $400 billion a year at stake, one might reasonably expect that some of the claims don't always square with the facts.

Milk, for example, may be nature's most perfect food for calves. But for people, especially blacks and some eastern Europeans who suffer from a lactose intolerance, milk can cause cramps and severe stomach distress. Whole milk also is a leading source of saturated fat, which should be avoided. Non-fat (skim) and low-fat milk, however, can be good sources of nutrition for the majority of people who can digest lactose.

For most people, particularly those over 30, the major problem having to do with food is simply that they are overweight. It's estimated that about 20 percent of all Americans begin a weight-reducing diet every year. Lots more "watch" what they eat with more or less ineffective results. (The trouble is, they do watch what they eat —every mouthful.) As a result of lifelong overindulgence in fatty foods, according to the American Heart Association, nearly half of all adult Americans are at increased risk of suffering from cardio-vascular disease.

Even those who measure up to the norms of height and weight published by insurance companies still may not really be fit. They may be overfat, if not necessarily overweight.

The Aerobics Center in Dallas has done fat-analysis tests on thousands of people, ranging from elderly women to the Dallas Cowboys. Their studies show that the average American male between ages 20 and 29 is toting around 16 percent of his body weight as fat. That's not necessarily bad. Fat provides energy stores needed for endurance sports, it cushions vital organs, it insulates the inner organs from cold, and it serves to shape and smooth the figure or physique. It's just that most people have far too much of a good thing.

The average woman in her 20s has fat that accounts for around 22 percent of her total weight, according to the Aerobics Center study. The percentage of fat tends to rise with age.

But no matter what the age, says Joe W. Priest, associate director of continuing education at the Aerobics Center, "we feel that you have an increased coronary risk with more than nineteen percent of body fat in men and twenty-two percent in women."

---

## *Fat Facts*

The Aerobics Center has studied the fat content in more than 74,000 American men and women and developed an extensive data bank of body-fat information. This chart shows the body-fat content of the average person in specified age ranges. But note that the recommended fat content never is higher than 19 percent for men and 22 percent for women, regardless of age.

| MEN Age | 20-29 | 30-39 | 40-49 | 50-59 |
|---|---|---|---|---|
| % Body fat | 16 | 19 | 21 | 22.7 |

| WOMEN Age | 20-29 | 30-39 | 40-49 | 50-59 |
|---|---|---|---|---|
| % Body fat | 22 | 23 | 26 | 29 |

---

*measuring fat*

To make a rough measure of body fat, squeeze a chunk of the side of your waist, just above the hip bone where it is fattest. Pull out the fold of skin and pinch it together. If you can hold more than an inch through the fold for a man, or an inch-and-a-half for a woman, you're probably too fat. Professional football players often have their subcutaneous skin fat measured with calipers in three different places and the readings are averaged.

There are a number of other methods for quick fat analysis, but they are not completely accepted as accurate. One of those is to use ultrasonic testers found in some sports medicine clinics, health clubs, and athletic organizations. These units bounce sound waves off the hard muscle underneath the skin, then measure the thickness of the fat between the skin and the muscle like radar. Another method works like a big galvanometer, running a weak current through the body and calibrating fat by how well the body conducts electricity. The military uses a simple tape-measure system that compares the ratio of certain body parts to total weight.

The consistent thing about all these measurement systems is that they are inconsistent, not only from one system to another but from day to day depending on who is doing the measuring.

The most precise body-fat readings are obtained by placing people on a scale and dunking them in a water tank. Their immersed weight then is compared to their dry weight. The bigger the difference, the porkier the person. That's because fat floats and muscle tends to sink. So the person who drops to the bottom of the tank when he exhales has a higher percentage of muscle than the guy who floats like a cork.

Prior to training camp a couple of seasons ago, William (The Refrigerator) Perry, Chicago's huge 300-plus-pound defensive tackle, was weighed in this manner. When Clyde Emrich, the team's weight coach, later was asked where he found a tank big enough to accommodate Perry, he replied, "Lake Michigan."

Big as they are, most NFL players these days are not fat. Outstanding running backs, receivers, and cornerbacks sometimes are as low as four or five percent body fat; NFL coaches want such speed and skill players to be less than about eight percent body fat overall. Even 270-pound offensive linemen rarely measure out at more than 18 percent body fat. Perry, by the way, was 20 percent that season.

*mirror, mirror*  Overall, the mirror may be the best, most infallible tool in determining body-fat level; if you appear overweight, you probably are. The high-tech equipment really is needed only if you require a precise reading. In fact, looks may be a better determinant than weight. Because muscle weighs more than fat, it is possible to diet, exercise, and look great, even though you weigh more than when you started calorie counting.

In a game of short sprints and violent clashes of strength versus strength such as football, the kind of energy that comes from fat doesn't count for much.

"Just look at what happens when [Chicago running back] Walter Payton takes on some overweight linebacker," explains Anjon's Anzelc. "Payton weighs 200 pounds and he's five percent body fat. The linebacker weighs 225 pounds, but he's twenty percent body fat. So who gets dumped when they collide? The big guy! That's because Payton actually outweighs him in lean body weight, which is the way you determine power. Payton is 190 pounds lean and the other guy is only 180 and lugging 45 pounds of fat."

# Putting It On

While most weekend athletes want to lose flab, many young athletes in serious training for their events are having the opposite problem. They can't seem to gain mass and strength because they're burning off so many calories in heavy training.

The basic concepts of an NFL-style diet program can help with weight gain as well as weight loss, if you keep these three precepts in mind:

- Eat a well-rounded diet, with at least 60 percent of the calories in carbohydrates, and reduce fat to under 20 percent.
- Don't skip any meals, especially breakfast.
- Get plenty of exercise and rest.

*long-range thinking*

Also, as in successful weight reduction, take a long-range view. Consider what adding less than a pound a week did for Cleveland Browns tackle Paul Farren. Says Browns conditioning coach Dave Redding, "Farren was quick and strong when he came here as a rookie in 1980...but a little under-sized at 235 pounds." By combining a consistent offseason program of lifting weights with a year-around high-carbohydrate diet that was designed to provide just a little more than his actual caloric needs, Farren added bulk each year. He now weighs a formidable 275, with less than 10 percent of that weight in body fat.

# Beating the Set-Point Spread

To lose weight—and keep it off—it is vital to exercise while restricting your calorie intake. Muscles that don't get worked tend to lose mass. The body is such an efficient machine that it sloughs off whatever isn't needed at the time and adds tissue only on demand. Muscles that are stressed get bigger and stronger. Muscles that are neglected tend to atrophy. After age 30, people generally lose three to five percent of their muscle mass every 10 years. That's one of the reasons for middle-age spread; fat takes the place of muscle, even if overall weight hasn't changed.

*diet plus exercise*

In order to maintain muscle mass while dieting, you've got to exercise what you've got. And that means more than just lifting a couple of light weights a few minutes a day or strolling down the beach on sunny weekends. What's required is a continuous workout of more than 20 to 30 minutes at least three times a week that creates an aerobic situation where oxygen is turning body fat into energy.

"People who diet without exercise actually can wind up in worse shape," says Watterson of the Oilers. That's because when food intake drops below what the body needs for minimal functions, the energy to survive is taken from stored fat and from the muscles. Fat is burned most efficiently during aerobic exercise. Thus, weight lost during inactive dieting comes mainly from the body's protein sources. In other words, it isn't fat pockets that get depleted; it's the muscle underneath.

The most obvious example of the effects of a sedentary diet program is what happens to women who try to lose fat on their hips. "Going on a strict diet will result in a woman losing some fat and mass on the hips," Watterson says, "but she also loses in the shoulders and bust. So, in proportion, she may look even more pear-shaped than before. If she would just exercise to increase the muscle mass in the shoulders and chest, and tone up the underlying muscles in the hips, she'll have more of an hour-glass shape when she does lose weight."

The same formula applies for men who've accumulated a roll of fat around the middle. "There isn't any such thing as spot reducing," says Phil Tyne, the conditioning coach of the San Diego Chargers. "However, if you tone the muscles in the area, the stomach won't sag, and if you can reduce overall body fat, it will come off the belly as well. By building up the shoulders, arms, and chest, the overall look will be very much improved."

There's another good reason why exercise must be a part of any reducing program: appetite. It goes out of control with inactivity. A study of thousands of people in India after World War II revealed that people who exercised more than 30 minutes a day ate proportionately more food. It's just what one would expect. But, below a half hour of good physical activity, the food intake increased as the exercise level went down. The less they worked, the more they ate. The study showed that there is a definite correlation between appetite and exercise. It also pointed to an appetite-control mechanism that goes haywire without enough physical activity. Anyone who has sat without exercise in meetings or lectures all day and emerged with a ravenous appetite can appreciate the theory.

*the set point*   Losing weight requires a more substantial change in habits to untrack the body's fat balance inertia. Ann Grandjean explains that the body has a kind of "set-point" mechanism that tends to maintain body weight despite fluctuations in calorie intake of as much as 10 percent.

"Over a limited time," she says, "if you take in too much food, the body just gets a little sloppy in processing and burns it off. If you don't have enough calories for normal operation, your metabolism slows a little so it doesn't have to cannibalize fat or muscle tissue."

That set-point theory explains why, for people who already have achieved a stable weight, cheating on dessert occasionally doesn't show up as a higher number on the bathroom scale. That's good news for them but not so good for people who want to lose weight.

It means that just dropping a doughnut from breakfast won't shrink the roll of fat around the midsection—it will take a net caloric change of more than 10 percent before you can expect to re-calibrate the body's set-point.

*avoid starvation diets*

Hence starvation diets, with or without exercise, are pre-doomed to failure. The body's metabolism adjusts to the new low calorie levels after several weeks. Your body becomes more efficient and requires less food to maintain weight. After enduring constant feelings of hunger and reduced energy, the dieter finally has pared his weight to an acceptable level and begins eating normally again. But the body's metabolism doesn't switch right back from the starvation mode. It can't process what used to be a normal amount of food. All those extra calories go back into fat, and the spare tire returns, generally much faster than it left.

Atlanta's Jorgensen gives his overly fat players a simple equation for losing lard. "A pound of fat equals about 3,500 calories of food value," he explains. "Reduce your caloric balance by 500 calories a day and you'll lose a pound a week."

Swinging the calorie balance could be done by jogging an extra hour, reducing food intake, or a combination of both. Jorgensen thinks it's all right to lose up to two pounds a week for an average-sized person or as much as three pounds a week for a big man. "But don't try to do more than that," he warns. "It can create undesirable side effects, including problems with the nervous system."

*lose a pound a week*

Most experts generally are more conservative. They contend that losing a pound a week is a good goal if you want to make the change permanently. By changing slowly, most of the increase is in added muscle and the reduction mostly is in fat. Quick weight-loss diets generally facilitate only a loss of water and muscle, and not much fat. And, by keeping the weight loss to only about a pound a week, the skin and other parts of the body can adjust to your new size and shape.

## Dieting the NFL Way

Here are some guidelines for adopting an NFL-style diet program:
1. Decide on an exercise program that fits your specific goals.
2. Estimate the average number of calories your program will require per day based on your size, sex, and exercise schedule.
3. Set a goal of how much weight you want to gain or lose, not to exceed two pounds per week. If you want to gain a pound a week, add 500 calories per day to your ideal calorie level. For losing weight, take 500 off that total. If you want to change weight by two pounds a week, make that 1,000 calories a day.
4. Make a daily diet plan that provides the calories you need and contains about two-thirds carbohydrates. Include plenty of variety so you'll enjoy it. Cut down on red meat, fatty foods, sugar, and salt;

replace them with complex carbohydrates and fresh produce.

5. When you get to your target weight, slowly readjust your caloric intake to a level that keeps weight and body fat stable. Be sure to continue exercising.

*don't skip meals*     Another tip from NFL conditioning coaches is never skip meals. Having something in your stomach reduces the perception of hunger. Research indicates the body uses calories from small frequent meals more efficiently than it does intake from one or two big meals. There also will be fewer excess nutrients to be stored away in deposits of fat. For athletes who want to gain weight, frequent small meals allow them to load up on calories during the day without feeling stuffed or putting a strain on the digestive tract.

Coaches warn overfat players never to eat after 7 P.M. Without exercise to work off a big dinner, the calories go to fat instead of being burned as energy. More than one hefty lineman has eaten his way into another job by an overwhelming fondness for midnight pizzas.

Getting something into your stomach at breakfast is important to prevent the metabolism from dropping back into a semi-starvation mode. That same theory relates to the problem with extremely low-calorie diets. If the metabolism has slowed down because there's been no breakfast and perhaps not much lunch, it is much slower at burning the energy you take in at night when you are tempted to make up for the lean day by gorging on a big dinner.

*eat natural snacks*     Whether working for gain or loss, have lots of natural snacks around. Weight losers will find low-calorie snacks help keep them from pigging out at dinner time. Items such as carrots, unbuttered popcorn, vegetables, and fresh fruit don't add many calories and provide extra vitamins and minerals.

For those seeking to add muscle and bulk, the snacks can be more substantial, such as breadsticks, low-fat yogurt, raisins, instant breakfast drink with skim milk, whole-grain rolls, and baked potatoes. But don't add fatty snack foods such as potato chips, peanuts, candy bars, and cheese.

"I can give you a great diet that will let you lose weight," says Attaway of the 49ers. "But it's much better if you let me teach you what you need to do for yourself. That way you'll change your lifestyle. Exercise and eating right have to become a habit."

# Liquid Assets

Drink water. Lots of it. It's an indispensible element of any nutrition program. Have six to eight glasses a day and be sure to drink during exercise. That's what every NFL team's conditioning coach recommends.

What about electrolyte replacement drinks and other high-tech fluids? They are okay, say most NFL coaches, if diluted with water. Electrolyte drinks are available on the field during practices and games in case players prefer the taste, but water still is the number-one choice. After a particularly hard workout during which the athletes have been sweating heavily and thus have lost minerals, the diluted drinks may speed recovery and mineral replacement.

Coaches say the problem with drinking anything except water is that it takes longer for a fluid to get through the stomach if it is mixed with anything. Cool water goes through the stomach and quickly makes its way to the working muscles. Other drinks with sugar and minerals take longer to be absorbed.

Soft drinks are not recommended. Sugar draws water into the stomach, increasing the possibility of cramps. The sucrose also upsets blood-sugar levels, bringing on an insulin rush that eventually can leave the athlete feeling fatigued. The only exception would be for diabetics who might sip orange juice or some other high-energy fluid replacement to balance their particular blood-sugar equation.

# Vim, Vigor, and Vitamins

Vitamins and minerals don't provide energy. They only serve to help regulate body functions and enable nutrients to work properly. In a way, vitamins and minerals are like the distributor and spark plugs in an automobile engine: There wouldn't be any power without them, though it is the gasoline that supplies the actual energy.

Not everyone agrees, however, over how much and what to take in the way of nutritional supplements. While most NFL conditioning coaches believe that vitamin and mineral supplements should not be necessary, they offer multiple vitamins to players anyway. A few coaches give vitamins regularly, and in sizable doses. Usually, that's to combat specific problems such as extreme heat, or to help promote healing. A few other NFL conditioning coaches are very reluctant to advise supplements at all unless a doctor determines that the player has a deficiency.

The NFL's vitamin-mineral consensus is summed up by Dean Bettenham, strength and conditioning coach for the New England Patriots. "Players shouldn't need supplements if they're getting a good diet," Bettenham says, "but who can tell for sure that they are? So we have multi-vitamins available if they want them."

Many diet counselors espouse the theory that all of the nutrients we need, including vitamins and minerals, are easily obtained by eating a balanced diet of fresh foods. They claim that until vitamins were discovered about 80 years ago, people on balanced diets did well without pills and supplements, and that a balanced diet contains more than enough of every vitamin and mineral known to be important in human nutrition. The Redskins' Riley is in this camp. "You can get everything you need from grocery-store shelves and you don't need to take vitamins or protein supplements," he says.

Nevertheless, advocates of vitamin and mineral supplements

point out that the way foods are grown, processed, stored, and cooked is different today than even 50 years ago. They claim that chemical fertilizers in the soil and genetically altered seeds produce fruits and vegetables that have a different complement of vitamins and minerals. Furthermore, they argue, more nutrients are depleted from the foods during extended storage, or during canning and freezing.

Necessary or unnecessary, does taking vitamins involve any risks? It varies with the vitamins. Vitamin C and all the B-complex vitamins are water soluble. Thus, if a higher dosage than needed is taken, the excess is excreted. That leads critics of the American vitamin habit to charge we have "the world's richest urine."

"I know about the expensive urine story," says Garrett Giemont, strength and conditioning coach of the Rams. "But I feel better and the players who take them say they feel better when they're taking vitamins and supplements."

*vitamin overdose*  While overdoing the water-soluble vitamins could be wasteful, overdosages of fat-soluble vitamins, especially vitamins A and D, can be toxic and even fatal. They accumulate in the fat tissues and, if present in overly large quantities, can interfere with normal body functions.

Minerals such as calcium and potassium are important links in the complex biochemical processes that keep human beings healthy and active. Again, most NFL conditioning coaches think that the diet should supply enough of these elements.

*protein supplements*  Bodybuilders who often take supplements of protein extracts because they believe supplements make muscles massive, are misguided; NFL conditioning coaches generally agree that there isn't much evidence to support that theory. What's more, coaches are trying to keep the total protein intake lower, not higher. Jones of the Bills says there is evidence linking too much protein to gout and other joint-related problems in athletes who put their joints under severe tension.

But some strength coaches think there are good reasons for occasional uses of protein supplements.

"I give amino acid supplements for easing pain and encouraging healing in bruised tissue," says Pittsburgh's Walt Evans.

Miami's Junior Wade provides mineral supplements, especially potassium. "It is hot down here," he says, "and when players practice they lose a lot of minerals when they sweat."

*salt tablets*  One traditional workout supplement no longer endorsed is salt tablets. They are taken on the premise that they replace salt—not minerals—lost through sweating. But many experts in sports medicine now say that salt tablets are useless, that their chief function is psychological in nature.

"Salt tablets are not part of the supplement plan at Buffalo," says Jones. "They irritate the stomach lining. They also can draw water *potassium*

away from cells where it is needed, and can cause cramping."

Rather than salt, which your body will crave in foods if it is needed, the most important mineral lost through perspiration is potassium. As Miami's Wade is aware, insufficient potassium can lead to muscle cramping in extreme situations. But don't rush out and buy a load of potassium pills. A balanced diet that prominently features fresh vegetables and fruits (especially the old standby favorite of marathon runners, distance cyclists, and triathletes—the banana) should provide what you need, whether you live in Tampa Bay or Green Bay.

Vitamin/mineral advice varies from team to team. What is constant throughout the league, however, is the belief that taking massive doses of any vitamin, mineral, or supplement is unwise without competent medical advice. Just because something, whether it be fish oil or calcium, is proven to be good for you doesn't mean that lots of it—especially in concentrated forms—will be better for you. NFL coaches also generally accept the idea that it won't do any harm to take a one-a-day supplement, just for insurance, especially for athletes who are in heavy training or are trying to lose weight.

For the weekend athlete, Grandjean, the Olympic Committee nutrition consultant, has a more global perspective. "We find that eighty-five percent of the people who have poor diets, and who could probably benefit from taking supplements, don't take anything," she says. "And almost all of the people who do take supplements are already getting everything they need from what they eat."

# Performance Enhancers

In a sport as fiercely competitive as professional football, in which teams can seem so evenly matched, coaches always are looking for an edge.

One place they looked was to endurance running, where marathon racers got the idea of boosting performance by radically modifying eating habits. The concept that interested the coaches is called "carbohydrate loading." Simplified, the concept entails making available more than normal levels of high-energy fuel for the muscles. The high-performance fuel in this case is glycogen, which is synthesized in the body mainly from carbohydrates.

*carbo loading*

How do you get the body to store more than the usual amount of glycogen? The same way you make the muscles stronger: stress the system. With carbohydrate loading, the athlete exhausts his glycogen stores by running a long distance, or by playing an exhausting game or doing a heavy workout.

Then, instead of eating a high-carbohydrate diet to replenish glycogen, he eats fats and proteins instead. The muscles and liver (where glycogen is stored) become starved for glycogen and become more efficient about collecting and storing it. After another three or four days of working out and depriving the body of carbo-hydrates, the program shifts. For three days before competition, large amounts of carbohydrates are consumed and the eager body accepts and processes much more than normal. So at the time of the race or the game, the athlete is over-charged with glycogen and theoretically is able to keep going longer and stronger than his un-loaded competitor.

That's the theory. Does it work? In some people yes and in others no. And sometimes athletes feel so pumped and overloaded with the extra glycogen that they're clumsy.

Nevertheless, on a modified basis, many NFL teams encourage players to boost their ratio of carbohydrates a few days before game day. And a few clubs do an actual formalized program.

Pittsburgh is one of the teams that occasionally urges players to take part in a carbohydrate-loading program. "We'll do it a couple of times a year for big games and for playoffs," says Evans. "We think it is useful, but we don't do it all the time. It could strain the system if you did it every week."

*caffeine*

What about caffeine? Some coaches believe a few cups of coffee trigger a body reaction that increases the availability of certain nu-trients. But others say caffeine is a diuretic, which reduces the re-tained fluids in a player's body at exactly the time, before a game, when they should be highest.

*steroids are deadly*

The only performance-improving substance about which NFL conditioning coaches unanimously agree is anabolic steroids: They are totally opposed to them. Anabolic steroids are artificial hor-mones that build strength and endurance in weightlifters and other strength-dependent athletes. The NFL and amateur athletic associ-ations have banned steroids and have instituted testing programs to enforce the ban.

Some athletes still take steroids under the assumption they build muscular mass and strength to a greater degree than they ever could attain otherwise, even with an ideal diet and disciplined workouts. But there is a very heavy price.

"Players on steroids don't tolerate heat well. They also tend to be more prone to injuries of the connective tissues," says the Bengals' Wood. "We are vehemently against the use of steroids for three rea-sons. First, steroid takers are essentially unhealthy, and we want to go to war with healthy people. Second, the long-term effects of ster-oids can be disastrous, including testicular atrophy, cancer of the testicles, sterility, arteriosclerosis, and chromosomal damage. Bad acne and swollen breasts also are common side effects of steroids, some of which may never go away. Third, and most important, you are a better athlete without drugs of any kind."

# Rusty Jones: Eating the Numbers

*Buffalo linebacker Jim Haslett and strength coach Rusty Jones go over diet options on a computer print-out.*

One bittersweet autumn evening in New Hampshire in the mid-1970s, two high school teams were playing the season's last football game. New assistant coach Rusty Jones was on the sideline watching his team finish the season with only two victories against seven defeats.

That disappointing season, though, marked a turning point in his life. For soon after that final game Jones began developing a nutrition and conditioning program that today is used by five NFL teams, a dozen universities, several professional hockey and basketball teams, and a distinguished list of corporations, medical facilities, and health clubs. Jones's diet and conditioning ideas eventually led to his current position as coordinator of strength and conditioning for the Buffalo Bills.

"I realized our kids were being overpow-ered," says Jones of his New Hampshire team. "We had no weight-training program. I knew that during the offseason we had to get those kids going."

Over the winter he scrounged some weights and made room in the gym for benches and mats. He began showing the players how to lift weights. Jones worked with many students in the spring and summer, beefing them up so well that the next season his team made it all the way to the state championship game.

Along the way, Jones realized he no longer wanted to be a head coach. "I learned that I liked the science side of conditioning."

Later, when he discovered that his players were not gaining strength the way he expected —even when they worked diligently in the weight room—Jones began asking them what they ate. He was appalled when he calculated what their answers meant in terms of nutrition.

"They were taking in lots of fats and proteins and not much in carbohydrates," he remembers. "Like most high school kids, even today, they thought it didn't matter what you ate as long as you ate a lot of it."

But Jones had been impressed by a book by Melvin Williams on nutrition and the athlete. "His ideas about emphasizing carbohydrates while cutting fats and protein made sense to me," says Jones. "So I started studying how nutrition affects performance." He also started suggesting diet changes to his players.

Suddenly, things began to happen. A young fullback agreed to stop eating bacon and eggs at breakfast and switched to cereal, fruit, and skim milk. He ate pasta instead of pork chops, and gave up high-fat foods such as sausage pizza and ice cream. Within weeks, the player's complexion improved, his body began filling out, and he began making significant gains in the weight room.

"All the kids were excited about how much he was improving and they wanted to try the diet, too," Jones remembers. So he started writing out an individual diet for each boy, basing his recommendations on getting at least 60 percent of daily calories in the form of carbohydrates. Jones was careful to tailor diet plans to the needs and the tastes of each person.

That system for customizing diet plans to meet individual preferences was the primary reason why the system worked so well at the high school level. It also is why Jones's system is having such success around the NFL. That, and results.

"Diets don't work if people don't follow them," Jones says. "So I wanted to be sure that there were things in it that the kids liked. And I felt it was important that they decide for themselves what they were going to eat. When a kid stayed with his daily diet, we said he was 'eating the numbers.'"

So many boys were asking for diet plans that Jones soon was swamped. He was spending hours every day calculating diet formulas for his players. Enter Bill Anzelc, a computer programmer from Indiana who had married Jones's cousin.

"I told him we needed a computer program to show what the numbers should be for our diets," Jones says. "After Bill wrote the program, I met Jerry Attaway [now with the 49ers], who then was an assistant coach at USC. Jerry was interested in our ideas so we sent him a copy of the software."

Attaway began experimenting with Jones's program at USC and also started seeing positive results.

Encouraged by the initial success, Jones went back to college, earning a master's degree in exercise physiology. He moved to South Bend, Indiana, after graduating, where he and Anzelc formed Anjon Systems. Anzelc handled the business and programming end and Jones provided the research and worked at sales.

Jones began making the rounds, selling the program wherever he could. "It's funny now to see our first list of foods," Jones says. "It was all on one sheet containing only about three hundred foods. Because it was a new idea, we wanted it to be easy to use."

Today, there are more than twelve hundred different foods in Anzelc's data base, including ing 33 different types of cheese, 43 cereal brands, and menu items from 11 different fast-food franchises, including McDonald's, Wendy's, Taco Bell, and Dairy Queen. The idea is to list all the possibilities so users can have their preferences accommodated. The vegetable list, for example, is so detailed as to include rutabaga, okra, chickory, and black-eyed peas. Nut fanciers can look up the fat content (surprisingly high) in varieties such as filberts, pecans, cashews, peanuts, and pistachios.

Explaining why the program has been accepted by such a wide variety of athletic organizations, Jones says, "We're just advocating a balanced diet. But the gimmick is that most

*With Jones's diet, Haslett now eats up the opposition.*

people are so far out of balance that this tool lets them get closer to the ideal range."

Jones left Anjon for a job as the conditioning coach of the Pittsburgh Maulers of the USFL. When the Maulers folded, the same management brought him over to coordinate conditioning for the Pittsburgh Penguins hockey team. Two years later, at the end of the 1985 season, the Bills hired the 32-year-old Jones to help rebuild the team in Buffalo. He brought his computer program with him.

How well has Jones's system worked at Buffalo? "I think you know you're doing a good job when you walk into the locker room and the guys don't say 'How are ya,' " Jones says. "Instead they ask questions about a workout or diet. Or they want to show you how well they've been eating and that they're down to nine percent body fat. If you've won the players' confidence, you know you must be helping them."

One of the players who got into Jones's program early was linebacker Jim Haslett. "When Rusty started, he didn't pressure us to make any changes," Haslett says. "But listening to him talk about nutrition made me want to change."

Jones explains that players adopt new diets mainly after they've hit a snag in their development, when they no longer get strength gains in the weight room or when their endurance begins to falter. In Haslett's case, the problem was keeping his weight up and keeping his body fat down.

"Rusty figured that during the offseason I was taking in only 3,500 calories and not eating the right proportions," Haslett says. "I also was skipping breakfast and not having much for lunch." Jones and Haslett came up with a 5,500-calorie diet that had very little fat and not much protein. Consequently, Haslett gained 15 pounds and played much stronger the following season.

Haslett's main focus is on improving his performance. Staying on a strict diet is just another element in his conditioning program, which is more rigorous than most non-professional athletes would care to endure. A bachelor, Haslett finds it easier to stick to the same breakfast and lunch every day. In the morning he has pancakes, waffles, or French toast, skim milk, and a can of instant breakfast drink. Lunch is even more structured: two turkey sandwiches on whole wheat with lettuce and tomato, 16 ounces of apple juice, and 20 Triscuits. "Sometimes I'll put mustard on the sandwich, but never mayonnaise," he says. For dinner, Haslett eats spaghetti or rice, flank steak, vegetables, and a low-fat dessert such as sherbet.

That diet has improved his play. "But," Haslett admits, "it does get kind of boring eating the same thing all the time."

Not that his diet never varies. Recently, Haslett went to see Jones for a little extracurricular diet advice. He was going to a hockey game with some teammates and didn't want to go off his diet. But he wanted to have a good time, too. Jones sat down at his computer, refigured the linebacker's daily eating plan, and came up with some revisions.

"We had a great time," recalls Haslett. "I had two hot dogs and six beers and I still came out that day almost eating the numbers."

# 5 Thinking Fit:

## *Mental Training*

One of the most significant aspects of fitness, mental training, also is the least evolved.

"Mental training now is about where weightlifting was in the 1950s," says C.T. Hewgley, strength coach for the Chiefs.

Mental considerations have gained such recognition in the NFL that some teams have consultants who help improve player attitudes and performance. The Patriots, for example, employ a psychiatrist from the Harvard Medical School, Dr. Armand M. Nicholi, Jr. The players were so impressed with his locker-room advice after one game, they awarded him a game ball.

To perform at levels that approach individual limits, the mind needs to be as well trained as the body. "In winning football games in the NFL," Dr. Nicholi says, "the mind and will play a more important role than the body and skill."

Dr. Nicholi believes there is a definite link between winning and positive attitudes. "The NFL draft," he wrote in the *New England Journal of Medicine,* "with winning teams choosing last, spreads talent evenly throughout the league. A critical factor in winning a game, therefore, is less a matter of talent than of mind—attitudes, confidence, motivations, desire, and will to win."

Physical factors are undeniably valuable in the NFL, as they are in any sport, pro or amateur. However, the hard work of physical conditioning doesn't get done without a strong mental effort. Getting up in the morning to jog, saying no to hot apple pie à la mode, and pushing muscles to the edges of pain require strong motivation and self-discipline.

"The hardest thing in my job," says Cleveland strength and conditioning coach Dave Redding, "is to convince a professional athlete that daily torture is good for him."

If it's difficult for athletes whose livelihoods depend on their physical fitness to develop the mind set needed to work out conscientiously, it's even tougher for ordinary people who have less pressure to excel and more good excuses to avoid the work and pain. But it isn't any less important.

# The Goal Line

Whether you're in the NFL or at the YMCA, coordinating the mental and physical sides of fitness is critical. Within the framework of your aims and abilities, make a list of what you want to accomplish.

"Set goals that challenge you a little, but don't make them too high," says Pittsburgh Steelers strength coach Walt Evans. "You have to be realistic about what you can accomplish. For most people, it is not realistic to expect to be in the Olympics or play in the AFC-NFC Pro Bowl."

People starting a conditioning program are, in many ways, like rookies in the NFL. They must work out with an eye to the future.

"It's especially important for new players to set goals because they haven't yet reached their potentials of speed, strength, and endurance," says Cleveland's Redding. "Unless they have goals, they don't have a target for improvement."

*make goals specific*

For any athlete, goals need to be clearly defined. Vague notions such as "I want to be in good shape," or "Lose weight" are too general to be useful. Your goals must be specific and detailed so you can chart progress toward achieving them.

The most successful goal-setting strategies are based on long-term targets that are combined with short-term and intermediate objectives that can be achieved in as brief a time frame as a week or a month.

Long-term goals might extend for a year or more, such as "Run a marathon next season in under four hours," or "Add an inch of muscle to my chest by next year." Short-term and intermediate goals would include all the steps along the road that leads to reaching the bigger objective.

*attach a timetable*

Time needs to be part of any goal. "Increase my total running mileage by half a mile per week over the next eight weeks," would be the kind of intermediate goal that can be accomplished and easily measured. If you don't attach a timetable to the task, you won't have the incentive to push yourself and don't have a deadline in which to evaluate your performance. You either did it or you didn't in the time you allowed. If you are motivated and have set realistic goals to be met in a workable time frame, you have maximized your chances for succeeding.

And if you fail to reach your goals? So what? This is training, remember. You won't be cut from your own team. Re-evaluate your goals, extend the time frame so it still presents a challenge, and resume working with a positive attitude.

# Getting—and Staying—Motivated

Along with selecting personnel and developing strategy, one of an NFL head coach's most important jobs is to motivate his players. The coach needs to get each player to deliver his best effort by whatever means he can use, be it tough talk, sweet-talk, or sweet reason. That's what many team meetings and individual conversations are all about—motivation.

The weekend athlete has the same need for motivation, except that he usually has to provide his own. The most powerful motivation to work hard at a conditioning program is a deep commitment to a long-term goal and an understanding of what steps must be taken to achieve it.

Atlanta strength coach Tim Jorgensen says athletes improve most when they are fully informed about the overall plan and its details. "We want them to know what we're doing, and why and how we're doing it," he says. "It is important because if they know why we do something, that helps with motivation. They work harder if they know where they are and where they're going."

*success motivates*

Following through on your own plan is easier if you keep stoking your motivation with success. "Do whatever is on your conditioning schedule every day you have something planned," says Rams strength coach Garrett Giemont. "Even if you're not feeling great and don't make any progress that day, you'll still feel good about having made the effort and succeeded in following your plan."

Evans agrees that motivation is boosted by success. He also stresses accentuating your strengths. "Whatever you are good at, you should build on," he says. "Whatever your interests are is what you should expand. First point to all the good things you have done in an activity. Then you can look at the places where you need improvement and figure ways to strengthen those weaknesses. But be sure you don't dwell on the things you can't yet do well."

While appeal to inner needs for personal accomplishment is what motivates the average athlete and most professionals, the baser instincts can play a role as well.

Athletes sometimes train hard because of fear. For instance, they can be afraid they'll get cut in favor of a new, more talented, or better-trained player.

"When there are a number of people competing at a position and they know that only one or two are going to get to stay on the team, they work pretty hard," says Raiders conditioning coach Bob Mischak.

Or they can be afraid they'll get hurt if they're not in shape. In fact, the motivation to avoid injury is what drives many players to devote extraordinary time to lifting weights, running, and performing stretching routines, especially during the offseason. They know that the best-conditioned athletes generally have less injuries.

When a player is injured, the need for motivation may be even greater. Seahawks trainer Jim Whitesel says that when he is working with injured players in rehabilitation, his job early in the process is to educate and supervise. But later, when the player understands what needs to be done and why it needs to be done, the trainer's job is to push him on to recovery. "It requires so much work out of a player to get through months of slow progress and very hard work that it almost burns them out," Whitesel says. "After they learn the routine, the main part of my job is to motivate them to keep going."

With professional players, motivation sometimes is as simple as money. "We're going to pay players to get into better condition," says the strength trainer for one team. "The more they can lift when they get to summer camp, the more they'll get paid."

That kind of wallet motivation is easy to understand. But it takes more than money to get people to consistently perform at a high level of excellence. Winning coaches in the NFL have known for a long time that pride, recognition, praise, team responsibility, and other internal factors are much stronger than money in motivating the best performance.

"When a player has just come to the sidelines after a great play," Dr. Nicholi says, "he doesn't hold up his paycheck."

*group motivation*

For amateur athletes, the desire to devote time and effort to a training program also can come from other sources. A friend or a training coach affiliated with a gym or health club may provide personal motivation. One of the reasons aerobics classes are so popular is that the leader provides encouragement and inspiration as well as providing instruction.

Friends can help maintain each other's motivation. Having a running partner makes you more likely to get out early in the morning and run the full distance. It is rare that both of you will feel like slacking off on the same day. And if you know there is someone waiting for you at the track, there's more reason to get out of bed on mornings when an extra hour of sleep might otherwise be an irresistible temptation.

A spotting partner in the weight room will help motivate a full effort. Besides playing an important safety role, your partner can observe to be sure your form is right, and he can urge you to make that one extra rep.

Proper diet, too, can aid motivation by keeping you alert and energetic. *(See Chapter Four for specific recommendations.)*

Among the many books on the role of motivation and mental fitness in athletics, one stands out: *Peak Performance* by Charles A. Garfield, Ph.D., with Hal Zinna Bennett. Garfield rates motivation (he calls it "volition") as one of the most important factors that contribute to achieving peak performance. He cautions that seizing control of your powers to boost performance is not always easy. According to Garfield, we often tend to think outside factors are responsible for our successes or failures. The truth is that usually our performance is directly related to our own actions.

"Your first assignment," Garfield writes, "is to focus completely on self, assuming responsibility and accountability for what you do. Make conscious efforts to see and acknowledge what it is that you do that is, indeed, significant and thus refutes all notions that your successes are pure luck."

While there are some differences in approach to the best ways to increase the levels of motivation, most coaches agree that any successful recipe for motivation begins, as stated earlier, with writing down your goals, both long-term and short-term, as honestly and completely as possible. When you know what you are after, and why you are after it, you have a better chance of getting there.

*reward yourself*    But whatever technique you use to motivate yourself, be sure you find ways to reward yourself when you achieve those intermediate goals on the way to the big target.

A reward can be taking a day off from the grind of training. Or maybe it is treating yourself to an hour of massage or tickets to a ballgame. Obviously, allowing yourself an eating binge after getting down to a target weight would be counterproductive. But something such as an ice cream cone could be an appropriate reward, if you offset the fats and calories during other meals in the day.

Getting yourself motivated actually becomes easier as your workouts become a habit. People start telling you how much better you look. You feel stronger, faster, and leaner. That kind of positive feedback is the kind that builds and maintains motivation.

And don't forget one of the best workout motivators of all—thinking about how good it feels, mentally and physically, when you're finished.

## The Confidence Factor

Great players exude a confidence others can feel. It's one of the things that make the difference between a competent quarterback with good physical skills and a great quarterback who somehow gets the team to come through in critical situations.

During the 1986 AFC Championship Game, the Broncos were on their own 2-yard line, seven points behind with only five minutes left, when quarterback John Elway walked into the huddle with a smile on his face.

Denver wide receiver Steve Watson vividly remembers the moment: "John said, 'You guys work hard and good things are going to happen.' I couldn't believe it. You figure we've got ninety-eight yards to go. And we haven't been moving the ball all day. He might as well be cool. I thought, if John is going to be cool, I can be cool, too."

Four minutes and fifty-five seconds later, the Broncos had scored the tying touchdown. With their confidence soaring, they beat Cleveland 23-20 in overtime.

Two weeks later, at Super Bowl XXI, Denver ran into another team with overwhelming confidence, the New York Giants. Running back Joe Morris has fond memories of the game, and not just because his New York team eventually won, but because of the matchup.

"Some teams play with an offense that feels no one can stop them," Morris says. "And there are teams where the defense knows that when they really need to hold, no team can score against them. When those guys really believe it, they're right. The fun is when you get two teams like that going against each other and see what happens."

On the other hand, Morris believes that when teams are psychologically down, they are beaten before they walk on the field. "You can feel when a team is ready to be beat," he says. "They don't have confidence that they can do it."

*confidence wins*

When dealing in matters of the mind, neat divisions are impossible to maintain. Confidence depends on interrelated factors that include preparation, concentration, visualization, and relaxation. Nevertheless, the general rule holds that people who succeed are the ones who are confident about their abilities. The runner who is accustomed to winning races usually will find strength at the end. He expects to win, and if he has trained well and is not out of his class, he probably will.

How do you get the confidence to lift a heavy weight, make a great catch under tough conditions, or play your best game against an obviously superior opponent?

*exercising for confidence*

For some people, the way to build confidence is to get into great shape. "Offseason conditioning is a confidence builder," says Broncos lineman Keith Bishop. "When you are not progressing along on the program you set for yourself it makes you uncertain. You don't have the extra confidence that you might have. But when you get the aerobic base and the strength and things are going right, you know you're going to do well during the season."

Bishop and his teammates clearly have plenty of confidence. But Bishop says that, like most rookies, he was shaken when he first came to the NFL. "The level of competition and contact is so much greater than in college," he says, "it was hard to perform up to my ability. When I was a rookie and first put on the pads and got out there and saw how fast they moved and how hard they hit, it was scary."

It took some time and a great deal of practice for Bishop to get his skills and his confidence to a level where he could be a contributor to a contending team. "Now, to keep it up," he says, "it takes working out until I know I'm ready."

Building confidence is one of the reasons Pittsburgh has its players run distances in the offseason. Evans says that along with promoting cardiovascular fitness, "distance running has something to do with mental toughness. Players look at distance running as torture. But done early in the preseason it is good for their preparation. We tell them to just get through it, even if they have to walk parts of it. Once they do run four or five miles without stopping, that achievement helps develop confidence in other areas as well."

All-time NFL pass receiving record-holder Charlie Joiner also depends on conditioning to build confidence. Now a coach with the Chargers, he figured that by going all out on every play, his teammates would come to rely on him. "I wanted the quarterback to have confidence that I'd be where I was supposed to be on every play," he says. In other words, Joiner went a step beyond; not only did he have confidence in his own ability, he tried to transfer some of it, as Elway did, to the rest of his team.

*maximize success opportunities* Confidence generally comes from establishing a personal history of success. It is axiomatic that success builds on success and failure upon failure. What you need to do is to be sure to maximize your chances for success every time.

Ski instructor John Alderson has made a career of teaching other instructors how to teach kids to ski. The key to Alderson's teaching philosophy is to emphasize building his students' confidence.

"I don't care that much about how well the kid skis when he finishes a lesson," Alderson says. "I care that he feels good about himself because he has set a goal and accomplished it. Even if he only learned a snowplow stop on a bunny slope, he accomplished something and I want him to be proud of it. The way to teach kids is to always set them up for success."

Alderson's techniques are just as valid for adults who want to build confidence. When you plan your training program, be sure to set goals you know you can reach. For example, in running, if you're just starting out, you might make a goal of running 10 minutes or one mile without stopping. But be sure you succeed in meeting that goal, even if you have to slow down while running. As your condition improves, push yourself further, as long as you stay within your ability to succeed each time.

Dieters build confidence with the same method. If you have trouble sticking with an eating program for a month, try doing it for a week. If even a week is too tough at the start, set your goals for just one day at a time. And don't try to lose all your weight in, say, a month. That can only lead to disappointment. Give yourself adequate time and work in attainable, healthy increments, such as a pound a week.

*discard negative thoughts* Confidence relies on the positive. Don't let negative thoughts stay in your mind. One technique for dealing with thoughts of failure is to visualize them in your mind on a photograph, then crumple the picture mentally and throw it in the garbage. When bothered by someone he dislikes, one athlete writes that person's name on a sheet of paper, puts the paper in a glass jar, and stores the jar in the freezer. The point is to make a positive step that deals with, and then dismisses, the negative thought.

Author Joe Hyams writes about an experience with positive thinking in his wonderfully instructive book, *Zen in the Martial Arts*. After a match against a stronger, more advanced opponent, Hyams's teacher summoned him for a private session. Hyams's frustration and anger was clear to the teacher in the way Hyams fought, trying to trick his opponent instead of relying on sound technique.

The master drew a chalk line on the floor, handed the chalk to Hyams and directed him to make the line shorter. After thinking for a moment, Hyams drew a perpendicular line in the middle, cutting the original line in half. That was the same kind of negative approach Hyams had used in the match. The master shook his head, then drew a longer chalk line next to the first. It made the first one shorter in a most positive way. "Lengthen your own line," he told Hyams.

*forgive yourself*

Getting angry with others is a minor problem compared with the more damaging habit of getting angry with yourself. If you make a mistake, forget about it. Concentrate on the next chance. A tennis player who shouts and berates himself during a match is more likely to lose than a player who puts his mind on the next point. Successful kickers are those who can forget about the missed field goals and have the confidence to remember the ones that sail straight through the uprights.

Even when you lose, look for the things you did right. Congratulate your opponents and congratulate yourself for the good points you won, the effort you made, the things that were positive. You have to review your weaknesses, of course, in order to work on them. But building confidence first requires giving yourself credit for what you did well.

## Visualizing Success

If you can see it in your mind, you can probably do it. If you can visualize a situation in vivid detail before you actually face it, bringing all your senses into play in your mind, your chances of being successful are that much greater. The idea of dreaming about something in advance is old. The idea of visualizing successful performance in sports isn't new either, but its use on a regular basis is a recent development.

*mental rehearsal*

Most NFL teams now expect their players to visualize success in some form during their training. The idea is to rehearse the action in your mind over and over with a satisfying ending. When the image is so well ingrained that you can almost feel the surroundings, your muscles actually begin to learn what to do. Research with athletes mentally rehearsing their activities showed weak nerve signals reaching the muscles at exactly the right times and in the same order as would be recorded in an actual performance of the maneuvers being visualized.

Visualization relies on spending time in a relaxed state thinking about how you want an event to happen. It works because the body is a complex machine that requires interaction between so many parts. Visualization provides a proven adjunct to training, without the effort of actually performing.

Even as simple a movement as walking requires a complex neuromuscular interaction that must be learned. Watch an infant as he struggles to master the first steps and it becomes obvious that there's a very involved relationship between voluntary muscles, the muscle sensors, the brain, the eye, and factors of balance and environment we still don't totally understand. Some physical movements, such as throwing a baseball or hitting a solid tennis backhand, require such extensive training of the neuromuscular pathways that if they are not learned in childhood they probably will never be fully mastered.

*imagery*

The key to success with visualization is a parallel technique called "imagery," which allows you to get as involved as you possibly can in what you are seeing in your mind. Concentrate on all the details of the image you are visualizing. Try to hear the sounds with your mind's ear. Smell the grass and the pine trees. Try to let your body feel the force of a fast turn, the weight of a ball, the minute sensory clues that affect your reactions. The more accurate the imagery of your mental rehearsal, the more likely it will lead to success when you actually try what you have visualized.

*videotape*

Another form of visualization, videotape, is a valuable teaching/learning tool, which is why NFL teams use it so extensively. Not only are tapes of upcoming opponents studied, but many practices and training sessions are recorded for later viewing, scrutiny, and evaluation by coaches and players.

Video is particularly helpful in learning sports such as tennis and skiing. Slow-motion videotapes of experts making the strokes and carving the turns are reviewed over and over. Soon, you can begin to see yourself in the picture. When you do go to the courts or the slopes, you have a head start in training the neuromuscular pathways that contribute to good technique. In other words, you let your mind do the work.

Videotapes of your own performance can be revealing. You can see what you are doing right and also see mistakes in form or technique of which you may not have been aware. It is important, however, that when you watch your mistakes you follow up by visualizing yourself doing the movements properly.

The wrong side of the visualization coin is negative rehearsal.

*avoid negative rehearsal*

Imagine before your second serve that you're about to double fault and that is exactly what you'll do. Worry about your ability to lift 250 pounds and you probably won't be able to complete a rep. Visualize yourself missing a crucial free throw and you've maximized your chances of doing just that.

In most people, expectations govern performance. Tell some weightlifters they have to do 10 repetitions of a difficult exercise and they will strain to finish the tenth. Tell the same person with the same weight that he needs to do 14, and he'll breeze through 10 and start straining only when he approaches the fourteenth. In the same way, runners in a 10-kilometer race (6.2 miles) are totally drained at the end. But put them in a 10-mile race and, because they know they still have four miles left, by the time they pass the 10k mark, they still are relatively fresh and may even be running a better time.

Under whatever name it goes—positive thinking, visualization, confidence, rehearsal for success— the process of thinking through a physical action in advance makes a great difference in the ultimate outcome.

Dr. Nicholi reports on the crucial role visualization played in a game the Patriots had to win—the last game of the 1985 season against the Bengals, with a berth in the playoffs at stake.

"The Patriots were hanging onto a 27-23 lead with less than two minutes in the game," he writes. "With fourth down and inches to go on the Bengals' 42-yard line, the coach decided to try for the first down: 60,000 hometown fans in the stands held their breath. If the play didn't work, it would be another year of frustration. A substitute running back who had been somewhat depressed about his play during the year, was put into the game, got the ball, bolted through the line, cut sharply to the right, and outran all of the secondary for a touchdown that clinched the game. When the player came off the field and broke through the back-slapping of his jubilant teammates, he rushed over and said, 'Doc, you won't believe this, but just before I went into the game I visualized myself running that very play over and over again. When I got into the game, I ran it step by step just as I visualized it!' "

## Concentration Pays

In any activity, keeping the mind on the subject at hand is tough. "Some people have short attention or concentration spans," Evans says. "They shift around and don't get a lot done. It is very hard to teach concentration, but we think it starts with conditioning. If someone will force himself to concentrate during training routines, we think it carries over into the performance of the actual task."

*focus to perform*

The more your mind is focused, the better your performance. There are physiological reasons for this as well as mental. The muscles are fired by signals from the brain. As discussed in Chapter One, the strength of a muscle contraction is determined by the number of muscle units turned on at any time. The more fibers recruited by the nerve signals, the stronger and faster the contraction. So in order to lift heavy weights or throw a ball to maximum distance, the brain has to get the highest possible number of fibers contracting at the same time. Concentrating your attention on the movement or muscles involved seems to focus the signals and make them stronger.

Thinking is not concentrating. In fact, thinking about playing may be the worst thing to do during a game or heavy workout. On the field, things happen so fast that there's time only to react. Athletes who can keep their minds strictly on the flow and rhythm of the game have the best chance of being in the right place at the right time. If you've trained your mind well, your body will know what to do.

Time and again, athletes who have had remarkable performances report that they were perfectly aware of what was going on and completely focused on their activity. Yet, the concentration they brought to the effort was such that they typically felt insulated from the distractions of personalities, crowds, or weather.

For the Oilers, the focusing process begins during the pregame warm-up and stretching. "The time each player takes prior to a game not only prepares the body for motion but is also when he prepares his mind," says strength coach Steve Watterson. "He lets go of all the things happening in the rest of the world, forgets about what happened during the week and focuses on the game. He tunes into what he is doing and what is going to happen."

*familiarity breeds success*  How do you achieve that kind of calm concentration? One way is to be so prepared in both mind and body that everything happening is familiar. Mental rehearsals in meticulous detail, going through familiar routines before play begins, and knowing your opponent (the way NFL teams do after studying game films) and the field or court you will play on can help make even a big game seem as if it were "just another game."

## Just Relax

The best athletic performances come when you are relaxed. Author John Jerome has called that relaxed moment when all your energies are focused "the sweet spot in time." Others have called it playing "in the zone" or "over your head." What it really is is playing within yourself and within your true abilities.

"All the great ones are the same," says the Bengals' Kim Wood. "They do it their own way. They get into their own world and don't let anything get in their way."

Because there are so many muscles and nerves in the body to co-

*relaxed power*

ordinate, the "sweet spot" isn't hit every time. But the closer athletes come to the ideal of relaxed power, the better they will perform.

That's why coaches exhort their teams to relax at the same time they urge them to get charged up. It seems to be a contradiction, but in fact the two must go together. An athlete must be giving maximum effort, but he has to be doing it without being tight.

From a psychological perspective, Dr. Nicholi says, "the ideal condition for top performance involves being intense mentally without being tense physically. Physical tenseness impairs coordination and interferes with concentration."

The reason why a relaxed athlete is better than a tense one has to do with the mechanics of the muscles. To move any limb, the agonist muscle contracts and the antagonist muscle relaxes. Do a chin-up exercise and it is your biceps muscles that are contracting while the triceps just loosen up. Jump for a slam dunk and it's your quadriceps that contract to spring you into the air. The hamstring muscle has to relax its tension to permit the quadriceps to develop full power.

A tense player doesn't relax the antagonist muscles completely. In effect, the tight player is like a car being driven with the parking brake on. Release the brake and the car goes faster with less effort. Relax the body and the muscles work to maximum advantage, giving you more speed, power, and endurance.

Relaxation also aids accuracy. The pitcher with everything working in synch feels relaxed, while one who tenses up when there are men on base throws wild because his muscles no longer are coordinated the way they were when he was loose.

"Being relaxed is mandatory when you are lifting weights," says the Rams' Garrett Giemont. "If you are tightening opposing muscle groups you are making an opposite effort. You can help prevent that by breathing properly. Inhale as the weight is coming down and exhale as you lift. In effect, think of blowing the weight up."

A deep breath is one of the most effective of all relaxation methods. Watch a basketball player as he lines up to make a free throw. He stands at the foul line, breathes deeply once or twice, bounces the ball a couple of times, and pumps the ball into the basket. The same type of breathing, relaxation, and focusing works wonders in any big-game or big-play situation.

Relaxation works not just for the muscles and vital organs, but also for the mind. It enhances your ability to interpret information —to think and to react. In sports terms, being relaxed keeps you from "choking."

*progressive relaxation*

It's so important that NFL teams invest a great deal of time teaching players better ways to relax. Pittsburgh uses a fairly common progressive relaxation technique. "We get the player to relax his whole body step by step, body part by body part," Evans says. Players lie alone in a dark room listening to soothing sounds of very soft music or the ocean playing quietly. Each player then clears his mind and begins the relaxation process.

Progressive relaxation usually starts with the outer limbs. You tense the hands and maintain the tension until it hurts slightly, then let go and keep letting go until they feel heavy. Then relax the arms in the same way, tightening until fatigued and then letting go. Continue progressively tensing and relaxing all the muscles in your body from head to toe. Focus your mind on each muscle being relaxed, and try to maintain steady, slow breathing. Once your body is in a relaxed state, shift the focus of your mind to your breathing. The whole relaxation process takes about 20 minutes. Sometimes you get so relaxed you fall asleep. If that happens, you probably needed the nap.

Among his assignments with the Patriots, Dr. Nicholi is charged with "teaching techniques for programming the mind for peak athletic performance." Included in those techniques are various methods for achieving a state of alert relaxation. New England players have learned relaxation methods that can be used in a variety of situations, even when they are on the bench waiting to go into the game. The purpose is to let players keep themselves mentally well balanced during the contest.

"A player can use the relaxation techniques if he finds himself too tense, or use visualization if he wants to raise his level of intensity," Dr. Nicholi says.

Relaxation away from the field is important, too. Houston's coaches try to help lighten the stress loads on players who are putting themselves under more emotional pressure than necessary.

*dealing with pressure*

"If a player can learn to relax himself when dealing with stressful everyday events," Watterson says, "then he can relax himself in difficult game situations as well, and be a more effective performer."

Most pressure, especially athletic, is self-generated. It comes from within. Once you deal with the pressure you put on yourself, there isn't much left. And don't confuse your performance with your self-image. No matter how important it is to you, you are not your golf game or your 10k time or your batting average.

The Rams' Giemont puts the need for good mental attitude in overall perspective.

"Fitness, whether mental or physical, is not exercise," he says. "It's lifestyle. You strive to be the best you can be. Because you'll never really know your ultimate potential unless you really push to reach your limits."

# *Performance Programming: Keena Turner and Riki Ellison*

With teams as evenly matched as they are in the NFL, athletes and coaches always are searching for an edge. At San Francisco, linebackers Keena Turner and Riki Ellison each has found his own unique path to consistent performance.

"When I came up to the 'Niners, I thought being a good athlete was all I needed," says Turner, San Francisco's second-round draft pick out of Purdue in 1980. "But I quickly learned that wasn't enough. When you look around the league, there is not that much difference in talent. So the edge has to be something mental. For me, it's all in the way I prepare."

Ellison agrees that mental and physical preparation is the key to success. But he and Turner go about it in different ways, and with vastly different styles.

Ellison is a favorite target of television cameramen. Before every play his forehead is intensely furrowed in concentration and his eyes have an almost crazed look. His body language seems to be daring the opposition to try another play. In fact, his appearance is an accurate reflection of his mental state: furious rage directed against the opposition. He uses it to keep himself focused during a game.

Turner is Mr. Cool by comparison, relaxed and remote, never talking with opponents and always playing within himself. Turner's forte is making the big plays. In Super Bowl XIX, for example, he had a team-high six tackles, including a hit against running back Tony Nathan in the second quarter that many consider a turning point in the game. Year after year he manages to be where the ball is, recovering fumbles, making interceptions, denying first downs. How does he do it?

"You have to think about it," Turner says.

"It doesn't just happen. You don't walk out there and think just your presence on the field will be enough. Before the game I have to see myself making plays. You have to visualize success. The night before a game, I dream about an interception with one second to go that wins the game. I am visualizing making big plays all the time. Most of the big-play guys are like that.

"Once on the field, there is no time to think. Everything has to be a reaction. You have to have thought about it already. When I see a runner like Eric Dickerson or Marcus Allen, I have to get him down. On the field it is just reaction because I already have visualized myself running through him. Sometimes the great running backs win the battles. But even if they do, you have to come back and believe that you will win the next one. I do what I have to do for us to win. I have to hold up my end of the chain."

The ability to react in critical situations is a combination of many factors: innate talent, experience, coaching, constant practice, and mental preparation—the factor that Turner feels gives him his personal edge. For him, the process of getting ready for a game begins months in advance. In early spring, Turner establishes some personal goals for the season. "I write them down and put them on the refrigerator door so I'm reminded every day," he says. "It helps me get up for training camp and the preseason."

Once the regular season begins, Turner follows a routine based on the team's weekly schedule that allows him to be relaxed on the field and stay mentally charged for action. Because he doesn't consider himself "an overemotional type of player," he requires a premeditated build-up of mental energy.

*urner: "The edge has to be something mental."*

"Monday I'm still consumed by errors I made in the game the day before," Turner says. "But by Monday night that's behind me and I start thinking about the next game. Tuesday is usually the rest day in the NFL, but I can't just shut down on my day off."

On Wednesdays and Thursdays the 49ers watch films of the next opponent and start getting into the offensive and defensive game plans. It means that Turner has to devote his attention to learning the defensive strategy and how he'll be expected to play.

"Our responsibilities change from week to week," he says. "Depending on who we're playing, there may be more emphasis on my watching the weakside [the side away from the tight end] or more on man-to-man pass coverage. I have to be able to adjust for the best matchups and I need to know where my help is all the time so I can play my man accordingly."

The team has hard practice on those two days, running the game plan and simulating both the offense and defense the opposing team is expected to run.

By Friday, the 49ers' game plan is finalized and committed to memory. They practice goal-line and other special situations, usually just running through the plays without pads. Saturday is even less strenuous, with a light workout and a review of any new plays.

"When I line up," says Turner, "whatever I do is a reflection of me alone. It has nothing to do with the team and who I'm representing. It is my goals, my pride, against whomever I am dealing with. It is me and that other guy. That is enough to keep me up.

"I have always wanted to be the best guy out there and I'm always striving. The ultimate compliment in this game is respect. And that is something you have to earn and prove you deserve on every play. That doesn't mean I don't get tired and down, but they are not part of my game plan.

"I don't think personally about the opposition. They don't even have numbers except that they are there. I'm in a tunnel. I respect them, but they don't have anything to do with what I have to accomplish. The only thing that can stop me is me. I don't talk to people on the field. If I'm talking, I'm not concentrating."

Between plays, of course, there is constant conversation with his teammates. "That's not chatter, that is business," says Turner. "That's encouragement and awareness. The more comfortable you are with other guys, the better the team is. I don't have to see [defensive end] Dwaine Board to know where he is. I just feel him there. When you get to that point, you know you are mentally prepared to play the game. You can feel those kinds of things."

Conversely, what Ellison feels is rage. "I work myself into a frenzy before every game," he says. "One time I even hyperventilated."

Ellison, however, is not nearly as crazy as he appears; there is distinct method in his self-induced madness. In fact, the entire emotional build-up he fosters is part of a carefully orchestrated program to develop the kind of mental edge he wants.

"I can get away with getting fired up, but a quarterback can't," he says. "That's one of the best things about being a linebacker. What I love about the game is getting myself psyched. I think about what the other team has done to me in the past. I find things to get me upset. And then I bring the whole stadium, all the excitement into it. I need to play with that kind of emotion."

When he was at USC, Ellison used the same techniques to prepare for big games. "I liked the whole thing with the Coliseum and the bands and the white horse," he says. "It would help get me charged up. I think if I lost that emotion I wouldn't be very good."

Stoking up his emotions is far from Ellison's only mental preparation. As the 49ers' defensive signal caller, he studies more game films and has a better grasp of the defensive game plan than perhaps any other player on the team. He also recognizes the need to relieve tension between games.

"On Sunday night," Ellison says, "I try to reflect on how I played. On Monday morning, I do flexibility exercises, running, and lift weights and then look at what my mistakes were the previous game. I grade myself on what I did right and wrong. Then I group all those things I have to work on and incorporate them in my practice. I'll do that extra practice on my own after team practice. If I didn't do pass drops right, I'll work on that. If my tackling was sloppy, I'll work on the tackling dummy for a while.

"But then on Tuesday, I get my mind completely off the game. I just get away out of town. Maybe take my wife somewhere, just as long as it has nothing to do with football. To keep your intensity level up you have to be very fresh. If I have too much on my mind, I can't be hungry in the game."

After practice on Wednesday Ellison stays late to watch more game films. "I try to study my opponent very well," he says. "I'll also try to watch one or two more films on lunch hours as well. Going through the defensive plan is like taking an exam. When I have to make adjustments in a game, they have to come to me right away. There is no time to think on the field. So you have to study and study and study.

"By Saturday I try to ease up physically on everything. I want to relax a little and be fresh again mentally and physically.

"On Sunday morning, I'm really fresh. I don't eat much and I start getting psyched up when I get to the stadium around 9:30. I organize my gear and get the taping out of the way. Then I get a playbook and isolate myself. I'll go in a corner somewhere away from everyone and lie down to do my concentration exercises."

It's during these exercises that Ellison builds his emotions. "Early in the week I put things in my mind of what I will see and how I will react," he says. "The night before a game I think of great plays I could make. I just picture the exact

*Ellison: "What I love about the game is getting myself psyched. I need to play with that kind of emotion."*

situation; the ground, the smell, the play in front of me. I do it in slow motion and fast motion and make myself do exactly the right thing in my mind.

"But you can't only think about making interceptions. You don't want to put too much pressure on yourself to make great plays.

"If you have studied how you are going to react, when it happens on the field it is very, very smooth—you already know how to do it. You've gone through it over and over in a dream-like trance. I think it is a great edge."

Ellison says that kind of concentration doesn't come easy, "especially in a pregame locker room with all the distractions. So on Sunday morning I'll sit there with a towel over my eyes and think about what I have to do. I get very intense. I let the stadium and the other things get me really fired up. If you're on the road, you use the crowd's hostility to your advantage. Let them get you even more angry to make you play harder. And when you're at home you let your own fans fire you up."

With all his rage and frenzy, Ellison recognizes very clearly the pitfalls of the process and attempts to keep himself in check. "If you are too high emotionally," he says, "wound too tight, you get yourself in trouble."

# 6 Playing Healthy:

## *Avoiding Injury*

"The better condition you are in, the less likely that you are going to be injured, especially in non-contact sports," says Don Clemons, Detroit's strength and conditioning coach. "When you train with weights, your muscle mass gets much bigger. That allows you to withstand more than if you didn't train.

"To get into the kind of condition that will help you resist injury, your overall program should include speed work, and flexibility, agility, endurance, and strength training. The smart guys in football work out in all those areas. The foolish ones think that only strength is enough or that they can get by without working out at all."

For the average weekend athlete, Clemons doesn't think it wise to put much effort into sprinting or explosive weightlifting routines. Those exercises should be reserved for pro athletes who need to develop specific muscle groups that will condition them for their sport. Clemons thinks that untrained people trying to do too much too soon are considerably more prone to injury; when that happens, conditioning has to stop before it ever really starts.

## Horsepower and Horse Sense

In any activity, failures are more frequent as the limits of performance are approached. For example, many of the race cars in the Memorial Day classic at Indianapolis break down before they complete the full 500 miles. Yet conventional automobiles are so reliable that most are warranted against major failure for up to 50,000 miles. It's not that the conventional cars are better built. They're not. The reason those race cars can't all finish even 500 miles is that they are being pushed beyond the absolute limits of their potential.

That same kind of push-to-failure breakdown is common with

championship-caliber athletes. Elite competitors train more and play harder, driving their bodies to new limits. But push your body like that and it sometimes pushes back in unpleasant ways, such as aching joints, sore muscles, and inflamed tendons. As you approach the boundaries of performance, injuries become more frequent and more serious.

*play within potential*

While work in training and a total effort during competition are necessary qualities in the pros, the average athlete should be prudent about staying within the limits of his or her own potential.

Train long enough and hard enough and sports injuries of some kind almost are unavoidable. The prescription is to reduce your chances of getting hurt and learn how to treat yourself when and if injury does occur.

*adapt gradually*

For example, when building a base of strength and cardiovascular fitness, let your body adapt to the new stresses slowly as you work into condition. But be aware that it's almost impossible not to feel some soreness if muscles are worked hard enough to make them stronger.

If you already are in good shape, learning a new skill can create the potential for injury. Expect at least some discomfort, such as soreness, from putting new demands on specific muscles.

Then, too, when you begin to perform closer to your ultimate potential, injuries also are possible from overtraining, overuse, or misuse caused by the demands of competition. Tennis elbow, shin splints, bone spurs, shoulder pains, and balky knees are maladies that commonly afflict pro and weekend athletes alike.

---

## Sports Toll

Some activities simply are more dangerous than others. Based on the number of injuries reported, the number-one cause of sports injuries is baseball, primarily a non-contact sport. And in some activities, particularly water sports, when an injury or accident happens, it is serious. Based on accidents per participant, boxing was the most dangerous, with nearly half of all participants suffering an injury of some sort during the year. According to the National Safety Council, selected sports-related injuries in the U.S. during 1985 were estimated as follows:

| | Injuries | Participants |
|---|---|---|
| Baseball | 474,261 | 13,556,000 |
| Basketball | 457,034 | 25,322,000 |
| Boating | 2,757 | 52,588,000 |
| Boxing | 7,926 | 16,000 |
| Football | 422,121* | 1,575,000† |
| Hang Gliding | 1,373 | 30,000 |
| Ice Skating | 19,431 | 18,032,000 |
| Roller Skating | 112,198 | 30,156,000 |
| Scuba Diving | 1,116 | 2,350,000 |
| Snow Skiing | 42,939 | 19,490,000 |
| Swimming | 136,329 | 102,286,000 |
| Tennis | 29,524 | 25,450,000 |
| Water Skiing | 29,620 | 18,032,000 |

*Includes all football — tackle and touch, organized and sandlot.
†Includes only organized tackle football; high school, college, and pro.

The goal is not to be so cautious as to lose the benefits hard training can bring, but to understand how to improve your odds of staying healthy, and to learn what to do if physical problems develop so you can get back to your sport as soon as possible.

# Hurt, or Just Sore?

Before treating an injury, you must determine its extent. What seems like an inflamed tendon might be only soreness caused by buckling your ski boot too tightly. And stiffness and minor bruises that will go away in a couple of days shouldn't necessarily mean a trip to a doctor. Conversely, numbness or tingling in your leg is the kind of annoyance that easily could be ignored but shouldn't be. If it persists and doesn't seem to have any identifiable cause, have it seen by a medical expert.

*evaluating injury*

Many sports injuries are pretty obvious. A pulled muscle in a tennis game feels like you've been hit in the calf by a rock. It hurts, and you start limping. That's something that should be wrapped, iced, and seen by a doctor. Harder to evaluate are the injuries that were unnoticed at the time but then sneak up hours later, becoming intense and very uncomfortable. Another injury that's difficult to judge is the kind that is relatively mild but doesn't seem to get any better over time.

Pains in the shoulder, knee, ankle, wrist, or hip can signal a real problem—but not always. Is the pain in a place on the joint where there is muscle? That's good news. It might be just a sore muscle. If the pain comes on suddenly, however, or you can feel a resistance inside the joint at any point, it may be more serious.

Swelling (from fluid build-up) always is a tip-off that something underneath has a problem. Puffy ankles indicate a strain or sprain someplace in the area that needs attention. Sometimes it's harder to tell whether a knee or elbow is swollen, so try to compare the right and left sides in a mirror. Pain, unusual squeaks or clicks coming from the swollen area, or discoloration are confirming indications that medical advice is in order.

You may have a problem if a muscle hurts when you touch a specific spot. Feel the area to see if there are any obvious holes or breaks or sharp ridges in the muscle under the skin. Try the same test on the limb on the other side of your body to be sure that it isn't a normal bump or just general muscle soreness.

When an arm or leg seems weak or you can't move it easily through its usual range of motion, that's a sign you have an injury that needs medical treatment. If you have weights or access to Nautilus equipment, try a few exercises with *extremely* light weights to check the relative strength and flexibility of the right and left body parts in question. Stop if anything hurts. You know there's trouble if you can't handle as much weight on one side as the other. All such information will help in later diagnosis by a medical expert.

Whenever there's a pain you can't easily treat or explain, stop the activity you think is causing it and get in touch with a competent health professional.

# Common Complaints

Sports injuries can result from activities as sedate as brisk walking or as obviously risky as rock climbing. Depending on which sport you play, different parts of the body are most susceptible to different kinds of overuse or accidental injuries.

"The most likely places to be injured in football," says Steelers conditioning coach Walt Evans, "are the hamstring, back, knee, and shoulder. Those same areas are most susceptible to injury outside of football, too, but it takes longer for those areas to break down in normal activities."

According to the American College of Sports Medicine, the most common sports injuries fall into four categories: tendinitis, strains and sprains, bursitis, and fractures.

### Tendinitis

Tender and swollen tendons usually are caused by long-term overuse of a particular muscle group. That would include activities such as jogging, aerobics, or baseball pitching. The stress inflames the tendon, the tough cord that connects the muscle to the bone. Shin splints, Achilles tendinitis, and tennis elbow are some of the more common tendon maladies.

In general, the cure is to determine what caused the injury, stop doing it, give the tendon time to recover, and then change whatever caused the problem in the first place.

To prevent tendinitis in general, experts suggest you warm up well before a workout, strengthen the muscles involved, and beware of repeated sharp impacts. To help avoid painful shin splints, be sure your shoes have enough cushioning, especially if you are working out or running on hard surfaces.

For Achilles tendinitis, the suggestion is strengthening calf muscles, limbering up completely before any activity, and wearing good athletic shoes.

Tennis elbow, known medically as lateral humeral epicondylitis, can result from a number of causes. Again, eliminate the cause and you have the cure. Have someone check your form to be sure you are not hitting ground strokes too late or too stiffly, and that you are using the momentum of your whole body in the swing, not just your arm. Have a pro evaluate whether your racket is the right size and weight and is properly strung. If those suggestions don't help after some rest, you may be playing people who put you under too much pressure, or you may need to consult a sports-medicine specialist about treatment.

**Strains and Sprains**

A strain is a stretch or tear in a muscle or tendon. A sprain is a stretch or tear in the ligament that holds the joints together. Strains and sprains are classified in three degrees, ranging from first-degree injuries that are painful but not debilitating, to third-degree injuries, which involve tearing of the muscle or connective tissue and definitely require medical attention, sometimes even surgery.

Muscle strains often are the result of failing to warm up before vigorous exercise or of not having complete flexibility through a joint's full range of motion. Putting sudden demands on a muscle also is a major cause of strains.

Ligament sprains most often occur in the ankle, knee, and shoulder. Sprains usually are a result of overuse, such as increasing running mileage abruptly. They also are caused by accidents that subject a joint to extreme stress, such as getting bumped just as you plant your cleat in a soccer game or falling awkwardly while skiing. Strengthening the muscles and ligaments surrounding the joints by regular workouts is the accepted NFL technique for reducing the chances for accidental injuries.

"It is not just the muscle that has to be enlarged," says Giants strength coach Johnny Parker. "It's also the connective tissue. Ligaments actually are thickened by working out."

**Bursitis**

The body's ball bearings are the bursa, fluid-filled sacs near the major joints. These bursa allow muscles, skin, and tendons to slide more easily over the bones. Any direct blow to the bursa may cause them to swell and become painful. Overuse or constant irritation, such as in baseball pitching or serving a tennis ball, also may bring tis. Rest is the only truly safe remedy. Cortisone shots can help in the short term, but long-term use of cortisone can produce dangerous side-effects.

**Fractures**

Put too much force on a bone and it will fracture. A complete fracture means the bone is broken in two. Complete fractures often are very painful and take months to heal completely.

A stress fracture is a hairline crack, usually in the leg or foot. Stress fractures are most often a result of overuse. Although they can be painful, they take less time for recovery. However, stress fractures in the lower leg are easy to confuse with shin splints, sometimes delaying proper treatment. Even x-rays don't always disclose the problem the first time.

Prevention is to avoid overstressing bone by wearing proper athletic shoes, playing within the limits of your ability, and making certain that ski boots and bindings are adjusted properly (the most common ski injury scenario is a slow, twisting fall that doesn't generate enough force to pop bindings set too high). In other words, prevention is based on a common sense approach to fitness.

# Do, but Don't Overdo

Training too much and too hard is one of the leading causes of sports injuries. The body needs to adapt to stresses. If a runner doubles his mileage suddenly or a pitcher begins throwing hard the first day in spring training, they can be pretty well assured the body will rebel. "It makes no sense to work out so strenuously to get yourself into good physical condition that you injure yourself or no longer feel good," the Giants' Parker says.

An athlete's natural competitive drive can get him into trouble. Trying to bench press more weight than the guy in the next locker is a good way to bring on a muscle sprain or worse. Following a more experienced mountain bike rider down a trail you can't handle also is an invitation to injury. Train and perform within your own abilities. Improve at your own rate; competition is competition, but training is *training*.

*use proper form*    Also, concentrate on using good technique. Form is not a matter of aesthetics; it's a question of safety. "Technique in lifting takes precedence over everything else to prevent injury," says Dave Redding, strength and conditioning coach for the Browns. "You don't want to bounce a barbell off your chest, for instance. It doesn't matter if you are working with machines or free weights, if you are using the wrong form, you could hurt yourself."

Dr. Donald Chu, director of the Ather Sports Clinic, agrees. "Most injuries are technique related," he says. "The problem often is overuse, like running too much or lifting too heavy with the wrong technique. The other problem is not having a balanced musculature. For a basketball player, for example, if he can't work off both legs, he's at greater risk of injury. Among other things, it could cause back problems."

*bilateral inequality*    "Many injuries occur," says Bengals strength coach Kim Wood, "when the body is out of balance. When one set of muscles is much stronger than the set that opposes it, problems are more likely to develop. Because muscles work in pairs, one extending a limb and the other contracting it, if there is an imbalance, the stronger one may contribute to a pull or tear in the other.

"We think bilateral inequality is one of the major reasons for injury in football. If the antagonistic muscle, such as the quadriceps, is much stronger than the agonist, such as the hamstring, you might have problems. For example, if a player does squats but not leg curls, he risks that kind of an imbalance."

Even the best balanced muscles can't prevent all accidents from happening. "There is not a lot you can do about some accidents," says Dolphins strength and conditioning coach Junior Wade. "They happen because you happen to be in the wrong position at the wrong time."

*fatigue*    However, fatigue, which often is a factor in sports injuries, can be recognized before it is too late. It is an axiom of the ski patrol that "all accidents happen on the last run." Of course, that is self-defining; you don't take any more runs after you're hurt. Fatigued muscles and a desire to do something memorable on the last run of the day combine to make late-afternoon runs more accident-prone than most. Tired weightlifters who lose their form to fatigue sometimes also lose their grip, which can cause serious injury in the training room.

# Easy Ways to Stay Healthy

Preventing injury is a primary concern at all NFL training camps, equally as important as improving performance. That priority should be the same for the average athlete as well. Here's a list of simple guidelines to help you avoid training ailments.

● *Know your limits.* A long-distance runner shouldn't start sprinting until he goes through a conditioning program to adapt his or her body to the different stress load. Trying to perform maneuvers you haven't practiced is dangerous. Push yourself to try new activities, but do it in increments so you can learn proper technique and your body can adjust to the new physical demands.

● *Avoid dangerous situations.* Work out with a buddy who can spot for you when lifting free weights. When swimming, stay away from riptides and rocky coastlines. Ski in-bounds, and even then look for possible escape routes whenever you're on or near avalanche-prone slopes.

● *Wear good protective gear.* Be sure it fits. Eye protectors for racquetball and squash are vital. Wear helmets for all kinds of biking—motor, mountain, and touring. Pads and protectors are required in football, hockey, and other contact sports. But wearing equipment, including knee protectors and shin guards, also is a good idea in sports such as soccer and roller skating. Preventing just one injury will more than make up for any inconvenience or costs you incur.

● *Use quality equipment.* Barbells with unsecured weights that can fall off can twist your back or injure your feet; they're also dangerous to people working out nearby. Skis should have calibrated safety bindings that release when you fall. Don't play racket sports in shoes with worn-out soles; your traction and balance depend on a non-slip grip. Keep the brakes and running gear on your bike upgraded and in tune.

● *Get enough rest.* Allow your body to regain full strength before going all-out on another heavy training session. Fatigue can be cumulative. Be sure to couple rest with adequate nutrition.

● *Drink enough fluids.* There is evidence that dehydration may be a factor in injuries. When the muscle cells don't have enough fluid in them, they become less elastic, which may contribute to certain kinds of muscle pulls.

# Working at Injury Prevention

"To prevent injury you have to have a good offseason program," says Eagles trainer Otho Davis. "It's not just building muscle. You have to do maintenance on the three major fitness aspects—flexibility, endurance, and strength."

*stretching*

Most NFL coaches agree that achieving flexibility means a regular stretching program. This usually involves a pre-workout stretch to prepare the body and a post-workout stretch to improve the range of motion in muscles. "The two areas in which a football player needs flexibility the most are hamstrings and groin," Packers strength coach Virgil Knight says. "Those are the areas most likely to have an injury that could be prevented by stretching."

Any good stretching program, including yoga or martial arts, can be effective in reducing injuries by making the body more supple and thus able to absorb sudden impacts. Take—or make—the time to warm up and stretch out before starting any hard exercise.

*strength*

At least as important as flexibility is increasing muscle power. "People at low levels of strength tend to have more injury problems," says Pittsburgh's Evans.

"We've kept our rate of injuries among the lowest in professional football by requiring all players to be involved in a regular balanced weight-training program," says the Bengals' Wood. "Players can prevent injuries by developing strength and mass."

In football, "the most important area of the body that has to be built up to prevent injury is the neck," says Washington's Dan Riley. Like many other teams, the Redskins do neck exercises every day they work out. "It's not so much the strength of the neck that counts," says Wood, "but the mass of the neck column." In any case, the way to build up both strength and mass in the neck is to work out with regular resistance training. Besides football and wrestling, however, few sports require bull-like necks, nor do most people want to develop them.

*endurance*

Because fatigue so often is a factor when an athlete gets hurt, developing endurance is the third important element of the injury-prevention process. The preseason is the time NFL teams build endurance. Some coaches want their players to have an aerobic base that will sustain them during the season. This means distance running or other aerobic exercise that will condition the heart and large muscles. Other coaches prefer to develop endurance by running numerous sets of short distance sprints, and by weight training with high reps and low weights.

The average athlete interested in overall fitness should include some kind of aerobic conditioning as a part of his or her program. It can be running, brisk walking, swimming, or another activity, but it should be something that helps build endurance, thus minimizing fatigue-induced injuries.

# If You Get Hurt

The first thing to do if you are injured is to stop playing or exercising. It sounds obvious, and it is, but athletes don't always heed their bodies' signals. Take a timeout to decide whether you need immediate medical help. Dealing with any health-related issue is serious business. In any case where there is doubt, always seek medical attention, even if it is just a telephone call for advice. For a detailed look at what can go wrong and when to call in the medics, read Dr. James G. Garrick's *Peak Condition*. It is one of the most complete and well-constructed books available on the causes and treatment of typical sports injuries.

Except for fractures and serious sprains that may require splinting or emergency medical treatment, most sports injuries will be strains, sprains, bruises, and tendinitis. The first aid for most of these is the same: mild compression with tape or elastic bandage; cooling with crushed ice in a plastic bag or towel to retard swelling; elevating the injured area above the heart to prevent pooling of blood; and rest.

The American College of Sports Medicine also recommends taking, if possible, an anti-inflammatory drug such as aspirin. They caution that ice should not be applied directly to the skin and should be moved every five minutes to prevent frostbite. The elastic bandage around the injured part shouldn't be so tight it cuts off the blood supply or causes numbness or swelling.

Elevating the injured arm or leg helps drain excess fluid from the affected area. The general rule is that reducing swelling and any pooling of blood at the outset of the injury will significantly increase the speed of recovery.

Unless you are sure that the damage is minor, make a quick visit to the doctor or emergency room for an expert appraisal of how to proceed. You'll want to begin some form of rehabilitation exercise as soon as possible to help the tissues restore themselves and to clear away by-products of the injury.

# Playing With Pain

One of the accepted myths of professional sports is the nobility of playing with pain. Bruises and bumps are just accepted as the price that has to be paid. It is not uncommon, for example, to see an NFL lineman play a ferocious game sporting a cast on a fractured hand.

*too much macho*   "A weekend guy has nothing to gain by going back too quickly," Evans says. "Lots of amateur guys are macho and want to get right back. But they don't have a pro sports career to maintain so they should wait. Sports at the pro level are all-out combat. However, weekend sports are supposed to be good for your health and relaxation. If you have an injury, take the time to let it heal."

Judging when it is safe to resume activity after injury is a critical decision. Go back too soon and you risk worse problems. Wait too long and your overall condition and muscle tone may deteriorate more than necessary.

To evaluate when a rehabilitating player is ready to go back to the field, some professional teams will test the strength of his injured muscle against the strength of his opposing muscle. For instance, if he has hurt his hamstring, they will put him on an isokinetic measuring machine and check the strength of both agonist and antagonist muscles. "If there is more than a ten percent difference between them, we won't let him go back on the field," Philadelphia's Davis says. Other teams test the strength of the right side and left side, using the same kind of judgment to assure he has regained equal power.

*listen to your body*

For weekend athletes, the best advice is to listen to your body. Test the injured area gently. If you have pain, don't push it. It is much better to wait too long. Give your body time to adapt to increased stress after an injury. Pushing too fast can cause reinjury that could prove chronic.

# Coming Back

The same principles of physiology that apply in building up the body also are in force when repairing injuries. The only difference is the level of intensity. The fibers in a muscle that is strained can't be worked out very strenuously. To do so would be counterproductive. But light exercise definitely is in order. It keeps the undamaged muscles from atrophying, and it brings more blood to the area to help repair the damaged fibers and wash away debris.

*isokinetics*

A tricky problem in promoting use of a rehabilitating muscle is determining how much stress to put on the muscle without causing additional damage to the fibers. One of the answers is working out on an isokinetic machine that resists only as much pressure as the athlete is able to exert. If, for example, his injury has weakened muscles at the contracted end of his range of motion, he still may be able to get a workout in the stretched range at good intensity; the machine automatically lightens the load to prevent strain on the damaged part.

*water therapy*

The swimming pool also is a favorite rehabilitation tool of some teams. For example, the Eagles use pool therapy to rehabilitate hamstring pulls. "Hamstring tears are more serious than many players realize," Davis says. "If a player doesn't recognize the problem and tries to push the rehab too hard, he just reinjures it, and then you really may have lost him."

Depending on severity, a hamstring can take a week or several months to return to normal. With pool therapy, the process seems to go faster and the chances for reinjury are much lower, according

## Heating Up After a Cold

Conditioning programs get sidetracked by colds, flu, and other minor illnesses. Your body will let you know in no uncertain terms when to stop working out, but problems can result from making the wrong decision about when to start back, and how hard work out when you do.

"When you get a bad cold or the flu, your body is under stress," says Dr. Ramon Ryan, a sports medicine fellow at Methodist Hospital in Indianapolis, and a consultant to the National Institute for Fitness in Sports. "If you work out when you feel sick, you are putting your body under extra stress and the weak link is going to break."

His advice: Listen to your body. Take off to rest and recouperate when you have a minor illness. Once you begin to feel better, start back slowly. Don't try to pick up where you left off. The body deconditions itself faster than it builds itself up. So after a week on the sick list, expect to take a week or more to regain your previous level of performance. Because dehydration is one of the symptoms of flu and colds, be sure to drink plenty of water before and after your post-illness workouts.

There's a rebound effect that athletes have noticed when they resume working out after a cold; lingering sniffles and congestion can be eliminated by the heat and increased blood circulation of exercise. "Moderate exercise may make you feel better faster," Dr. Ryan says, "but that's only after the major symptoms have broken up. A workout definitely is not a cure for a cold."

to Davis. The player is immersed in a deep pool, wearing a flotation collar and tethered in place. He does walking, jogging, and then running motions in the pool. The water provides resistance against which his muscles push, but not so much resistance that reinjury can occur. There is no weight on the leg, which makes it useful in treating fractures as well. Among the unique benefits of the rehab pool is that after a long period in a cast, doing running or walking motions in the water re-educates the muscles and nerves without imposing undue strain. Later, after recovery, many athletes contin-

*take your time*   ue their water workouts, running in shallow water along a shoreline as a strength-building resistance exercise.

In any rehabilitation situation, the key is to take your time coming back. If you get hurt, find out exactly what your injury is and then get sound advice on how to treat it. The information in this chapter is only a basic guide—it is not sufficient for treatment of any but minor injuries.

More important, try to prevent injury. Strengthen your muscles and improve your flexibility and endurance. Whatever conditioning routine you develop, stick with it. The Giants' Parker points out that the workout method you use is not nearly as important as the effort you make. "The worst program that everybody on a team does," he says, "is much better than the best program that nobody does."

# Adequate Compensation

Sometimes, no matter how good your medical treatment or how well you heal, there will be some residual problems as the result of an injury. It could be a slight impairment of range of motion, or persistent soreness in a joint when it is stressed heavily, or any number of complaints. You may have to learn to work around these things, adjusting your conditioning program and, perhaps even your athletic form, to compensate for them. But a trick knee or restricted reach shouldn't keep you from being fit.

For example, Pro Football Hall of Fame quarterback Joe Namath was almost as famous for the "zippers" on his knees, the scars from numerous operations, as he was for his passing arm. When running became too painful, he switched to swimming to maintain his aerobic fitness and extended his career.

Certainly, you should have an awareness of limitations caused by previous injuries. But use them to your training advantage, not as an excuse. When you've been injured badly, its almost as if you are in continuous rehabilitation. Keep working on the injured area to keep it strong and help resist reinjury.

# *Curt Warner: All the Way Back*

Curt Warner was 15 yards from Cleveland's goal line with a clear shot at a touchdown when it happened.

"I planted my right foot, started a cut toward the end zone, and my right knee blew out," Warner says. Without being touched, the Seahawks' running back snapped the anterior cruciate ligament in the middle of his right knee when his cleats snagged in the artificial turf early in the first game of the 1984 season.

"I went from being in the best shape and having the best time of my life to zero," he says.

Within seconds of Warner's collapse, Seahawks trainer Jim Whitesel and the team doctor were on the field. They already had a good idea of what happened. In the locker room, further examination confirmed that the knee ligament was ruptured.

There was no delay in treating the injury. The knee was wrapped and iced to keep swelling down, and surgery was scheduled for the next day. By operating immediately, there was less chance that the torn ligament would grind into other parts of the knee, causing further damage, or that there would be excessive swelling and pooling of blood in the lower leg.

Warner's surgery was extensive, requiring doctors to "harvest" tendons from two other areas of his body and use them to reconstruct ligaments in his knee. Specifically, the surgery was a combination repair that replaced the torn interior ligament with a piece of tendon from a superfluous muscle. The 1½-hour operation also used a section of tissue from another leg tendon to reinforce the outer knee ligament.

Warner stayed in the hospital for five days, his right knee immobilized by a splint. During that time he was recovering from the anesthesia and was monitored to assure there were no infections or complications from surgery.

Rehabilitation started the day after surgery, when Warner was asked simply to tighten the

*Curt Warner's knee injury ended his 1984 season early.*

muscles in this injured leg. After another five days at home, the sutures where removed, he was put in a brace to restrict the range of motion in the joint, and he began hobbling around on crutches.

"That's when I found out what rehabilitation really means," Warner says. "It's not just a word. You can't wish your leg back. You have to work your leg back, and I mean work. It took everything I had and by the time it ended I was totally drained."

What makes the process tough is not so much the pain or the boredom of doing the same exercises over and over. It's the slow pace.

"It took me three months just to get the medicines out of my body and get the swelling in my knee to go away," he says. "For weeks and weeks it seemed like nothing was happening and I began to think that I was never going to play again."

Whitesel says that after knee surgery, it generally takes at least 20 weeks before players can do any running. In some cases it can take as long as 30 weeks. In Warner's situation, the first four weeks of rehabilitation were spent massaging the leg and doing isometric contractions with the knee still locked to maintain some muscle tone. Then, about five weeks after Warner's surgery, the stops on the brace were loosened somewhat to permit more bending in the joint and specific exercises were begun, five days a week.

More than two months after the accident, Warner still was on crutches, but the brace was loosened a little more and he was able to use a stationary bicycle and an isokinetic exercise machine. Then he went into a therapy pool, floating to keep weight off the knee, flexing the joint to approximate the motions of walking and running.

"There were lots of days when I had to force myself to go to the training room. I just didn't want to do it," he says. " But after a while, you begin to see some progress and then you can feel that you're getting better."

Warner began working his knee on a Cybex machine, which automatically adjusts the amount of resistance it provides to compensate for weakness at any point throughout the range of motion of an exercise. "I hated it," he says. "But that machine probably helped make

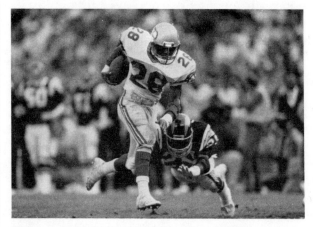

***Warner returned to lead all AFC rushers in 1986.***

the most improvement."

All during the time he was using the Cybex and Nautilus equipment at light weight set tings, Warner was working out his upper body and doing exercises for the hip and groin areas that did not involve using his knee.

Finally, five months after the accident, long after the season was over for the team, Warner was able to begin to do some jogging. That was allowed only when tests showed there was less than a 20 percent difference in strength between his injured right leg and his left.

When he tolerated jogging well, Warner went on to running figure-eight patterns and then easy agility drills. It took nine months before Warner was able to get back on the practice field and run full out. He had to wear a brace until about halfway into the 1985 season. That may be one reason why he didn't return to the rookie-of-the-year form he displayed in 1983. He had one great game. Then his ankle was injured in an accident, forcing more rehabilitation after the season.

Warner persevered.

In 1986, all his rehabilitation behind him, Warner showed he had come all the way back. He led the AFC in total rushing with 1,481 yards, had the highest rushing production of any back in a single game, gaining 192 yards against Denver, and had 13 rushing touchdowns, more than any other running back in the conference.

But what may be the most telling statistic of all was his 319 rushing attempts, the most by any AFC runner.

Warner wants to relegate his injury to the past. "I don't like to talk about it," he says. "It's over and I'm as good as new."

He has made some changes in style, however. "During training," he says, "I don't pound the knee as much. I save it for the games. And all those months of hard work of six hours a day of rehab doing the same exercises have made me less cocky. I think that I see the game and my life in better perspective."

# 7 Aging Vigorously:

## *Tips for the Older Athlete*

"Use it or lose it" may be a tired cliche. But it's such an accurate prescription for growing older athletically that it's worth repeating.

"Conditioning is as close to the fountain of youth as anything I've ever seen," says Chargers conditioning coach Phil Tyne. "Regular exercise and good nutrition in a consistent program will improve the cardiovascular system and retard the aging process."

Even if it doesn't lengthen life, staying fit will put more life into the years you have. Evidence is clear that those who engage in vigorous physical activity enjoy their maturity with less illness, more strength, and a more positive attitude than their sedentary peers.

What's more, because so few people ever develop even close to their physical potential when young, a new, more vigorous workout program could make your athletic performance better than ever. Inactivity is what blights your body. Give up your conditioning at middle age and you'll soon begin to feel older. Stop jogging or walking briskly and stairs will begin to seem steeper. Don't go to your health club and notice how your shirts begin to hang around your shoulders. Keep eating the way you did in college and that same shirt will get tighter around the neck and middle.

The big surprise is how soon physical decline begins. The aging process starts as early as the mid-20s, and begins to accelerate sometime after the mid-30s. A blow-by-blow description of the progression is provided by Dr. Roy Shephard, director of the school of physical and health education at the University of Toronto and a member of the American College of Sports Medicine. "Aerobic fitness starts to decline in the early twenties," he says. "Flexibility of the tendons starts deteriorating at about twenty-five and bone strength declines starting at around thirty-five. Muscular strength plateaus until about thirty-five or forty, and after forty you see less elasticity in the skin."

# The Over-the-Hill Gang

The National Institute on Aging has studied a group of more than 1,700 adults for the past 30 years attempting to measure and understand what actually happens in the aging process. The effort, officially known as the Baltimore Longitudinal Study, is important to the average person because it focuses on what happens to healthy, educated people who are aware of the basic concepts of diet, exercise, and stress.

The results of the Baltimore study can be seen as predicting how the general population will age, not just what happens to sick people or those suffering from some special problem. The data still are being evaluated, but already there are some well accepted results. The NIA's current understanding of some specifics of how the aging process begins and how fast it progresses is summarized below.

Declines in performance noted here are based on individuals who engage in an average amount of exercise, well below what is recommended by most experts of fitness and aging. The rate of decline for those who are involved in vigorous exercise several times a week is known to be slower, but definitive data are not yet available.

**Static Muscle Strength**

There is little or no decline due to aging until the 50s, and then the decline is relatively slight all the way to 80. A total reduction in strength of about 25 percent occurs between the ages of 30 and 80, most of it in the last 20 years.

**Coordinated Muscle Strength**

Measurable declines begin in the early 30s. By age 80, strength drops to only about half of peak performance. While the same muscles are involved as in static strength, the fall-off here is much faster, probably because the reserve capacity of the muscles declines with age. A coordinated strength test involves hand-cranking a bicycle attached to a measured load.

**Raw Reflexes** (Nerve Conduction Speed)

Measured by the speed at which a signal moves up the arm when the funny bone is tapped, this performance factor stays relatively unchanged up until age 80, declining only about 15 percent over a lifetime.

**Bone Loss**

In men, thinning of the bone mass, which indicates declining strength, begins to be evident in the early 40s. Between 45 and 69, men lose an average of 14 percent of long-bone mass. Comparable figures for women have not yet been tabulated in the Baltimore study, but other research indicates the figure is higher.

**Renal Function** (Kidney)

The kidneys lose half of their ability to clear the organic compound creatine from the body between the ages of 30 and 80. However, in otherwise healthy subjects, the kidneys have enough spare capacity to handle all normal functions.

**Cardiac Output**

The pumping capacity of a normal human heart at age 20 is seven liters per minute. At age 80, it is down to only four liters. Nevertheless, the heart has an ability to compensate for its own deficiencies. During exercise, an older person's heart will pump just about as well as someone much younger. Obviously, other factors such as lung capacity, the vascular system, and ability of muscles to utilize oxygen affect overall performance.

**Visual Acuity**

Sharpness of vision begins to decline in most people in the mid-20s. There is an acceleration of visual loss in the late 60s and 70s.

**Hearing**

The ability to hear high-pitched sounds begins to drop off in the 30s, especially in men. Over 65, few people can hear tones that are higher than 10,000 cycles per second. By age 70, about a third of all men have a measurable loss in hearing. Over the age of 75, more than half of all men have a substantial loss.

The ages at which all of these changes in human performance take place are approximations based on measurements extending across a large sample of the population. What happens to individuals is often quite different from the averages described, and the differences between individuals become more pronounced with advancing age.

# Early Retirement?

Although the aging process affects everyone differently, it *does* affect everyone. Usually the process is very subtle. "Very rarely does anyone notice the initial effects of aging," Dr. Shephard says, "unless they are engaged in high-performance athletic competition."

For athletes, the impact can be clear and dramatic. In the NFL, most players have retired from active participation in the sport well before the age of 30. With greater demands for quickness, consistency, and intensity than anything else in the athletic world, professional football is too competitive for players who can't deliver the ultimate performance.

In competitive sports, the first effects of aging show up as a half-step loss of speed, a slight hesitation in reaction time, or slower recovery from injury. The mental and physical effects of this aging process were sensitively described recently by NHL goalie Ken Dryden in his book, *The Game*: "For each of us, it's a race, a short, quick race we don't know we're in until we start to lose. We build up our bodies, break them down, and build them up again; it is the natural, unconcerned rhythm of our careers, until one day they break down faster than we can build them up and the end is not far away. Though we know that it's coming and can feel its symptoms, the effects, we pretend, are much less clear, and the time always seems months and years off, except for others. I'm not there yet, at least I don't think so, but what every other year was a slump can suddenly become the irreversible status quo. And desperately preoccupied with redeeming myself and proving others wrong, like everyone else I would be the last to know."

Andy Robustelli, a member of the Pro Football Hall of Fame, remembers the end of his 19-year career with the New York Giants. "When it's time to retire," he says, "nobody has to tell you.

"For me it was that I wasn't willing to go through what you have to do in order to be able to play like you should."

In the NFL, the players who last beyond age 30 generally are either overpowering physically or extremely smart. Physically dominating players are so good at their positions that even playing at 5 or 10 percent less power and speed than at their peak, they're still better than anyone else. Other players still are effective well into their 30s because they've made up in savvy or technique what they've lost in strength or speed. Redskins conditioning coach Dan Riley says that "you can have a guy who is slower but who has over the years picked up so much in game smarts that he can more than compensate for the slight physical decline."

Robustelli says that he didn't begin to play his best football as a defensive end until he turned 36. "That year I became a player-coach. I was much smarter because I studied game films all the time so I could teach the others how to play. I didn't look as spectacular on the field, but I did a much better job."

The effects of aging are different for each position. Outstanding quarterbacks and kickers can have long careers because so much of their performance depends on mental factors. Linemen usually can maintain their on-field skills longer than running backs because sheer strength generally doesn't begin to decline as early in life as agility and speed.

## Getting More Out of Less

A medical definition of the aging process comes from Dr. Nathan W. Shock, of the National Institute on Aging's Gerontology Research Center in Baltimore. "Unlike diseases, which affect only selected members of a population," he says, "aging ultimately occurs in everyone, resulting in a gradual systematic reduction in adaptability that is a normal part of the life span. The essence of aging is an increasing vulnerability to all stresses."

*room for improvement*

The essence of fitness training is to delay the aging process by conditioning the body so it is better able to resist those stresses. In many ways, the average weekend athlete has a better chance to maintain youthful performance than the championship player. Because most amateurs never have operated at anything close to 100 percent of their potential, they have more room to grow.

You can step up your training intensity and get stronger, relative to your potential. The champion player already is at his best when he is young. As his potential declines with age, he can expect less performance in those peaks skills no matter how hard he works. Ordinary people who start from a lower base and work harder every year may be able to more than maintain their levels of speed, strength, and endurance. For example, say your overall physical potential declines at five percent a decade, and you started out operating at only 75 percent of your capacity at age 30. You actually could be able to perform better athletically at 50 if you trained hard enough to achieve 90 percent of your potential. At some point, of course, the underlying potential will decline so much that even a 100 percent conditioning effort won't completely counteract the effects of age.

## Lessons From the Masters

There is some evidence that there's more to vigorous exercise than just holding the line. Studies of masters runners show some amazing results. Masters competitors, long-distance runners and race-walkers who range from 55 to 75 years old, generally possess aerobic capacities higher than healthy, untrained 25-year-olds. However, those masters runners are not as fit today as they would be if they still were 25 and doing the same conditioning, nor are they as fit as young men who train equally hard. The masters' ability to perform is better, and their loss of function over the years is smaller than normally would be expected from people of their age. That's the conclusion of Dr. Andrew Goldberg, an endocrinologist and gerontologist who is running the study for the General Clinical Research Center at the Francis Scott Key Medical Center in Baltimore. Dr. Goldberg says the masters runners in his group have a significantly lower risk of developing heart disease and diabetes than other people of their age. The conclusion simply is that people who

*exercisers live longer*

have stayed in good condition all their lives have a better chance for a healthy and longer life than their more sedentary counterparts.

"Although you can to some extent get it back if you start working on conditioning at any age," Dr. Goldberg says, "your ability to add muscle mass and strength decreases after about age fifty. So, the better conditioned you are before the older years, the better and longer you'll be able to perform."

To get into the lowered risk category, Dr. Goldberg suggests vigorous exercise at least three times a week. That could be a competitive sport, jogging, or brisk walking, or working out in an aerobics program or doing calisthenics. The workouts should last about an hour and should maintain the heartbeat at least 50 percent over the normal rate at rest for 30 minutes.

Evidence that masters runners maintain their vigor longer than normal lends credibility to the opinion of Russ Paternostra, strength and conditioning coach of the Saints. He believes age can be pushed back almost indefinitely, at least in the game of football. "If you want to keep the hounds off your heels, you have to keep getting stronger every year," he says.

"With professional football players it's possible to keep getting stronger every year and getting better as long as you are willing to pay the price of working hard at conditioning all year around. You can keep doing that until your mind starts accepting that you're getting older. It's when you start backing off that it's over."

## Taking the Long View

Some players agree that the mind plays a pivotal role in aging. Robustelli said he retired for reasons that were more psychological than physical. At the end of his career, he found the running, practicing, and constant tension ultimately more than he was willing to endure. He also recognized that older players take more criticism. "Everybody makes mistakes in a game," Robustelli says. "But when you are thirty-nine years old, even if you're doing the job, you make a mistake and people say you're too old to be playing." And pretty soon, you may begin to believe them.

No matter how much we consciously try to push it, the body does react differently at 40 than it did at 20. Otho Davis, the trainer for the Philadelphia Eagles, observes that "the older he gets, the longer it is going to take a player to stretch out after a game . . . to return the muscle fibers to their original condition."

Athletes just beginning to feel the effects of aging may be most vulnerable to the temptation to deny the very real effects of the aging process. Davis is concerned that people prevent problems later in life by proper care in their youth. "With a player," Davis says, "I want him to take care of himself and keep strong enough for two reasons: so he prevents injury and is an asset to the team, and also so when he is through playing football and living the rest of his life he can be able to get up in the morning and feel decent. You want him still to be able to play tennis or handball. You don't want him to have arthritis or some kind of nagging injury that could have been prevented."

Author and running guru Dr. George Sheehan provided this advice in his book, *Dr. Sheehan on Fitness:* "Most people live nowhere near their limits. They settle for an accelerated aging, an early and precipitous fall. They give aging a bad name. Too many people entering their forties are performing at physiological levels more appropriate to somebody sixty years old. It's time to elevate our consciousness of normal aging. Normal is the best you can be at any age."

# Easy Does It

Obviously, the same training regimen won't apply to all people at all ages. And even people of the same age need different programs.

Overall, the key to improving fitness after 35 is to decide what you want to accomplish and then make a plan to achieve it. But set realistic goals for yourself. Otherwise you may impose too tough a regimen on yourself. If rigorous workouts appeal to the tough guy in you, forget it. Training too hard leads to staleness, injuries, exhaustion, and eventually just giving up on the whole idea of fitness. But do make your goals at least a little challenging.

In the scheduling and goal-setting department, be sure to allow enough time for recovery after running or lifting. Especially after 35, it takes longer for cells to regenerate after being worked hard. Two days between weightlifting sessions would not be inappropriate. And alternating hard with easy and medium intensity running and strength training definitely is recommended.

Cleveland's Dave Redding advises older athletes to start out easy "and set small goals you can reach. Then set your goals a little higher and reach them. Don't strain yourself at the start so you get so burned out that you quit. Get into something aerobic and keep on with recreational sports that are going to keep you positive."

Gymnastics was the sport in which Jim Williams, the Jets' conditioning coach, competed when he was younger. That required a great deal of weightlifting. Now, he still works out regularly. "But," he says, "I no longer lift competitively and have trained myself more into endurance."

*make aerobics a priority*

Williams believes the cardiovascular system should be a priority for aging athletes. "As you get older," he says, "you need to get more concerned about your aerobic conditioning. People with a weightlifting background don't worry as much about the condition of that big muscle that beats inside their chests as they do about their biceps. That is a mistake."

When Bob Mischak played guard for the Raiders, he was a formidable presence. With his playing days more than a decade behind him, he's now a Raiders coach. He's still big and strong, though, and moving with the kind of agile lightness that marks an athlete. As an active player, Mischak worked out with heavy weights. Now, he spends more time doing yoga stretches and aerobic jogging. He weighs 220 pounds, 10 pounds less than when he was playing. While weightlifting still is part of his conditioning program, he uses lighter weights and does more repetitions. He also spreads out the workouts more and includes more stretching exercises. Well into his 50s, Mischak no longer feels obligated to follow a set exercise pattern. "It gets boring doing the same thing every day," he says. "So maybe I'll skip rope or use a machine for lifting instead of weights."

That laid-back attitude doesn't mean Mischak is casual about his workouts. "I always set a number of reps and sets that will be a challenge and then work out until I meet that goal," he says.

What advice does this tough former player from one of the league's roughest, toughest teams have for older athletes? "Don't hurt yourself," Mischak says. "Moderation is important. Don't always follow the fads. It isn't always necessary to have fancy equipment or be enrolled in an organized class. Just be sure that you are consistent in whatever you do."

## Goodbye Ribs, Hello Pasta

It's ironic that after living as an adult for years, the best dietary advice sounds like your mother's tired refrain: "Eat your vegetables so you grow up big and strong."

*diet gains importance*

For the aging athlete, that dietary admonition is best expanded into: Eat more vegetables, fruits, and complex carbohydrates so you won't get big around the mid-section and so your heart, lungs, and vital organs stay strong. Rusty Jones, the nutrition-minded conditioning coach of the Bills, says, "As you get older, the first thing to kill your conditioning is diet. The second thing is aerobic capacity."

Unwanted weight gain almost always is the major problem for aging athletes. "A lot of our players blimp up by thirty pounds the year after they stop playing," says John Macik, sports medicine coordinator for the NFL Players Association. "The biggest problem with players after they retire is couch potato-ism. It's tough out there, looking for a job after the glory and money of playing pro ball. After years of being taken care of by coaches, some of them have trouble taking charge of their own needs. So a lot of them turn to the refrigerator."

Food is often a form of solace. Allowing big eating binges to continue for very long is well recognized as a mental problem that needs to be understood and faced squarely. What's not so well recognized is the need, as we get older, to actually reduce food intake. "It happens to a lot of football coaches," says Williams of the Jets. "We go from playing football into coaching football and we continue to eat like the players. That's usually because the training table is available to coaches as well as players. You see a guy who had a great build when he was playing and now, wow!, he's carrying forty extra pounds."

The body's basal metabolic rate, the level of energy we burn just to maintain minimum functioning, goes down as we get older. "For the exercising person," says Olympic Committee nutrition consultant Ann Grandjean, "the metabolic rate doesn't go down as fast."

*reduce caloric intake*

In other words, if you want to keep eating like a horse, you'll have to work like one. Still, no matter how much exercise you get, there comes a point where you have to decrease your intake of calories. It may come suddenly at age 26 if you've just retired from the NFL, or it might come gradually in your 60s when your jogging mileage has declined and your pace has slowed. As your metabolism changes, whether sudden or subtle, the trick is to reduce the caloric intake without losing nutrients.

"We're beginning to think that as we get older, there is a decrease in our ability to absorb some nutrients,'"Grandjean says. It makes sense as we get older to think about taking some vitamin and mineral supplements. "The rule of thumb," says Grandjean, "is that if your total caloric intake is less than 1,800 calories a day of a good balanced diet, then maybe take a vitamin-mineral supplement. A good one-a-day, but *not* megavitamins. Take one that will provide 100 percent of recommended daily requirement, but no more."

A less obvious nutritional complication of increasing age is that the thirst mechanism becomes less accurate. We don't recognize that we need water as soon as we previously did.

Not getting enough fluids can lead to heat exhaustion and constipation, a common problem with older adults. So be sure to drink water frequently, especially before and after exercise.

Overall diet recommendations for older athletes are very similar to what's recommended for younger athletes: a balanced diet that includes plenty of carbohydrates and very little fat and protein (see Chapter Four).

"Go easier on high-calorie foods such as barbequed ribs, butter, and gravies," Grandjean says.

Also limit intake of alcohol. After fat, which contains nine calories per gram, alcohol has the most calories per unit—seven calories per gram. Headaches, morning fuzziness, and other effects of drinking are worse for older people because the body can't dispose of the toxins created by alcohol as quickly as when they were young. The secret, as for anyone, is to adjust the intake of calories and nutrients to match your body's present needs.

Changing your food habits doesn't have to be that difficult. Robustelli has had good results over the years. He says that after twenty years in retirement he still is only about six pounds over his playing weight of 233 pounds. That relative trimness is mainly the result of becoming more careful about his diet. "I started to stay away from red meat and fried foods," Robustelli says. "I eat chicken and vegetables and a little veal." He worries about eating too much bread, but that actually is a very desirable food—as long as you're exercising. Bread, pasta, cereals, fruits, and vegetables all fit neatly into current NFL diet preferences to reduce fats and proteins and increase complex carbohydrates.

Former all-pro Atlanta Falcons center Jeff Van Note also shifted his dietary patterns when he retired recently. "Like anybody should who is moving on in life," Van Note says, "I started to eat better, cut down on sweets and salt. I don't eat chocolate fudge sundaes anymore. I try to keep cholesterol intake down and don't drink whole milk or use cheese anymore. But I still stop in and get a burger once in a while."

# A Strong Second Wind

Without question, the cardiovascular system is the most important factor in maintaining good athletic condition as we age. The heart, lungs, and circulatory system are vulnerable as much to misuse as disuse. Tobacco, a high-fat diet, mental and physical stress, inadequate rest, obesity, excessive drinking, and consumption of certain kinds of drugs all are things that have serious impacts on fitness at any age. Those abuses of the body are particularly ill tolerated by an aging cardiovascular system and can lead to heart disease, hardening of the arteries, strokes, emphysema, or worse.

Disuse of the body from a sedentary lifestyle accelerates the aging process. That's why health experts advise aging athletes to do aerobics that fit their age, health, and fitness goals. Aerobic exercise (*see Chapter Two*) is popular because of convincing evidence that it boosts lung capacity, improves anti-coronary factors in the blood, and strengthens the heart muscle itself.

The benefits of aerobic activity are not lost on savvy NFL retirees who stay in shape for life after football. They keep interested in their aerobic fitness by keeping it in perspective. They let exercise improve their lives, not take over their lives. For example, Mischak's aerobic exercise is not predicated on running a certain distance in a certain time. "It's a combination of running, then walking at a good pace when I don't feel like running anymore," Mischak says. "I run to a point where it is exhausting, but not quite. Then I walk for ninety seconds or until I feel comfortable and start running again. I don't feel you have to kill yourself. If it's raining and you don't want to run in the rain, walk."

Says the 61-year-old Robustelli, "I'm in nowhere near as good shape now as I was in when I was playing. But I don't have to be, either.

"You have to get your blood flowing enough so it is getting enough oxygen and I do that regularly. A lot of people are of the opinion that jogging is the best thing to do, but I somewhat disagree. I think brisk walking is the best exercise. If you do it every day for a couple of miles in, say, thirty or forty minutes, that should be enough. It is for me."

*vigorous, non-impact activity*

Riding bicycles or exercise bikes also will provide that kind of non-impact, but vigorous, activity. Rowing machines, cross-country skiing, swimming, or hiking also are good aerobic activities, though more strenuous. The important thing is to try to schedule at least three aerobic workouts every week and have each session be no less than 20 minutes. The large muscles of the body need to be working rhythmically for that length of time to get the aerobic mechanism working fully. If you run slowly, the time should be extended. In fact, for running and walking use mileage, not time, as your guide. Jogging three miles might take 25 minutes and will provide enough aerobic work for almost anyone. Walking that same distance might take twice as long, but will produce about the same aerobic benefits, if it is done at a brisk pace. Your level of activity should be determined by your age, your personal goals, and your doctor.

For NFL players who retired only a few years ago, and other middle-aged athletes who like their aerobics more rigorous, relaxed attitudes such as Robustelli's and Mischak's might not be

*customize your schedule*

appropriate. And they needn't be. The rule is to fit your schedule to your personal needs and preferences. For example, former Chargers special teams standout and running back Hank Bauer, at 33, has reshaped his exercise program and reshaped his body along with it. During his NFL career he had to eat constantly and work out regularly with very heavy weights to maintain his 208-pound build. Now, with a low-fat diet and a stepped-up aerobics program, Bauer is down to 180 pounds. At 5 feet 11 inches, he feels he is now at his natural body weight. He's lifting only half the weight he did as an active player during resistance training sessions, but he's running a great deal more. "I run every other day, about twenty-five or thirty minutes for as fast as I can maintain over the distance," Bauer says. "That generally works out to a total of three-and-a-half to four miles each workout."

In addition, on the days when he does weight training, he begins with a light aerobic workout on an exercise bike. When his work schedule permits, he also plays racquetball or surfs off beaches near San Diego.

Even active NFL players find that adding aerobic training to their conditioning programs can help. Jeff Van Note was the Falcons' starting center when he first realized, at 37, that he was getting older. It was March, 1983, and he had been selected after the previous season to play in the AFC-NFC Pro Bowl. "But I hadn't been able to train much and I was twenty-three percent body fat," he says. "I wasn't in very good shape. I felt like I wanted to play longer and that I could contribute to the team."

He also knew that in his condition he wouldn't be able to contribute much, and might not even make the team. So he went to see George Dostal, then the strength and conditioning coach for Atlanta, and asked for some help.

"I knew I could no longer rely on a young man's quicker recovery," Van Note says. "Developing a good aerobic base became of prime importance. We did fartlek and aerobics and agility drills and I got to training camp in very good condition."

His body fat had declined by more than half, to 11 percent. He maintained his expanded aerobics training program, and it helped him play another four years before he retired to devote full time to his trucking business.

## New Twists for Older Bodies

*emphasize flexibility*

As you age, the need to warm up more and do more stretching increases. The muscles, the skin, and the connective tissues lose a little of their elasticity. That's why the skin gets wrinkles; your skin doesn't snap back as smoothly after it is stretched. Neither do your muscles. So any conditioning program for older athletes has to have an emphasis on flexibility.

The first rule is to warm up completely. Light activity of the muscles and joints that you're going to use will limber the muscles and will actually bring a lubricating fluid into the joints. Your cardiovascular system will get a chance to prepare for the higher demands, too, instead of being forced to full speed in a stress-inducing jackrabbit start. If you're biking or running or using an exercise machine, start out with a very easy setting for the first 5 or 10 minutes. Then get off and do a complete stretching routine *(see Chapter Three)*. When you've finished exercising, whether it was aerobics, weightlifting, or a recreational activity, take another 10 minutes and stretch again.

It's important to remember that because of the effects of aging, just maintaining flexibility requires more effort every year. "As you get older," says Mischak, "keep a balance in everything you do. Make sure the agonist muscles are as fully developed as the antagonist muscles and that they are equally stretched out as well."

For his part, Mischak does some of his stretching in the form of yoga exercises. "It is really quite rigorous," he says. "You can get your heartbeat moving really fast and I feel my body is under better control." The exaggerated stretches of certain forms of yoga are not for everyone, however. Be sure to work with a well-trained instructor and be sure to inform your doctor of your activity.

## Full-Strength Living

Raw muscle power is one of the last physical performance factors to be affected by the aging process. The ability to develop strength for simple motions such a curling a barbell or picking up a bag of cement usually stays constant until well after age 40, as long as you've been doing it consistently. Working the muscles with regular progressive resistance exercises can keep aging athletes quite strong, relative to their peak years. Strength that's involved in complex motions, such as cranking a bicycle, or pitching a baseball, generally does decline sooner. That's probably because complex muscular activities are more affected by aging of the neuromuscular system that coordinates muscle movement and the synchronization of agonist and antagonist muscles as they contract and relax.

Increasing and maintaining muscle strength is a basic part of any conditioning program. What has to be adjusted for age and condition is the kind of strength training equipment used and the intensity. Packers strength and conditioning coach Virgil Knight says, "Don't try lifting a weight that is too heavy for you. Do something you can handle."

*weightlifting and blood pressure*

A more specific recommendation comes from Ben Hurley, an exercise physiologist at the University of Maryland who has studied the effects of progressive weight training on older individuals. "The older you get, the more cautious you should be," he says. "The act of lifting weights increases blood pressure during the activity. While that eventually may lead to a lowering of blood pressure, during the exercise it can get quite high. Anyone with a higher than normal blood pressure should be extremely cautious about weight training. And if you are older, lift lower weights with more repetitions. Above all, don't hold your breath and strain against the weight. That really boosts the pressure."

Despite those cautions, Hurley finds evidence that weight training can improve the health of older adults. "There's no question it increases strength and muscle tone and can increase lean body mass if done properly," he says. The exciting part of his research is that "there is a possibility that weight training can reduce risk factors related to heart disease and age-onset diabetes."

*work out with machines*

Most NFL strength coaches, even those who prefer free weights for their teams, suggest that people over 40, particularly those unaccustomed to free weights, should consider using machines to provide their progressive resistance. Nautilus and Universal machines generally are much safer than barbells because the weights are stacked inside the machine. Only the specific muscles being exercised are involved and you don't have to balance the load in potentially dangerous positions.

"With age you have to rest more," says San Diego's Tyne. "You also should go slower and expect less change in weights as you progress. Start off very, very light and progress upward. Read your body and let your body tell you what to do. There's no need to go through excessive effort and pain."

A specific strength training plan is provided by Mischak. "Pick out apparatus that cover the body parts," he says. "Exercise the legs first. Then you'll have energy left to work out the upper body. In my routines, I have cut back on total weight. I'll start with a relatively light weight and then maybe do another set with a little more weight. If it is light, I'll do more reps. But I won't use a lot of weight at any time because I don't want to build my upper body that much."

The only free weights Mischak recommends is a set of light dumbbells for fine-tuning strength and for a full range of motion.

# Mastering Macho

There's a great macho tradition in sports of playing hurt, sacrificing yourself for the team, and making a valiant effort even at the risk of injury. Everyone admires the players who have that kind of determination and loyalty. But those values don't apply to athletes who are just trying to stay in good condition. Your goal is to stay healthy, not make yourself feel worse. Don't work out or compete if you're hurt. There's no stadium crowd cheering for you to get into that game or run in that race. As Dr. Sheehan writes, "There will always be another race, another marathon. . . .it is possible to miss the race next Sunday and survive."

The Packers' Knight believes ordinary people need to keep exercise activities in perspective. "You are competing with no one but yourself," he says. "You are trying to get better in some phase every time you work out or play. Maybe you want to lose weight or get stronger or be able to run longer or faster. You do want to record some sort of improvement every time. But you don't want to push yourself so hard that you're literally killing yourself."

As an older athlete, how do you know that you are overdoing it? An objective way to evaluate whether you are getting enough rest or doing too much exercise is supplied by Dr. Donald Chu, director of the Ather Sports Injury Clinic, Castro Valley, California. "If your pulse when you wake up in the morning is ten percent higher than normal, that's an indication that your body is under stress. It might just be that you're getting a cold or it could be that you are working too hard on your training program. In any case, take it easy until the early-morning resting heartbeat goes back to normal."

A more down-to-earth gauge comes from ex-player Mischak. "When you start taping ankles and putting on liniment to ease sore muscles," he says, "that's when you know you're doing too much."

# *Working Out in the Real World: Charlie Joiner, Alan Page, Bill Bergey*

## *A Players' Coach*

It's 9:30 A.M. on a Tuesday in early January. Weight rooms of NFL playoff teams are loud with the clanking of iron and the grunts of big men pushing themselves to prepare for the critical games on Sunday.

It's different in the white concrete room under San Diego Jack Murphy Stadium. The season is over for the Chargers. When the room was opened at 8, the loudest sound was the humming of fluorescent lights. Wall mirrors reflected deserted machines and dumbbells and free weights piled neatly on a row of mats.

But now the Nautilus circuit is clattering with the exercises of a lean man in gym shorts who looks more like a jogger who lost his way to the health club than a pro football player. It's wide receiver Charlie Joiner, who caught more passes (750) for more yards (12,146) in his career than any player in the league's history. He retired at age 39 after 1986, his eighteenth season (a record for the position), and is staying on with the team to coach receivers.

Joiner moves to the free weights and begins pumping iron. He has entered the growing ranks of retired NFL veterans who stay in first-class shape with a postseason workout program that fits athletes who no longer have to perform at peak levels. Joiner lasted as long as he did in the NFL by staying in exemplary condition. He is beginning his post-football life with the same disciplined, professional attitude and logical personal game plan that kept him among the receiving leaders for so many years.

"My approach," he says, "was to try to get into the best possible condition so I could play hard every down. If you do that, you cut down on injuries and everyone on the team knows they can trust you to get the job done. Now I'm approaching my coaching career the same way. I want to be in good shape as a coach and develop the bond between coach and players."

Known for years as a quick, clutch receiver, much of Joiner's training regimen involved sprints and interval running. Now, he's changing his workouts to meet the needs of his new job. "I'm doing more weight work to firm up my body and doing less running," he says. "Not too many guys want a coach to show them up, so they'll have to try harder if they want to keep up with me."

*Joiner retired in 1986 as the NFL's top receiver.*

## Lawyer on the Run

**Page was the NFL's most valuable player in 1971.**

Former all-pro defensive tackle Alan Page approaches his post-NFL workouts much differently than Joiner. A lawyer in St. Paul, Page's program involves almost nothing but running.

Page is a special assistant Minnesota attorney general specializing in labor laws, a job he's held for more than two years. He knows all about labor—for 15 seasons, 11 with the Vikings and 4 with the Bears, he took on opposing offensive linemen. In 1971, he was one of the first defensive players ever to be named the NFL's most valuable player.

Now in his early 40s, Page lives a pretty normal middle-American life, considering he's a guy who stands 6 feet 3 inches and weighs 220 pounds, who played in four Super Bowls, and was named to the AFC-NFC Pro Bowl nine times. He has been married for more than 20 years, has four children, a desk job in the city, and a house in the suburbs.

What's unusual is the intensity Page puts into everything he does. His running, for example.

In summer, he averages 60 miles a week. Even in the freezing Minnesota winters, he still runs a brisk 30 miles a week, most of it at 5 or 6 o'clock in the morning before work.

"I still think I'm improving," he says. "I've been working on running shorter distances faster and I just broke sixty seconds in the 440 for the first time." After 40, making substantial gains in speed takes great effort. But Page goes for distance as well. He has run a number of marathons, finishing in about three-and-a-half hours. That is a respectable time for any amateur his age, and extraordinary for a big man who is the antithesis of a sinewy, narrow-shouldered endurance runner.

Most big people don't find distance running comfortable. But Page enjoys the sport and appreciates how running improves and maintains cardiovascular function. "When I was a rookie," he says, "I weighed two hundred and fifty pounds and my heart rate at rest was about seventy. Now, with all the running and the lower-fat diet I've adopted, my resting heart is about fifty beats a minute."

His eating habits have changed over the years, too. He sharply restricts red meats, soft drinks, sweets, and butter. "I haven't had an ice cream in a year," he says. And asked if he had tried low-fat ice milk deserts, he dismissed the notion by saying, "I may be a little rigid about this, but if you're going to do something, you might as well go all the way or not do it at all. If I have ice milk, I'll want the real thing."

Page is attracted to "the real thing" in athletics, too, so when he was interested in running an endurance race, he entered—and finished—a competition called "The Ultimate Runner," staged in Jackson City, Michigan. Each contestant is required to run in a series of races: a 100-meter sprint, a 400-meter dash, a 10-kilometer run, a one-mile race, and a standard 26-mile marathon —all in the same day.

His advice for other aging jocks: "Stay active. Find something that you enjoy and that you can do every day, rain or shine, snow or heat."

# The Biking Bergeys

Pedaling through Nebraska on an 18-speed bike, former Eagles all-pro linebacker Bill Bergey was beginning to hate his choice of activity.

What bothered him was pushing against an unusual and persistent east-to-west headwind through a landscape that was composed primarily of blacktop and soybean plants. His brother, former Chiefs tight end Bruce Bergey, was pumping just a few yards ahead; his wife and kids were following them in a truck towing a big house trailer.

"Pretty soon I was beginning to hate them and myself, too," he says. But the Bergey brothers don't give up when the going gets tough. It's part of the ethic they developed playing football. They rode another three days before there was a shift in the wind and in their mood. Eventually, they completed the trip—3,100 miles on bicycles from Lincoln City, Oregon, where Bruce has a summer home, to the New Jersey shore and Bill's summer home.

The cross-country trip had taken more than three weeks and was part of a fund-raising effort for handicapped children sponsored by the Philadelphia Variety club. Another purpose of the grueling ride was to relieve the Bergeys' pent-up energy.

"Ever since my brother and I left football we've done something a little crazy at the time when NFL training camps open," Bill says. The first summer after they retired, they joined a party of river runners and rode rafts down the treacherous and little-known Illinois River in Oregon. The next year they did the river run again, but alone in one-man white-water kayaks.

The Bergeys are in their 40s now, partners in a successful contracting and development company. They work hard at their jobs for 10½ months of the year, then take off on a physical challenge when the itch to play football strikes in early summer.

*Bergey was an NFL standout during his 12-year career.*

Bill Bergey stays in shape mainly by cycling, using an electronically controlled stationary exercise bicycle when the weather is poor and his 18-speed mountain bike for tooling through the lush Eastern Pennsylvania countryside when the days are pleasant. He also plays racquetball several times a week.

Even with that exercise, Bergey finds the demands are not as tough as during the 12 years he played for Cincinnati and Philadelphia. So he has to be diligent about his diet to keep from ballooning up beyond 250 pounds, about the weight he carried during his career. "I really have to watch what I eat," he says. "I can't pig out with second and third helpings anymore."

The Bergeys' latest summer vacation scheme is to traverse the entire western hemisphere from Pt. Barrow, Alaska, to the southernmost point of Argentina, all by bicycle. In a concession to good sense, they expect the journey to take four or five summers.

# 8 Putting It All Together:

## *The Fitness Game Plan*

No matter what your present condition is, *The NFL All-Pro Workout* program is designed to improve your overall level of fitness and performance. You reach that goal by following *The NFL All-Pro Workout's* three simple steps:

(1) Take stock of your current state of fitness.

(2) Decide what level of conditioning you want to reach and maintain.

(3) Develop a specific plan based on *The NFL All-Pro Workout's* strength training, cardiovascular conditioning, flexibility exercises, and diet guidelines.

Adhere to your plan faithfully, making adjustments as your condition improves.

Be realistic about what you can do. By all means make the program challenging, but don't expect more of yourself than you can deliver. Keep confidence high by setting goals you can reach. Giants strength coach Johnny Parker believes success is so important to confidence that he spends months during the offseason calculating individual weight loads for each of his players. He wants them challenged by the exercise, not defeated.

"Players should develop a habit of succeeding at whatever they try, so I don't want anyone to miss even one rep," says Parker.

It's natural to want to perform like professionals. But most amateur athletes don't have as much time to devote to training. What's more, very few people have the genetic potential to duplicate the strength and quickness of world-class athletes. However, hard work, proper attitude, and a disciplined approach to training often can more than compensate for physical shortcomings.

Your conditioning goals should be subjective and appropriate for your own abilities and interests. Develop your own potential and don't bother comparing yourself with others. Work within yourself and for yourself. Begin with exercise activities you enjoy and build up your strengths. Shore up your weaknesses after you've established confidence in your overall fitness training.

If you are over 35 or just getting started in a conditioning program, get a medical checkup before you begin.

And, above all, give yourself and *The NFL All-Pro Workout* time; don't expect results overnight.

# Taking Stock

For most people, a glance in the mirror is enough to begin the evaluation process. It doesn't take long to see where fat has accumulated or which muscles need development. You also can see where you are trim and well developed.

*self appraisal*

Mirror imaging is the method of choice when the Oilers' Steve Watterson counsels professionals or amateur athletes. "We have them strip down to shorts and do a self-evaluation by looking in the mirror," Watterson says. "Self-evaluation works because it's honest. When another person tells you what should be improved, he will usually temper the truth. But it does help to have someone around to direct the criticism or soften the self-judgment."

When it comes to evaluating your athletic skills, recent performance is a good indicator. If you're having trouble bringing down rebounds even though you're as tall as other players, you may want to strengthen the jumping muscles with squats and plyometrics. If you're feeling stiff and tight with backhand shots in racquetball, you may need to spend more time stretching and doing flexibility and mental focusing exercises.

In addition to remembering your last few games and spending a few minutes in front of a mirror, you'll want to carefully measure and evaluate all your major body systems: cardiovascular fitness, strength, speed and agility, and flexibility. You need to calibrate your current performance and fitness levels to pinpoint where improvement is required. Most important, you'll also have a starting point from which to measure progress.

Write down your mirror image evaluation. If you want to add some muscle on your chest or take away some fat on your midsection, this is the time to commit your observations to paper. A rule of thumb on body fat for men is that if you can pinch a fold of skin from your side, just above the hip bone and below the ribs more than an inch thick, you probably are too fat. Ask your doctor or fitness center if they can use calipers or one of the other methods to make a more precise estimate. Consider taking a photograph of yourself for reference later on.

*pinch an inch*

Have someone help measure your height, weight, and the circumference of arms, legs, chest, waist, and hips. Go out to a track and, after a thorough warm-up and 10 minutes of stetching, time your speed in the 40-yard dash, the 100-yard dash, and the quarter-mile run. Remember, you are trying to establish your present level of conditioning, not compete with anyone or with any predetermined standard.

Then gauge your strength by lifting some moderate weights to exhaustion. See how many times you can press a barbell over your head, how many times you can press it off your chest while lying on a bench, and how many times you can curl it with your biceps.

Pick a weight you can handle. It doesn't matter whether you use a 50- or 100-pound barbell as long as you keep going until your muscles fail. What is important is that you have a record of your prelimi-

## The 1½-Mile Test

A simple way to measure aerobic capacity is to time yourself over a measured distance, such as this jogging test adapted from Dr. Kenneth Cooper's book, *The Aerobics Program For Total Well-Being*. Test your aerobic fitness by timing how long it takes to run or jog exactly 1½ miles on a level surface. Measure off the distance with a bike or car odometer or do six laps around a standard quarter-mile track. If you are over 35 or haven't been working out lately, get a medical checkup before trying this test. Run or jog as fast as you can, then find your relative aerobic fitness by matching your time with those in the chart below, factoring in your age and sex.

### THE AEROBICS CENTER CARDIOVASCULAR FITNESS TEST
*Minutes and seconds required to cover exactly 1.5 miles*

| FITNESS LEVEL | AGE 20-29 | AGE 30-39 | AGE 40-49 | AGE 50-59 |
|---|---|---|---|---|
| **VERY POOR** | | | | |
| Men | ▶16:01 | ▶16:31 | ▶17:31 | ▶19:01 |
| Women | ▶19:01 | ▶19:31 | ▶20:01 | ▶20:31 |
| **POOR** | | | | |
| Men | 14:01-16:00 | 14:44-16:30 | 15:36-17:30 | 17:01-19:00 |
| Women | 18:31-19:00 | 19:01-19:30 | 19:31-20:00 | 20:01-20:30 |
| **FAIR** | | | | |
| Men | 12:01-14:00 | 12:31-14:45 | 13:01-15:35 | 14:31-17:00 |
| Women | 15:55-18:30 | 16:31-19:00 | 17:31-19:30 | 19:01-20:00 |
| **GOOD** | | | | |
| Men | 10:46-12:00 | 11:01-12:30 | 11:31-13:00 | 12:31-14:30 |
| Women | 13:31-15:54 | 14:31-16:30 | 15:56-17:30 | 16:31-19:00 |
| **EXCELLENT** | | | | |
| Men | 9:45-10:45 | 10:00-11:00 | 10:30-11:30 | 11:00-12:30 |
| Women | 12:30-13:30 | 13:00-14:30 | 13:45-15:55 | 14:30-16:30 |
| **SUPERIOR** | | | | |
| Men | ◀9:45 | ◀10:00 | ◀10:30 | ◀11:00 |
| Women | ◀12:30 | ◀13:00 | ◀13:45 | ◀14:30 |

▶ *means "more than."* ◀ *means "less than."*

nary capability so you can measure progress.

The most important element in any workout program is cardio-vascular conditioning—aerobic fitness—the ability of your heart and lungs to deliver oxygenated blood to the muscles. A stress test on a treadmill with your breathing closely monitored is the best way to get an accurate measurement. This must be done at a doctor's office or sports medicine facility.

*pulse rating*

A crude method of judging aerobic fitness is to measure your pulse recovery rate. That's the speed with which your heart rate drops back toward normal following vigorous aerobic exercise. Measure your pulse rate (the beats counted in 10 seconds multiplied by six) immediately after finishing a run or other strenuous activity. Wait exactly 60 seconds and take the pulse again. If your heartbeat has dropped more than 40 beats per minute in that time, you probably are in good shape. If it has declined less than about 10 beats per minute, you should ask a doctor to double-check your condition.

# Fitness Equations

Calibrating fitness is a critical activity in the NFL. NFL training camps are full of returning veterans, rookies, players who had been on injured reserve, and free agents seeking a chance to make the team. It's like a game of musical chairs with about 100 players trying out for only 45 jobs. It takes more than simply timing players in the 40-yard dash and measuring how much they can bench press for coaches to get a good idea of their real athletic potential. That's why teams such as the Detroit Lions have engaged consultants to help identify which players are most likely to be productive. The Lions' consultant is Dr. Donald Chu of the Ather Sports Injury Clinic.

*five tests*

Dr. Chu has developed a set of five tests, described below, to determine flexibility, potential speed, usable agility, body strength, and endurance, as well as the ability to coordinate those factors into useful athletic movement and learn new skills quickly.

For the average citizen, these tests can indicate strengths and weaknesses and remain a personal benchmark against which to measure future progress. These tests are included here for their reference and interest value, not as a critical standard. Your main concern always should be to improve yourself, not to compete with professional athletes.

### 30-Second Quick Foot

A player stands on two squares and alternately picks up one foot at a time as fast as he can for 30 seconds. The squares are connected to an electric timer that counts the steps. The more steps he can make in the 30 seconds, the faster and more agile he is likely to be. By timing the rate in the first five seconds and comparing it with the rate in the last five seconds, a player's endurance, his ability to keep run-

## Average Performance of NFL Players

| Position | 30-Sec. Quick Foot (steps) | 90-Sec. Box Jump (cycles) | Triple Jump (ft. and in.) | Medicine Ball Put/ Throw (ft. and in.) | Vertical Jump Stand/Bound (inches) |
|---|---|---|---|---|---|
| Quarterback | 273 | 77 | 23-5 | 18-3/36-8 | 22.5/21.3 |
| Running Back | 301 | 74 | 26-1 | 20-6/38-6 | 27.5/24.1 |
| Wide Receiver | 284 | 85 | 28-4 | 18-7/36-1 | 27.7/25.5 |
| Def. Back | 253 | 79 | 24-6 | 19-1/38-5 | 26.1/27.1 |
| Tight End | 270 | 75 | 25-3 | 21-1/37-7 | 24.6/23.4 |
| Def. Line | 279 | 56 | 25-2 | 21-5/39-7 | 21.5/21.3 |
| Off. Line | 254 | 65 | 22-7 | 23-2/39-6 | 25.8/20.6 |
| Linebacker | 269 | 75 | 25-9 | 19-7/38-3 | 27.5/25.1 |

ning fast for 30 seconds, can be judged as well. The best score ever recorded by Dr. Chu was 336 steps by an NFL linebacker. Because the feet move faster than most people can count, this test is very difficult to perform on your own.

**90-Second Box Step**

A wooden box 12 inches high, 20 inches wide, and 30 inches long is the instrument in this test. Players stand on the right side of the box and jump sideways to the top, then jump down to the other side and back up to the top and down to the other side as many times as possible in 90 seconds. Count one every time you land on top. This is a very good indicator of anaerobic endurance. Because leg muscles get completely drained of energy in this test, a player's willingness to drive himself in the last seconds gives coaches a tip-off to his intensity and desire. The best score achieved was 110 by a college quarterback.

**Standing Triple Jump**

A test designed to rate the ability to learn new skills quickly and measure running and jumping potential. From a standing start, the player does a standing jump, landing on one foot, strides for one more step, and ends a third step on both feet. The best distance in this test was achieved by an NFL wide receiver, 30 feet, 6 inches.

**Medicine Ball Put/Throw**

Upper body strength is measured by this test. The player is strapped in a chair so only the muscles in his arms and shoulders are used. A 10-pound medicine ball is pushed off from the chest with two hands mostly using the arm muscles. The second half of the test is an over-the-head two-handed throw that allows more shoulder and chest muscles to be employed. An NFL offensive lineman holds the record with 25 feet, 10 inches in the put, and 48 feet in the throw.

**Vertical Jump**

Another two-stage test, this one measures explosive leg strength and muscle resiliency. The player reaches as high as he can with his heels on the ground. That height is marked and he then leaps as high as possible from a standstill, recording that point on a wall or a set of tabs on a pole set one inch apart. The distance between the flat-footed reach and the top of his leap is the vertical jumping measurement. The player also does the same test by jumping off a two-foot-high box to start the leap. These tests measure rebound reflexes and indicate degree of muscle reactivity. The best result was 35.5 inches in the standing jump by an NFL rookie wide receiver. The rebound jump record is 34 inches.

# Making Decisions

Once you've established your benchmark performance figures and physical measurements, you must decide what level of conditioning you want to reach and maintain.

The decision should be based on your athletic activities and interests. If you want a great-looking body at the beach, you will work out differently than if you're aiming to become a better baseball pitcher. If you want to get in condition to play football, you will go through a different workout program than if you're trying to maintain a more resilient body for basketball. The idea is to train for specific activities while maintaining a high level of all-around fitness.

Cleveland's Dave Redding says the Browns focus their training efforts on specific objectives. "We don't get too carried away with how many pounds we're pumping," he says, " because we're training to be better football players, not power weightlifters."

*typecasting*   Be specific about what needs to be improved so that your body is trained for those activities that are important to you. Recently, some NFL players spent several days in the mountains on a promotion that featured a ski race against state police association skiers. In the weight room, on a football field, or even on a track, the big, muscular NFL players would make the cops look like the amateurs they were. But on the ski slopes, where they had little training, the NFL players were obviously outclassed by athletes trained to ski.

Every body is different and the differences are important in determining your potential to succeed in certain sports. For example, lean athletes with long legs and underdeveloped upper bodies usually make the best distance runners. Muscular people with shorter legs often make good downhill skiers. And so on in each sport. But we are talking ideals here, not everyday reality.

However, an excellent guide for determining which sports are best suited for your particular build and skills is *Sports Selection*, by Dr. Robert Arnot and Charles Gaines. Arnot uses a variety of body proportion, strength, and agility tests to identify the sports in which you would be most likely to succeed. Although his book provides testing and training tips for only seven sports (tennis, windsurfing, running, swimming, cycling, and both alpine and nordic skiing), the tables of performance and explanations are useful in establishing your relative strengths and weaknesses and how they affect various sports activities. No matter what sport you favor (or that favors you), use the training concepts in *The NFL All-Pro Workout*.

# Charting the Course

The best way to make your conditioning program work is to make an ironclad contract with yourself. You meet the terms of the deal by working hard and staying on schedule. In return, you get stronger, healthier, better at your chosen sports, and better looking, too. Like any contract, make sure you put it in writing. On a weekly basis, list all the elements of your program as completely as you can. Use the chart provided on the last page of this book, or design a chart of your own.

*train seasonally*

A unique aspect of *The NFL All-Pro Workout* is that the workouts change with the season, correlating to the way you change the sports that you play. Just as NFL players adjust their training schedules so they will hit stride just when the playing season begins, you should plan your conditioning schedule with your activities in mind.

"They play championships in January, not July," says the Giants' Parker. "There's not much reason to be strong in July if you don't plan to be as strong or stronger in January. Our goal [in the NFL] is to peak for the Super Bowl."

Suppose you are a downhill skier and tennis player. Begin to get in shape for ski season with special balance and lower body strength exercises in the early fall, even while you're still playing a lot of tennis. Work hard at your skiing all winter. Then, around March, while the ski season is winding down, start working on the twisting moves, short bursts of speed, hand-eye coordination, and arm and shoulder exercises that will prepare your body for tennis again. Remember, though, the seasonal changes in workout are *in addition to* a core program that by itself will produce and maintain a strong and supple body for any sport or activity.

# Basic Training

*The NFL All-Pro Workout* is based on a weekly schedule of a *minimum* of two days of aerobic exercise, one day of strength training, and another day of optional sports activity. A high-carbohydrate, low-fat diet is part of the plan; so is stretching every day you exercise. While the minimum maintenance schedule requires only half an hour a day, four times a week, *The NFL All-Pro Workout* can be tailored to fit your own schedule and activity preferences.

Following this four-day-a-week schedule will help you get and stay fit, lose weight (in conjunction with a diet plan), and maintain good muscle tone. But it will not help you make significant gains in strength, aerobic capacity, or specific sports skills. To do that requires a larger investment of time on your part. Adding another strength training session is highly recommended to compensate for the loss of tone that naturally begins to occur three or four days after a weight workout. Adding a second day of practice in your specific sport(s) also will hasten improvement.

# Timing

Alternate weight training days with aerobic days so your muscles have at least 48 hours to recover. Design your schedule to fit your own needs and be sure you don't heavily stress the same muscles on consecutive days. For example, if you want to lift weights two days in a row, concentrate the first day on the upper body and work on the lower half the next day. If you want to run two days in a row, you might do one day of long slow distance, and do fartlek, or intervals, the next.

# Aerobics

In designing your plan, start with aerobics. If you scored excellent or better in the fitness test on page 143, you can stay with a maintenance program of at least 30 minutes of aerobic activity at least twice a week. If your aerobic fitness level is low, you'll want to spend more time on the aerobics activities at first, working slowly and progressively up to higher levels.

Though running or jogging is the first aerobic activity that usually comes to mind, walking also is good (it just requires twice as much time), as is cycling (road or stationary), and swimming.

Distance running conditions you specifically for only one sport—distance running. Few NFL teams ask players to run more than three miles. But they do put players through workout sessions in the offseason using exercise bikes, intervals, and some distance running to assure that the players have a good aerobic base when they begin the tough contact work at training camp.

*foundation of fitness*

Athletes with strong aerobic systems can do the same work as poorly conditioned athletes and have a lower heart rate. Their cardiovascular systems work more efficiently. What's more, athletes with a strong aerobic system can recover from the oxygen debt faster when they do work at high intensity. In other words, aerobic training has to be the foundation of your overall conditioning program. It is true that most of the effort in playing football is anaerobic, but without strong cardiovascular systems, NFL players would not have the endurance required to keep going when the going gets tough in the fourth quarter.

As athletes age, the necessity to maintain cardiovascular conditioning becomes even more important. It doesn't matter which activity you choose as long as you can maintain a training-level heart rate for at least 30 minutes.

## Exercise/Calorie Ratios

| Activity | Calories/Hour (approximate) | Activity | Calories/Hour |
|---|---|---|---|
| Sleeping | 60 | **Football** | 600 |
| Sitting | 120 | **Swimming** (40 mtrs./minute) | 600 |
| Walking (20-minute mile) | 300 | **Tennis** (vigorous) | 600 |
| Golf | 300 | **Biking** (5-minute mile) | 600 |
| Dancing (vigorous) | 400 | **Jogging** (10-minute mile) | 600 |
| Volleyball | 600 | **Downhill Skiing** (10 mph) | 650 |
| Basketball | 600 | **Handball, Racquetball** | 900 |
| | | **Running** (5-minute mile) | 1200 |
| | | **Cross Country Skiing** | 1200 |

# Strength

The goal is to increase strength and endurance. From that flows greater speed and the ability to perform at higher levels. Progressive resistance training is the recommended method to boost the number and efficiency of muscle fibers. *The NFL All-Pro Workout* recommends a two-stage system of strength training: core fitness exercises to condition the whole body, and specific exercises designed to improve performance in specific sports.

*one-day minimum*

At least one day a week, you should do a strength workout that stresses all the major muscle groups. That schedule will maintain a certain level of tone and strength, but won't do much to improve your performance. To significantly increase the size and strength of your muscles, you'll need to work out two or three days a week. Every so often, do an aerobic weight workout (high reps, low weight) to improve muscle endurance. And don't forget the importance of giving your body time to recover between workouts. It is possible, and even likely, that you actually will set back your conditioning program by working out too long or too often.

"You can't keep going hard and heavy all the time," New York's Parker says. "For every player in weight training who doesn't do enough, there are a dozen who do too much."

The rule in strength training, as with all the other aspects of *The NFL All-Pro Workout*, is patience. Set your priorities and live with them. Work hard to accomplish your goals, but don't expect miracles to happen in a couple of weeks. Training takes time. Trying to rush your conditioning is a common way to become injured. The body adapts to stress and makes itself stronger only if the stress is applied gradually and progressively.

# Specific Agility

As the season for your primary sport gets closer, emphasize those exercises that correspond to the sport. When you get through with your aerobic activities, add some dashes or intervals in the distances that you run most often in your sport (e.g., the length of a basketball court or the side-to-side distance of a tennis court). In the weight room, give added time to the muscles that you'll be using most. Throughout the year, include skill sports such as racquetball, baseball, soccer, or handball in your workout schedule. The agility and eye-hand coordination they require are important for your overall conditioning. The variety, competition, and challenge they provide are important to your mental conditioning.

# Flexibility

Stretch before every workout. Flexible athletes are the ones who resist injury best. Do your stretching after you have warmed up. The general rule is that if you'll be doing very strenuous activity such as sprinting or weightlifting, you should stretch before *and* after. If you are only jogging or walking, waiting until afterwards when your muscles are warm is fine. A complete stretch sequence takes about 7 to 10 minutes, so leave time for it in your workout plans. Be sure you include the neck, back, and hamstrings, body parts that are sensitive to overuse and also are commonly neglected.

# Common-Sense Considerations

Vary your programs. In running, take different routes that include hills and flats. Change your speed; run faster some days and slower others. Take a break from distance and do intervals. If you are a sprinter, occasionally run some long, slow distance.

In the weight room, follow the advice of successful NFL strength coaches such as the Giants' Parker and the Redskins' Dan Riley and work out your muscles with different exercises as often as you can. As you will see in the exercises in Chapter Nine, there are many ways to work out each muscle group. Variety is what keeps your interest up and keeps your muscles constantly adapting to new stresses. Wear gloves and a support belt, when necessary, and remember to use good form. Err on the side of using weights that are too light rather than straining with a weight that is too heavy.

Don't tax yourself by working out in heavy smog, sizzling heat, snowstorms, or other potentially dangerous weather. That doesn't mean you duck for cover anytime it drizzles, but do use good judgment. If your back hurts when you run, switch over to biking or to brisk walking for a few days. If the pain persists, see a doctor.

When you're sick, be sure you have recovered from the illness be-

# Sample Weekly Training Schedules

Here are examples of four weeks of training with *The NFL All-Pro Workout*. Of course, you can customize your own training schedule given the basic minimum maintenance requirement of two days of aerobic conditioning, one day of strength training, and one day of specific sports activity.

Training for athletic competition will require a more intensive schedule, with additional strength training and sports days. People just beginning a fitness program may have to work up to the minimum. Note that a varied exercise schedule helps prevent injuries by limiting stress on vulnerable body parts.

## Week 1

**Monday:** Running *(30 minutes sustained, minimum)*
**Wednesday:** Tennis *(1 hour singles, minimum)*
**Thursday:** Weight Workout *(full body)*
**Saturday:** Bicycling *(30 minutes sustained, minimum)*

This is a basic workout week. The running and cycling provide the necessary aerobic activity days. The full-body weight workout fulfills the minimum maintenance strength training requirement. The tennis is an example of adding in a session of your favorite sport; any sport you enjoy, such as basketball, volleyball, racquetball, etc. will do. How long and how far you run or bike, for example, is up to you. The key is to keep your heart at or near the training level for a minimum of 30 minutes—or as close as you can come to that ideal given your physical condition. At a standard running/jogging pace, 30 minutes translates to running approximately three to four miles.

## Week 2

**Monday:** Weight Workout *(upper body)*
**Tuesday:** Weight Workout *(lower body)*
**Thursday:** Running *(30 minutes sustained, minimum)*
**Saturday:** Hiking *(one hour sustained, minimum)*

This week illustrates two things. First, it shows how to split up weight workouts on consecutive days into upper body and lower body sessions. This is a good way to work out if your daily schedule does not permit enough time for a full-body weight workout. Second, it shows how an optional activity, such as hiking, may do double duty as a sports day and an aerobic day—if the activity is strenuous enough. If you wish, a session of your specific sport or another strength workout can be added late in the week. As an adjunct to your physical conditioning, work on mental training. Practice relaxation and visualization techniques as if they were as important as your baseball swing or volleyball serve—they are.

## Week 3

**Monday:** Exercise Bike *(20-60 minutes sustained)*
**Wednesday:** Aerobic Weight Workout *(full body)*
**Friday:** Running *(30 minutes sustained, minimum)*
**Sunday:** Aerobic Dance *(30-60 minutes)*

An exercise bike is a great way to get an aerobic workout. Be sure to ride at a high enough resistance setting to raise your heart rate into the training zone. The aerobic weight workout (high reps, low weight) serves both as an aerobic session and a strength session. Because it takes less time than a progressive weight workout, it is a good alternative if your weekly schedule is tight, or if you are interested more in building tone and endurance than in adding strength and size. Try to schedule a rest day after an aerobic weight workout, which can be exhausting. Aerobic dance provides a good, low-impact aerobic workout, but any aerobic activity could be substituted. This week is exclusively aerobic; you may want to add a specific sport session to keep your playing skills sharp. If increasing strength is a primary goal, add another full-body weight workout (progressive).

## Week 4

**Monday:** Weight Workout *(full body)*
**Wednesday:** Running *(intervals)*
**Thursday:** Swimming *(30 minutes sustained, minimum)*
**Sunday:** Bicycling *(30 minutes sustained, minimum)*

This week shows how to vary your activity if you simply are trying to maintain an overall level of fitness as opposed to training for a specific sport. After the basic progressive strength workout and a rest day, give yourself a change of pace with a session of interval work instead of aerobic distance running. Using swimming as an alternative aerobic workout also adds something new. The cycling gives you another day of aerobic activity. If you have the time, add a second strength workout and/or a session of your sport.

fore you resume your workouts. However, you shouldn't stop your running program for a week because you have poison ivy on your hands. But, in that case, you might want to let up on weight work that requires a lot of gripping.

Use good equipment in constructive surroundings. Work out in a place that you enjoy being in and that is conducive to steady progress. And, stay within your ability. Macho is fine when you are on the field and competing. In practice and in fitness training, you don't have to psyche yourself out. Push yourself, surely, as long you keep it within reasonable bounds. You are working out for you, and you alone.

# On the Road

You don't always need a gym to get a good workout. When you travel on business or for pleasure, you still can exercise. You can run anywhere you travel. And many hotels now have fitness centers and workout rooms. Use them.

*room service*

Even in your room you can maintain a minimum of fitness. Sit-ups and leg lifts provide good conditioning for the abdomen. Side leg lifts also are good conditioners. Pushups and dips between a couple of chairs also will work out the upper body.

With a little forethought, you can get some very good workouts with very little equipment. Jump ropes are easy to take along in a suitcase. A length of rubber surgical tubing can provide a marvelous assortment of resistance exercises in a very lightweight package. Use your imagination for fitness maintenance while you're away.

# Following the Plan

The Rams' Garrett Giemont has a favorite aphorism: "Press on." He says persistence and determination are the important elements in success in anything, especially conditioning.

Giemont believes that people who don't improve their level of fitness usually are those who engage in what he calls a "locker room workout."

"Some people get dressed for a workout, drive down to the gym, and then just hang around and talk," Giemont says. "At the most, they'll pick up a weight and put it right back down. Without effort, there is no gain. If you're going to take all the trouble to be there, you might as well do the work."

The Packers' Virgil Knight agrees. "The best workout plan in the world is useless if it doesn't get done," he says.

# The Consummate Athlete: Walter Payton

*Bears running back Walter Payton races teammate Dennis Gentry, a wide receiver, in a grueling hill run.*

Chicago Bears superstar running back Walter Payton has no offseason. He's always training, always studying, always trying to improve. Except for the Bears' preseason training camps, Payton's workout program is of his own design, directed and motivated only by himself.

"I'm very comfortable with that," says Chicago strength and conditioning coach Clyde Emrich. "Walter is one of the smartest people I know in terms of knowing how to take care of himself."

Payton also is his own most demanding coach. "What I do on my own to stay in shape actually is harder than what we do when we're in training during the season," he says.

Rule number one for Payton is intensity. Everything in his workout is done at full throttle. "There are times when I work out and feel like if I take one more step, I'm going to die," he says. "But if I don't take that step, I don't stay sharp. I lose my edge."

The other major rule in Payton's conditioning program is working to completion. It sometimes takes as much as seven hours a day to include the elements he believes are needed to perform at top level: strength training, aerobics, interval running, flexibility, and agility. Although he doesn't exercise every part of his body every day, during the course of a week every muscle gets a complete workout.

Payton's training routine is anything but routine. Every day is different because he wants his fitness workouts to remain fresh. He avoids doing the same exercises and workouts and is constantly looking for new ways to push himself.

Payton has no set pattern for exercise except

that he tends to work out with weights in the morning and do his running later in the day. His main running exercise is sprints of less than 40 yards. He jogs three miles or so to loosen up, with an occasional 12-mile run as distance work.

Lately, Payton has been sprinting against an automobile for more challenge. He and a friend will find a deserted road or a parking lot and take turns running and driving. They'll pick a spot 20 or 40 yards away and then, one running and the other driving, race to get there first. A man's acceleration is faster, but the car's top speed is higher, so they have to adjust the distance to provide a good contest.

Some days during the spring, Payton will drive to a high school field near his home and measure off distances against which he can test his quickness. "I've changed my routine over the years," he says. "I work more on things now that I'll use in a game. If you just run for long distances, you still aren't in shape for going in quick bursts like you'll need when you're carrying the ball. So, I'll do a few one hundred-yard dashes, then fifties, then forties and tens. I do them all against the clock. You have to do them against the clock or they aren't as effective."

His toughest aerobic challenge, though, is a steep hill in Arlington Heights, Illinois, near his home. There, Payton's runs are a study in dedication and precision. He runs straight up the hill, runs down backwards, runs up and down sideways, and then turns around to run up backwards and straight back down full blast. Then it is more dashes, agility drills, and, finally, stretching exercises.

Often, Payton is so worn out by his running workouts that he just collapses in the grass. "If somebody came along and saw me," he says, "they'd think I was a corpse."

Payton's emphasis in the weight room is on his legs and chest. Lifting for lifting's sake is not on his agenda. What he wants to do is build stamina and quickness.

He works out every day, and stretches before and after his workouts. While he has used free weights, most of his weight training is done with machines. As with his running program, the emphasis is on variety and intensity. Some days he'll work the entire Nautilus circuit pushing himself about equally on each muscle group. More often he will concentrate on one particular area of his body one day, such as shoulders, and go to legs or arms the next.

With so much time and effort invested in physical conditioning, Payton is careful to provide the other three necessities for championship performance: adequate rest, good diet, and a positive mental attitude.

*Flexibility and tenacious training are keys to Payton's NFL longevity and practically injury-free career.*

*Payton has one of the NFL's most-feared straight-arms.*

Payton is a night owl. He owns a string of night clubs and he sometimes stays out past midnight monitoring his business. He makes up for the late nights by sleeping in, but doesn't let that stop his conditioning program. He begins every morning with a workout, whether at ten o'clock at a Chicago health club in the off-season or at dawn during the season at the Bears' practice field.

He avoids late nights once team workouts begin in the early summer. With team practice and his own additional workouts, Payton is so focused on football and so tired out that he usually gets home in the early evening and falls asleep right after dinner.

At 5 feet 10 inches and 206 pounds, Payton is not the biggest running back in the league. But with only three percent of his body weight in fat, about the minimum possible in healthy humans, Payton's ratio of strength to weight is better than that of most athletes. Part of his exemplary physique is due to genetics, of course. The other part is hard work and good diet.

Payton is as tempted by junk foods as anyone else, and allows himself to nibble on chocolate and potato chips once in a while. Most of the time, however, he sticks with more nutritional fare. In fact, he recently gave up hamburgers and barbequed ribs, long-time favorites, because they contain too much fat.

Meals for Payton are light, and snacks are frequent, mainly fresh fruit, especially bananas and grapes. Close friends describe him as "a very picky eater," favoring chicken, crab, shrimp, pasta, and salads.

His breakfasts generally include a bowl of cereal, with an occasional indulgence in one of the high-sugar brands. An athlete like Payton with otherwise excellent diet habits doesn't have to exclude *everything* that might be considered junk food; he just has to keep those things in moderation.

For lunch, Payton generally has a sandwich or two. He doesn't drink much alcohol, just a wine cooler once in a while. During the season, however, he won't even drink a beer.

Payton doesn't take vitamins or supplements, preferring to get his nutrition from natural foods. He also doesn't use aspirin or other commonplace medicines.

For players with Payton's discipline and drive to succeed, giving everything on the field is second nature. What is harder, for weekend athletes as well as professionals, is to keep giving that effort during the drudgery of practice. "Every time I'm on the field," he says, "every time I touch the ball, I play as hard as I can. Every play's a Super Bowl for me."

Payton has had a dozen years of excellence at a position where the average career lasts just five. Entering the 1987 season, he is the NFL's all-time leading rusher and holds or shares nine league records. So how can he still feel he needs to prove himself on every play and in every practice?

From anyone else, Payton's answer would sound trite. "You're only as good as your last game," he says.

# 9 Customized Workouts:

## *Illustrated Exercises*

"There are two kinds of strength," says Pittsburgh Steelers center Mike Webster. "There's strength relevant to playing and there's weight training strength. Basically, I train to keep my strength up, but not to lift weights. I train with weights to be more efficient.

"But," adds Webster, long considered one of the strongest players in the NFL, "there's only one way to get strong—you work at it."

On the pages that follow are the illustrated stretching and strength exercises of *The NFL All-Pro Workout*. These exercises can be combined into customized workouts to help achieve your personal fitness goals. The exercises are organized and divided into groups by the area of the body they work. They are subdivided under each body area heading by type of exercise: Resistance, requiring little apparatus besides your own body weight; Free Weights, i.e., barbells and dumbbells; and Machines, such as those made by Nautilus and Universal. Those two lines of exercise machinery are featured because they are the machines most used by NFL teams and commonly are found at local fitness centers. However, there are many other comparable machine systems, sometimes based on completely different principles (such as Polaris, Kaiser, and Cybex), that will complement any workout program, if used properly.

Most exercises aimed at developing a specific muscle or muscle group are interchangeable. So it really doesn't matter whether you do a bench press, for example, with a barbell or with dumbbells, or on a machine. "The muscle does not know what type of equipment is being used," Washington's Dan Riley says. "It is not the type of equipment that is being used that will produce the results. It is how the equipment is being used and what takes place between the first and last repetition of each exercise that produces results."

# Anterior

## Major Muscles and Muscle Groups

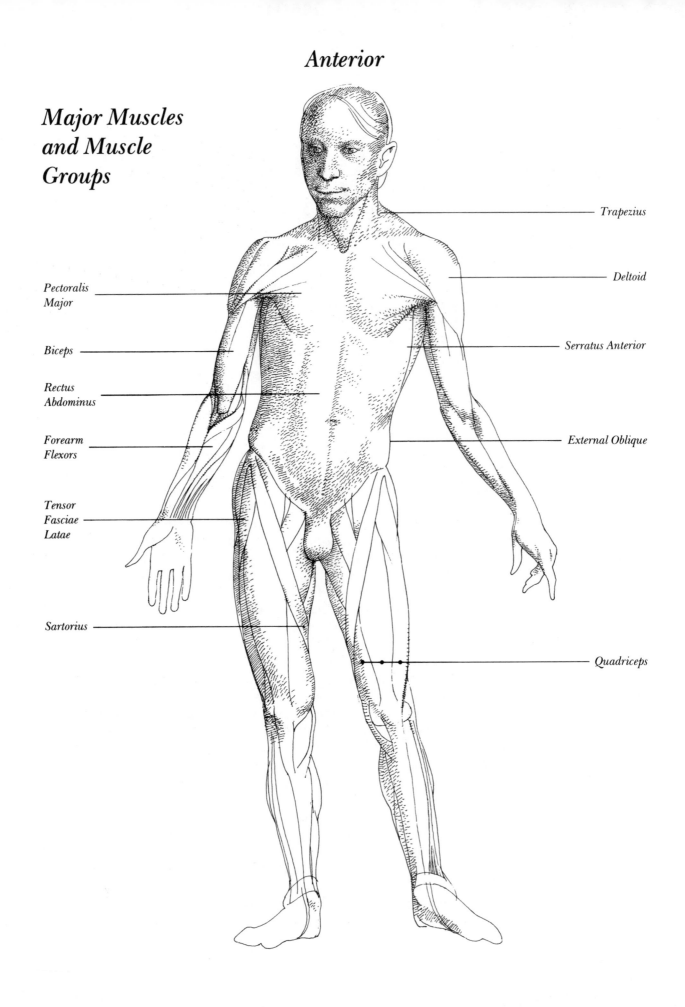

Trapezius

Deltoid

Pectoralis Major

Serratus Anterior

Biceps

Rectus Abdominus

Forearm Flexors

External Oblique

Tensor Fasciae Latae

Sartorius

Quadriceps

# Posterior

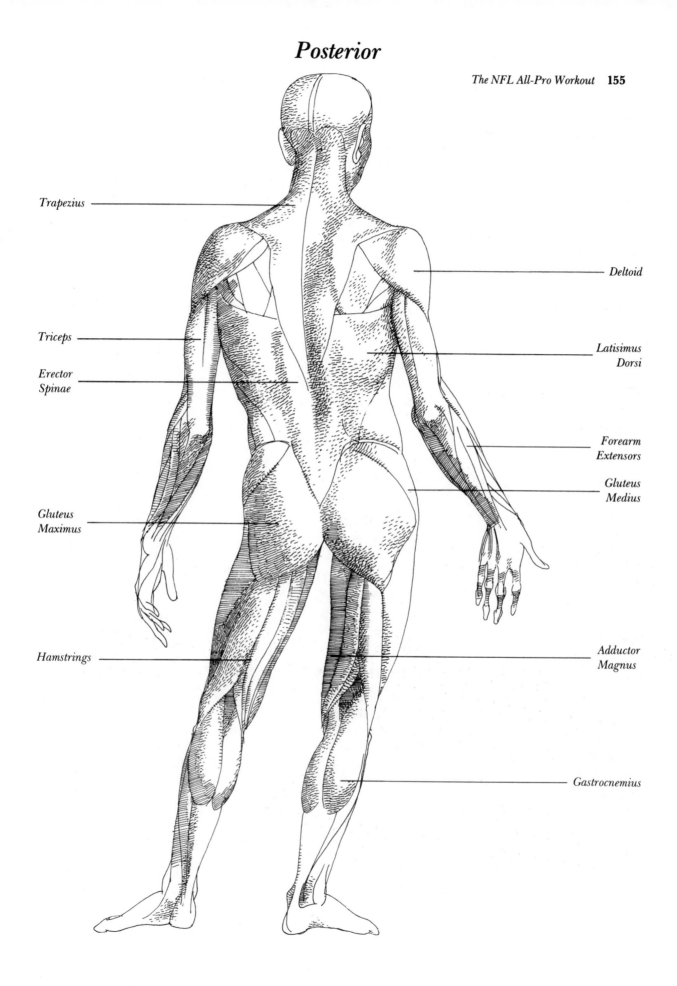

Trapezius

Triceps

Erector Spinae

Gluteus Maximus

Hamstrings

Deltoid

Latisimus Dorsi

Forearm Extensors

Gluteus Medius

Adductor Magnus

Gastrocnemius

# Suggested Exercises

## Stretches

Neck Roll
Arm Circle
Standing Crossed-Leg Toe Touch
Straddle Leg Stretch
Forward Lunge Stretch
Leaning Hamstring Stretch
Seated, Spread-Leg Reach
Seated Groin Stretch
Seated One-Leg Toe Touch
PNF Hamstring Stretch
PNF Quadriceps Stretch

## Legs

*Quadriceps*

**Free Weights**
Squat
Lunge

**Machines**
Leg Extension (N) (U)
Leg Press (N) (U)

*Hamstrings*

**Free Weights**
Lunge

**Machines**
Leg Curl (N) (U)

*Calves*

**Free Weights**
Calf Raise

**Machines**
Calf Raise (N)
Leg Press (N) (U)

*Hips/Thighs*

**Free Weights**
Leg Lift
Side Leg Lift

**Machines**
Hip and Back (N) (U)
Cable Side Leg Lift (U)

## Back

**Resistance**
Wide-Grip Chin-Up

**Free Weights**
Pullover (bench)
Dumbell Row
Barbell Row
Hyperextension

**Machines**
Pullover (N)
Torso-Arm Front Pulldown (N)
Behind-Neck Pulldown (N)
Behind-Neck Pulldown (U)
Behind-Neck Lats (N)
Seated Pulley (U)

## Chest

**Resistance**
Push-Up
Dip

**Free Weights**
Bench Press
Dumbell Fly
Dumbbell Press (inclined/declined)

**Machines**
Arm Cross (N)
Decline Press (N)
Pec Deck (U)

## Shoulders

**Free Weights**
Overhead Press
Upright Row
Lateral Raise
Bent Lateral Raise
Frontal Raise
Shrug

**Machines**
Lateral Raise (N) (U)
Overhead Press (N)

## Arms

*Biceps*
**Resistance**

Close-Grip Chin-Up

**Free Weights**
Preacher Curl
Standing Curl
Reverse Curl
Seated Dumbbell Curl
Seated Concentration Curl

**Machines**
Cable Curl (U)
Multi Biceps (N)

*Triceps*

**Resistance**
Triceps Push-Up
Dip

**Free Weights**
French Curl
Triceps Extension
Triceps Kick-Back

**Machines**
Cable Push-Down (U)

*Forearms/Wrists*

**Free Weights**
Wrist Curl
Reverse Wrist Curl

## Midsection

**Resistance**
Abdominal Crunch
Bicycle
Reverse Abdominal Curl
Partial Sit-Up with Reach
"V" Sit-Up
Side Bend Sit-Up
Side Crunch
Trunk Twist

**Free Weights**
Side Bend with Dumbbells

**Machines**
Abdominal Crunch (N) (U)
Forward Torso (N)
Rotary Torso (N)

# Sample Weight Workouts

Here are six weight workouts designed to strengthen and tone the entire body. The workouts increase in difficulty from number one to three, which all are full-body progressive workouts. Number four is a special aerobic workout. Numbers five and six are split workouts, meant to be done on consecutive days. No matter which workout you do, precede it with a 10-minute warm-up (such as jogging, jumping rope, or riding a stationary or road bike), followed by a stretching session. Try to stretch after every workout as well.

Sets and reps for each exercise are indicated, but are flexible. If you are new to weight training, do as many sets and reps as you can without straining. Weights for the various exercises generally are not indicated; you must determine how much weight you can lift, given the target number of sets and reps. Nautilus exercises are designated (N). Universal exercises are designated (U). In some cases, both (N) and (U) appear, meaning the machines for that exercise are interchangeable. (Be sure machines are adjusted properly for your body before using them; if you don't know how to adjust or use them, ask for help.) If a machine is not specified, the exercise is to be performed with free weights, or is a resistance exercise such as a push-up.

The same exercise can be made to hit different areas of a muscle group simply by changing or reversing your grip (e.g., wide- and close-grip chin-ups, and forward and reverse-grip curls) or exercise angle. Flat, inclined (head angled up), or declined (head down) positions are specified for some exercises, particularly dumbbell presses and flies. If no position is specified, perform it flat (on your back).

Another exercise variation is doing "negatives." Rather than stressing muscles in the positive lifting (or concentric) phase of an exercise, negatives stress during the lowering (eccentric) phase. To do a negative dip, for example, step up on a box or support to get into the fully-ex-tended position. Then, lower your body as slowly as you can. Repeat, doing the same number of reps that you normally would do if you were working positively. You also can shift to negatives when you no longer can continue with a positive exercise. Say you hit failure after 7 chin-ups and you wanted to do 12. Rather than stopping, switch to negative (lowering only) chin-ups and finish your set.

It is suggested you begin with workout number one and stick with it for three or four weeks. Then move on to workout number two, adjusting your weights accordingly, and do it for a few weeks, perhaps adding in the aerobic weight workout (number four) once or twice. (However, any workout can be made more aerobic by shortening rest periods between sets and exercises.) By the time you get to workout number three, which is strenuous, you should begin noticing a significant improvement in your strength, tone, and definition. Note that in workout number three the number of reps per set decreases, reflecting an increase in weights.

(Keep in mind that the reps and sets specified in all six workouts are goal figures. Do as many reps as you can in each set, adjusting reps up or down, rather than weights, until you gain strength and experience.)

After you've worked up to program number three, there's no reason that you can't go back to workout number one and simply raise the weights and increase the sets. Or, you can "pyramid"—add weight and do fewer reps each consecutive set.

If you already are an experienced weightlifter, or are working out for a specific sport, perform the workouts in whatever order you choose, or modify them by adding and substituting exercises as desired.

# ONE:
# Basic

| Legs | sets | reps |
|---|---|---|
| Leg Extension (N) (U) | 2 | 15-18 |
| Leg Press (N) (U) | 2 | 15-18 |
| Leg Curl (N) (U) | 2 | 15-18 |
| Calf Raise (N) (U) | 2 | 20 |
| **Back** | | |
| Pullover (N) | 2 | 12-15 |
| Behind-Neck Pulldown (N) | 2 | 12-15 |
| Wide-Grip Chin-Up | | to failure |
| **Chest** | | |
| Arm Cross (N) | 2 | 12-15 |
| Decline Press (N) | 2 | 12-15 |
| Bench Press | 2 | 12-15 |
| Dip | | to failure |
| **Shoulders** | | |
| Lateral Raise (N) | 2 | 12-15 |
| Upright Row | 2 | 12-15 |
| Overhead Press | 2 | 12-15 |
| **Arms** | | |
| *Biceps* | | |
| Standing Barbell Curl | 2 | 12-15 |
| Seated Concentration Curl | 2 | 12-15 |
| *Triceps* | | |
| Triceps Extension | 2 | 12-15 |
| Triceps Push-Up | 2 | 15-18 |
| **Midsection** | | |
| Abdominal Crunch | 2 | 25 |
| Reverse Abdominal Curl | 2 | 25 |
| Trunk Twist | 2 | 25 |

# TWO:
# Intermediate

| Legs | sets | reps |
|---|---|---|
| Lunge (no weight) | | 20 each leg |
| Leg Curl (N) (U) | 3 | 15 |
| Hip and Back Machine (N) | | 20 each leg |
| Leg Press (N) (U) | 3 | 15 |
| Calf Raise | 3 | 15 |
| **Back** | | |
| Barbell Row | 3 | 12-15 |
| Pullover (N) | 3 | 12-15 |
| Behind-Neck Pulldown (N) (U) | 3 | 12-15 |
| **Chest** | | |
| Bench Press | 3 | 12-15 |
| Dumbbell Fly (inclined) | 3 | 12-15 |
| Decline Press (N) | 3 | 12-15 |
| Push-Up | | to failure |
| **Shoulders** | | |
| Frontal Raise | 3 | 12-15 |
| Lateral Raise (N) | 3 | 12-15 |
| Overhead Press | 3 | 12-15 |
| **Arms** | | |
| *Biceps* | | |
| Preacher Curl | 3 | 12-15 |
| Reverse Curl | 3 | 12-15 |
| *Triceps* | | |
| Cable Push-Down (U) | 3 | 12-15 |
| Triceps Kick-Back | 3 | 12-15 |
| *Forearms/Wrists* | | |
| Wrist Curl | 3 | 12-15 |
| **Midsection** | | |
| Abdominal Crunch | 2 | 25 |
| Partial Sit-Up with Reach | 2 | 25 |
| Side Bend with Dumbbells | | 50 each side |
| Side Bend Sit-Up | 2 | 25 |

# THREE: Difficult*

| Legs | sets | reps |
|---|---|---|
| Leg Extension (N) (U) | 3 | 10-12 |
| Squat | 3 | 8-10 |
| Leg Curl (N) (U) | 3 | 8-10 |
| Lunge (with dumbbells) | | 15 each leg |
| Cable Side Leg Lift (U) | 3 | 8-10 each leg |
| **Back** | | |
| Wide-Grip Chin-Up | 2 | 8-10 |
| Torso-Arm Front Pulldown (N) | 3 | 8-10 |
| Dumbbell Row | 3 | 8-10 |
| Seated Pulley (U) | 3 | 8-10 |
| **Chest** | | |
| Dumbbell Press (inclined) | 3 | 8-10 |
| Dumbbell Fly (inclined) | 3 | 8-10 |
| Dip | 3 | 8-10 |
| Bench Press | 3 | 8-10 |
| Dumbbell Fly | 3 | 8-10 |
| Dumbbell Press (declined) | 3 | 8-10 |
| Dumbbell Fly (declined) | 3 | 8-10 |
| Push-Up | | to failure |
| **Shoulders** | | |
| Upright Row | 3 | 8-10 |
| Frontal Raise | 3 | 8-10 |
| Lateral Raise (N) | 3 | 8-10 |
| Overhead Press (N) | 3 | 8-10 |
| **Arms** | | |
| *Triceps* | | |
| French Curl | 3 | 8-10 |
| Cable Push-Down (U) | 3 | 8-10 |
| Triceps Push-Up | | to failure |
| *Biceps* | | |
| Seated Dumbbell Curl | 3 | 8-10 |
| Close-Grip Chin-Up | | to failure |
| *Forearms/Wrists* | | |
| Wrist Curl | 3 | 8-10 |
| **Midsection** | | |
| "V" Sit-Up | 3 | 25 |
| Bicycle Sit-Up | 3 | 25 each leg |
| Reverse Abdominal Curl | 3 | 25 |
| Rotary Torso (N) | 2 | 25 |

*\* This is a good workout to do with a partner. Because it is a lengthy and strenuous workout, the third set of many of the exercises may require a spotter for safety purposes, and also to help the lifter perform maximum reps.*

# FOUR: Aerobic Weight Workout*

| | reps |
|---|---|
| Wide-Grip Chin-Up (negative)† | 15 |
| Push-Up | 25 |
| Hyperextension | 15 |
| Abdominal Crunch | 30 |
| Dip (negative)† | 15 |

*Pause 15 seconds. Check pulse; if too high, rest until it stabilizes in target area.*

| | |
|---|---|
| Wide-Grip Chin-Up (negative) | 10-12 |
| Push-Up | 25 |
| Hyperextension | 15 |
| Abdominal Crunch | 30 |
| Dip (negative) | 10-12 |

*Pause 15 seconds. Check pulse.*

| | |
|---|---|
| Wide-Grip Chin-Up (negative) | 8-10 |
| Push-Up | 15-20 |
| Hyperextension | 8-10 |
| Abdominal Crunch | 30 |
| Dip (negative) | 8-10 |

*Pause 20 seconds. Check pulse.*

| | |
|---|---|
| Wide-Grip Chin-Up (negative) | to failure |
| Push-Up | to failure |
| Hyperextension | 8-10 |
| Abdominal Crunch | 30 |
| Dip (negative) | to failure |

*Rest one minute. Check pulse.*

| | |
|---|---|
| Leg Press (N) (U) | 25-30 |
| Leg Curl (N) (U) | 25-30 |
| Leg Extension (N) (U) | 15-18 |

*Rest 30 seconds. Check pulse.*

| | |
|---|---|
| Leg Press (N) (U) | 25-30 |
| Leg Curl (N) (U) | 25-30 |
| Leg Extension (N) (U) | 15-18 |

*Rest one minute. Check pulse.*

| | |
|---|---|
| Standing Biceps Dumbbell Curl (alternating arms) | 18-25 each arm (10-15 lbs.) |
| Triceps Kick-back (both arms simultaneously) | 18-25 (7-10 lbs.) |

*Rest 30 seconds. Check pulse.*

| | |
|---|---|
| Standing Biceps Dumbbell Curl (alternating arms) | 18-25 each arm (10-15 lbs.) |
| Triceps Kick-back (both arms simultaneously) | 18-25 (7-10 lbs.) |

*Stretch well.*

*\* Reps, weights, and rests may have to be adjusted up or down to compensate for heart rate and physical condition. If you become dizzy or light-headed, stop exercising.*
*† As you get stronger, you may have to perform these negative exercises with weight added (using a machine such as the Nautilus Multi-Exerciser) to raise your heart rate into the target zone.*

# FIVE: Split Workout

| Shoulders | sets | reps |
|---|---|---|
| Lateral Raise | 3 | 8-10 |
| Frontal Raise | 3 | 8-10 |
| Upright Row | 3 | 8-10 |
| Overhead Press | 3 | 8-10 |
| Shrug | 3 | 8-10 |
| **Chest** | | |
| Bench Press | 3 | 8-10 |
| Decline Press (N) | 3 | 8-10 |
| Dumbbell Fly (declined) | 3 | 8-10 |
| Arm Cross (N)/Pec Deck (U) | 3 | 8-10 |
| Bench Press (inclined with dumbbells) | 3 | 8-10 |
| **Arms** | | |
| *(Triceps)* | | |
| French Curl | 3 | 8-10 |
| Cable Push-Down (U) | 3 | 8-10 |
| Triceps Extension | 3 | 8-10 |
| Triceps Push-Up | 3 | 8-10 |
| **Midsection** | | |
| Forward Torso (N) | 2 | 25 |
| Reverse Abdominal Curl | 3 | 25 |
| "V" Sit-Up | 3 | 25 |
| Side-Bend Sit-Up | 3 | 25 each side |

# SIX: Split Workout

| Back | sets | reps |
|---|---|---|
| Pullover | 3 | 8-10 |
| Barbell Row | 3 | 8-10 |
| Seated Pulley (U) | 3 | 8-10 |
| Dumbbell Row | 3 | 8-10 |
| Wide-Grip Chin-Up | 3 | 8-10 |
| **Arms** | | |
| *(Biceps)* | | |
| Standing Barbell Curl | 3 | 8-10 |
| Preacher Curl | 3 | 8-10 |
| Seated Concentration Curl | 3 | 8-10 |
| Close-Grip Chin-Up | 3 | 8-10 |
| **Legs** | | |
| Leg Extension (N) (U) | 3 | 8-10 |
| Leg Press (N) (U) | 3 | 8-10 |
| Squat | 3 | 8-10 |
| Leg Curl (N) (U) | 3 | 8-10 |
| Lunge (with dumbbells) | 3 | 8-10 each leg |
| Calf Raise (N) | 3 | 15 |
| **Midsection** | | |
| Abdominal Crunch | 3 | 25 |
| Partial Sit-Up with Reach | 3 | 25 |
| Bicycle | 3 | 25 |
| Reverse Abdominal Curl | 3 | 25 |
| Side Bend with Dumbbells | 1 | 100 (15 lbs.) |

## Dan Riley's Weightlifting Tips

Following are five weightlifting precepts advocated by Washington Redskins strength coach Dan Riley:

1. Whenever possible, exercise the potentially larger and stronger muscles first. Do not, however, sacrifice training efficiency to maintain a predetermined exercise order.

2. To maintain full flexibility in your joints, raise and lower the weight through your full range of motion. It may be harder to do, but it is more beneficial in the long run.

3. Take about two seconds to raise the weight, and about four seconds to lower it. When you throw the weight into position or let it fall quickly, you are relying more on momentum than muscle fibers.

4. Once you have gained weightlifting experience, try to reach the point of total muscular fatigue sometime between 8 and 12 repetitions. ("If an athlete can properly perform another repetition and doesn't," Riley says, "he has not gained as much from the exercise as he could have. A subpar effort will produce subpar results.")

5. Have supervision when training with free weights. When working to failure, a spotter should be on hand to prevent accidents if the lifter has trouble handling the weight. The spotter also can encourage the lifter to make maximum effort.

# Stretches

### Arm Circles

*Stand with feet shoulder-width apart and arms outstretched, parallel to the floor. Keeping arms straight, begin making small circles (in a forward motion) with your hands. Increase size of circles with each rep. After a few reps, change direction of motion, beginning again with small circles.*

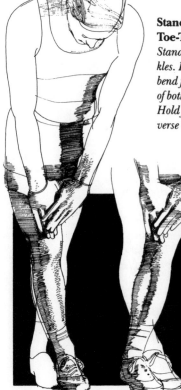

### Neck Roll

*Standing with feet shoulder-width apart, slowly roll head in a 360-degree arc. Repeat three times, then change direction for three reps.*

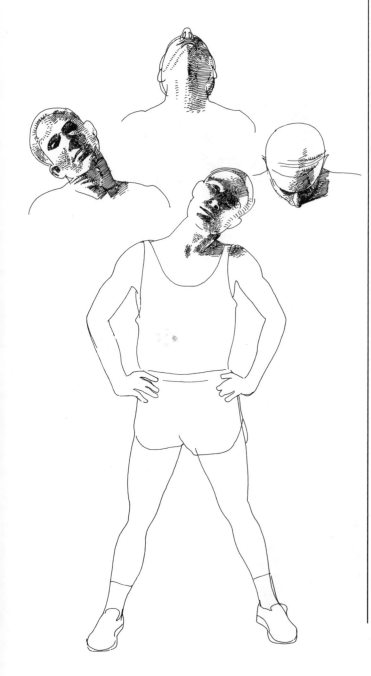

### Standing Crossed-Leg Toe-Touch

*Stand with legs crossed at the ankles. Keeping knees locked, slowly bend forward and touch fingertips of both hands to toes of forward foot. Hold for 20-30 seconds; repeat. Reverse legs and repeat twice.*

### Straddle Leg Stretch

*Stand with legs far apart. Lean right knee outward and slowly stretch inner thigh muscles of left leg. Stretch as far as you can, and hold for 30 seconds. Repeat, trying to relax further into the stretch. Reverse stance and repeat stretch.*

### Forward Lunge Stretch

*Stand with feet shoulder-width apart. Lean forward, leading with your right knee. Keeping back straight, lower torso as far toward floor as possible. (Do not touch rear knee to floor.) Hold for 30 seconds. Repeat, trying to relax further into the stretch. Repeat stretch twice leading with left knee.*

### Leaning Hamstring Stretch (b)

*Same as Leaning Hamstring Stretch (a), but on this one you stand farther from the wall and extend one knee forward as far as possible. Hold for 30 seconds. Repeat with other knee forward.*

### Leaning Hamstring Stretch (a)

*Stand about three feet away from a wall (or tree, telephone pole, etc.) Lean forward, extending arms and placing palms flat against wall. Gradually lean closer to wall until hamstrings feel tight. Make sure that your heels stay flat on ground. Hold for 30 seconds. Repeat, standing farther away from wall.*

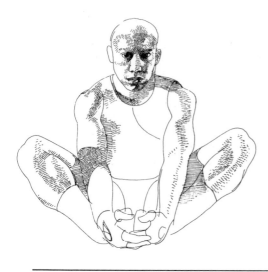

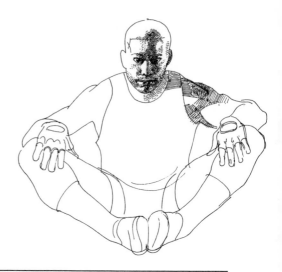

**Seated Groin Stretch (a)**
*Sit with soles of feet together. Slowly lean forward and grasp toes. Hold for 30 seconds. Repeat.*

**Seated Groin Stretch (b)**
*Sit with soles of feet together. Gently push knees downward as far as possible. Hold for 30 seconds. Repeat.*

**Seated One-Leg Toe-Touch**
*Sit with left foot drawn in toward inside of right thigh and right leg extended. Gradually lean forward and touch right toes with both hands. Hold for 30 seconds. Repeat. Exhaling slowly as you lean forward helps maximize your reach. Switch positions so that left leg is extended. Repeat stretch twice.*

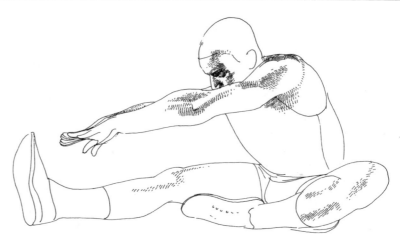

**Seated Spread-Leg Reach**
*Sit with legs extended and spread. Gradually lean forward from the waist as far as you can. Hold for 30 seconds. Repeat twice more, exhaling slowly as you lean into stretch.*

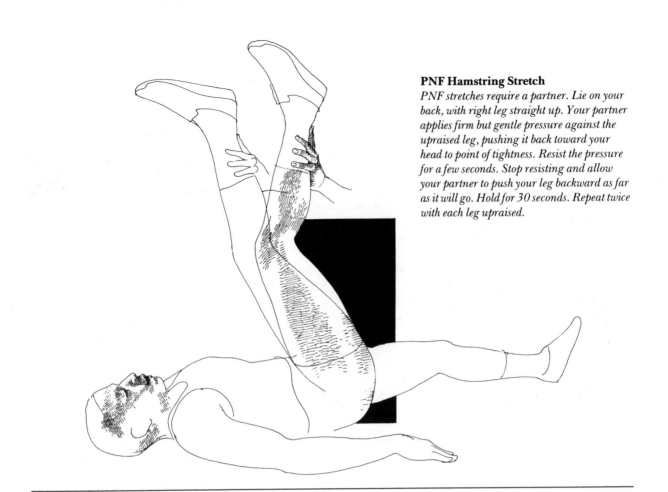

## PNF Hamstring Stretch

*PNF stretches require a partner. Lie on your back, with right leg straight up. Your partner applies firm but gentle pressure against the upraised leg, pushing it back toward your head to point of tightness. Resist the pressure for a few seconds. Stop resisting and allow your partner to push your leg backward as far as it will go. Hold for 30 seconds. Repeat twice with each leg upraised.*

## PNF Quadriceps Stretch

*PNF stretches require a partner. Lie on your stomach with knees bent and heels toward buttocks. Your partner applies firm but gentle pressure against your ankles, pushing your heels toward your buttocks to point of tightness. Resist the pressure for a few seconds. Stop resisting and allow your partner to push your heels as far toward your buttocks as they will go. Hold for 30 seconds. Repeat twice more.*

# Legs

### Calf Raise

*Stand holding a barbell across your shoulders, behind your neck. Put the toes and balls of your feet up on the edge of a weight plate (or thick board). Raise up on your toes, lifting your heels as far off the floor as possible. Lower your heels to floor. Repeat.*

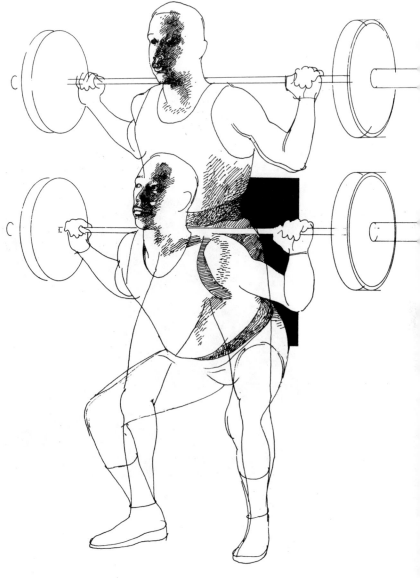

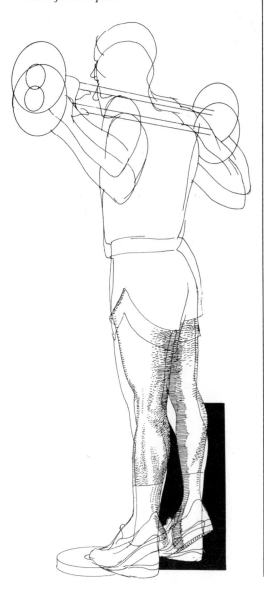

### Squat

A wide leather support belt should be worn to perform this exercise. *Place barbell on squat rack and adjust weight. Stand under the barbell so that it rests across your shoulders and behind your neck. Grasp the barbell with your hands, palms up, wider than shoulder-width apart. Stand up, balancing the barbell on your shoulders, and step away from squat rack. Keeping your back as straight as possible, bend your knees and lower your body into a squatting position. Slowly stand up straight again. Repeat. Depending on the weight being lifted, one, sometimes two, spotters may be required for safety. Deep squats are not recommended for people with knee problems.*

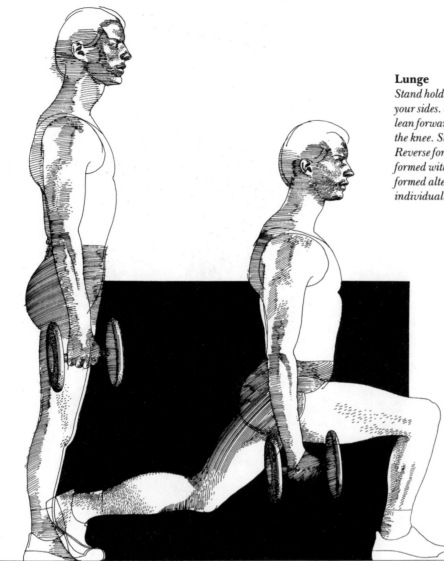

## Lunge

*Stand holding a dumbbell in each hand, arms at your sides. Step forward with your right foot and lean forward with your back straight, bending at the knee. Step back to starting position. Repeat. Reverse for left leg. This exercise also can be performed without dumbbells. Sets can be performed alternating legs or for each leg individually.*

## Side Leg Lift

*Lie on your left side on the floor, with a weight strapped to your right ankle (or a weight boot on your right foot). Keeping your right leg straight, lift it as far as possible in a scissors-type movement. Lower your leg slowly. Complete the set. Switch weights and repeat exercise with left leg.*

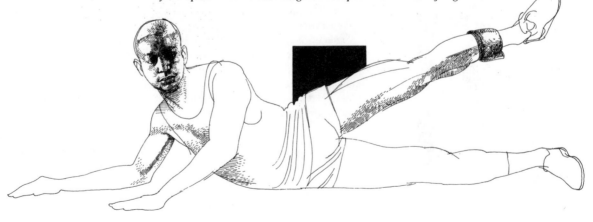

**Leg Lift**

*Lie on your back on the floor, with a weight strapped to each ankle (or a weight boot on each foot). With your arms at your sides (hands palms down), lift both feet about six inches off the floor. While keeping your feet elevated, lift your right leg straight up toward your head. Lower your right leg slowly to level of left leg. Complete the set. Repeat with left leg.*

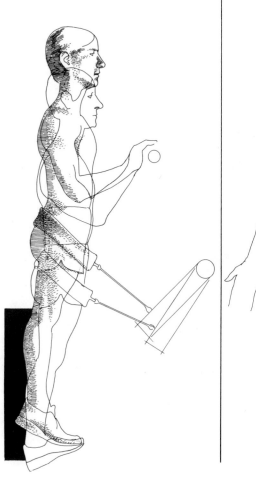

**Calf Raise (N)**

*Set weight level. Attach padded hip belt to Multi-Exerciser and adjust it around your hips. Put the toes and balls of your feet on the front edge of the lowest step. Holding the horizontal bar in front of you, raise up on your toes as high as possible. Slowly lower your heels as far as possible. Repeat. This exercise can be performed with both legs at once, or, by crossing one leg behind the other, with one leg at a time.*

**Cable Side Leg Lift (U)**

*Set weight level. Attach the ankle strap of cable to your right ankle. Stand with your right side toward apparatus. Lift your right leg up and to the side as far as possible, across the front of your left leg. Slowly return your leg to starting position. Complete set. Attach the ankle strap to your left ankle. Standing with your left side toward the apparatus, perform the set with your left leg. This works the muscles of the inner thigh. To work the outer thigh, attach the ankle strap to your left leg. Stand with your right side toward apparatus. Lift your left leg up and to the left as far as possible. Reverse position to exercise right leg.*

**Hip and Back (N) (U)**

*Set weight level. Lie on your back in the apparatus, placing both legs over the roller pads so that the pads are just behind your knees. Fasten the seat belt and grasp the handles loosely. Extend both legs, pushing against the roller pads. Keeping your left leg extended, allow your right leg to come back toward your chest as far as possible. Re-extend your right leg, arching your back slightly and pointing your toes at full extension. Complete the set with your right leg. Then, keeping your right leg extended, perform the set with your left leg. People with lower back problems may not want to do this exercise. Also, women using this machine may find the muscles it develops (top of buttocks) unattractive.*

**Leg Press (N) (U)**

*Set weight level. Fasten seat belt. Sit in apparatus with your knees up toward your chest and your feet against foot pad (toes slightly turned in). Pushing against the foot pad, extend your legs smoothly. Allow the foot pad to return slowly to the starting position. Repeat.*

### Leg Extension (N) (U)

*Set weight level. Sit in apparatus with your feet behind the roller pads and your knees just over the front edge of the seat. Fasten seat belt. Hold handles loosely. Using the fronts of your ankles, smoothly push roller pads up until your legs are fully extended. Lower roller pads slowly. Be sure to keep your back against the seat pad. Repeat. This exercise also can be performed one leg at a time.*

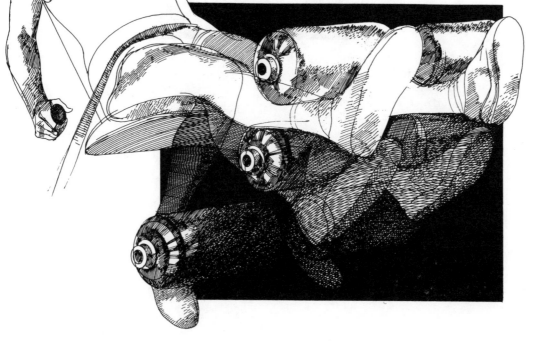

### Leg Curl (N) (U)

*Set weight level. Lie on your stomach on the apparatus with your knees just beyond the edge of the main pad and your heels under the roller pads. Hold the handles loosely. Pushing against the roller pads, bring your legs up over your back toward your buttocks as far as possible. Slowly allow the roller pads to return to starting position. Repeat. Try to keep your pelvis against the main pad as you perform the exercise; an additional pad beneath, and slightly elevating, the pelvis helps. This exercise can be performed with both legs or with each leg individually.*

# Back

### Wide-Grip Chin-Up

*With hands wide apart (palms out) on bar, raise body so that chin is level with bar as in a standard chin-up. Lower body slowly. If you can't complete your set, switch to negatives. This exercise also can be done behind the neck, as shown.*

### Hyperextension

*This exercise requires a Roman Chair, or a high bench or table and a spotter to hold down your lower legs. Lying on your stomach with head down toward floor, raise upper body. Lower upper body slowly. This exercise can be made more difficult by holding a weight plate behind your head.* Do not attempt hyperextensions if you have a history of lower back problems.

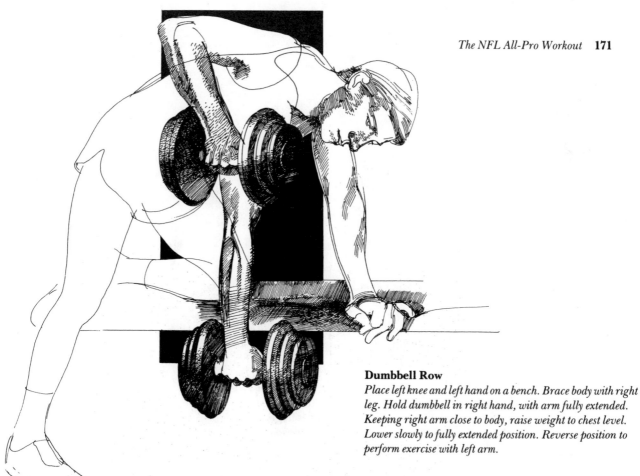

## Dumbbell Row
*Place left knee and left hand on a bench. Brace body with right leg. Hold dumbbell in right hand, with arm fully extended. Keeping right arm close to body, raise weight to chest level. Lower slowly to fully extended position. Reverse position to perform exercise with left arm.*

## Barbell Row
*Bend forward with back parallel to floor. Grip barbell, palms down, with hands outside shoulder width. With legs shoulder-width apart and knees slightly bent, raise barbell to chest. Slowly lower to fully extended position. Wear a wide leather support belt during this exercise.*

## Pullover
*Lie on a bench with head just at edge. Grip dumbbell between thumb and index fingers of both hands, with arms extended fully above chest. Slowly lower weight in backward arc over your head, bending your elbows slightly. Raise weight slowly to fully extended position. If working to failure, use a spotter.*

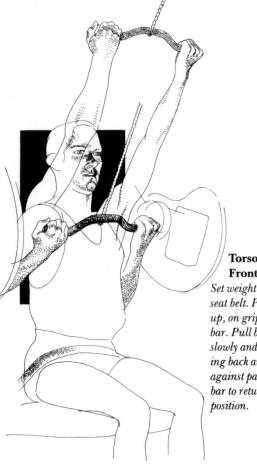

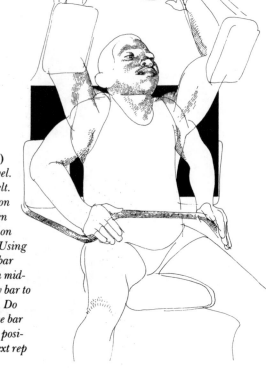

### Torso-Arm
### Front Pulldown (N)
*Set weight level. Fasten seat belt. Put hands, palms up, on grips of overhead bar. Pull bar down to chest slowly and steadily, keeping back and shoulders against pad. Slowly allow bar to return up to starting position.*

### Pullover (N)
*Set weight level. Fasten seat belt. Place elbows on pads, and open hands loosely on curve of bar. Using elbows, push bar down to touch midsection. Allow bar to return slowly. Do not pause once bar returns to top position; begin next rep immediately.*

### Seated Pulley (U)
*Set weight level. Sit on floor facing apparatus, with legs extended and slightly spread. Lean forward from the waist and grip bar. Lean back, pulling bar toward chest using a rowing motion. Allow bar to return to starting position slowly and smoothly.*

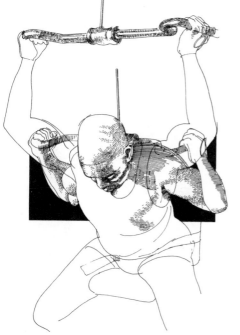

## Behind-Neck Pulldown (N)

*Set weight level. Fasten seat belt snugly, but not tightly. Grip bar and lean forward at a 45-degree angle. Maintaining lean throughout exercise, pull bar down slowly and smoothly, keeping elbows back, until padded central portion touches nape of neck. Slowly allow bar to return to starting position. Concentrate on pulling with lats and back muscles.*

### Behind-Neck Pulldown (U)

*Set weight level. Grip bar with hands wide apart. With a slight forward lean, and keeping elbows back, pull bar down until it touches nape of neck. Slowly allow bar to return to starting position. Concentrate on pulling with lats and back muscles.*

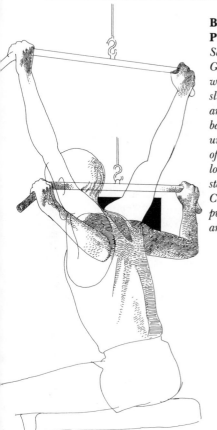

## Behind-Neck Lats (N)

*Set weight level. Fasten seat belt. With arms bent at the elbows, forearms crossed behind head, and palms facing out, put back of upper arms on padded rollers. Keeping arms back, push down on rollers with upper arms until rollers touch sides of body. Slowly allow rollers to return to starting position. Do not pause in top position; begin next rep immediately.*

# Chest

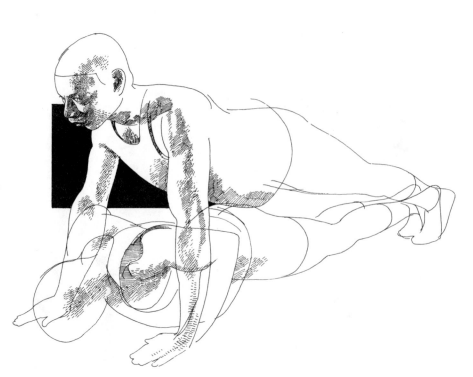

### Push-Up

*Lie face down on the floor with your hands, palms down, under your shoulders and your feet together, toes down. Keeping your back and legs straight, raise your body off the floor by extending your arms completely. Slowly lower your body so that your chest almost touches the floor. Raise body again by extending arms. Repeat.*

### Dip
(See "Arms")

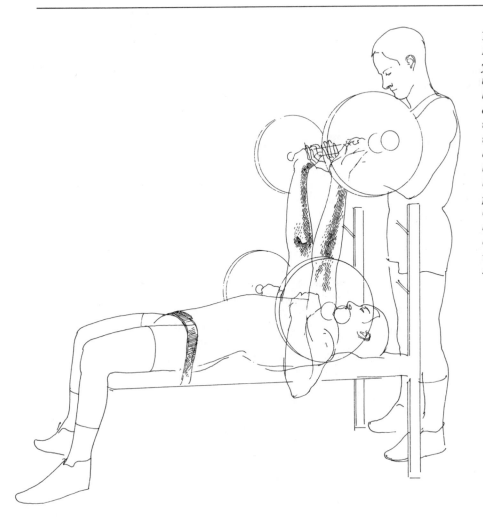

### Bench Press

*Lie on your back on a bench with your feet flat on the floor. Grasp the barbell with your hands slightly wider than shoulder-width apart. Begin the exercise by holding barbell so that it is just touching your chest. Keeping your elbows close to your body, raise barbell straight above mid-chest level by extending your arms completely. Be careful not to raise the barbell too far back toward your head. Lower the barbell slowly to chest. Repeat. If working to failure or new to weightlifting, have a spotter help you with this exercise.*

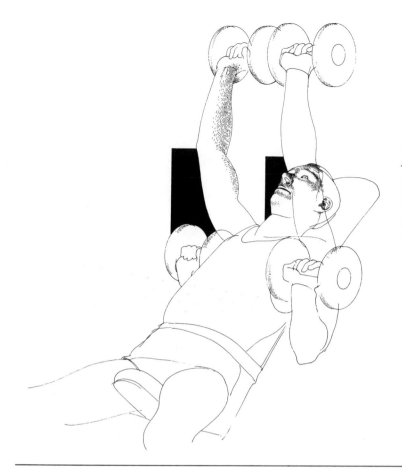

**Dumbbell Press**

*Lie on your back on a bench with your feet flat on the floor on either side. Hold a dumbbell in each hand (at right angles to your body) at chest level. Keeping elbows close to body, press the dumbbells up until your arms are fully extended and dumbbells meet end-to-end over your chest. Slowly lower dumbbells to starting position. Repeat.*

**Dumbbell Fly**

*Lie on your back on a bench with your feet flat on the floor on either side. Hold a dumbbell in each hand (palms up), arms bent with elbows held out to the side as far as is comfortable. Keeping elbows bent, raise dumbells in an arc so that they meet over your chest. Lower dumbbells slowly to level of bench. Repeat.*

### Arm Cross (N)

*Set weight level. Fasten seat belt. Place your forearms against the arm pads and grasp handles above pads loosely. Keeping your back against the seat, push with forearms against pads, trying to bring your elbows together in front of your chest. Slowly return to starting position. Repeat.*

### Pec Deck (U)

*Identical exercise to Arm Cross, except that exerciser sits in a more upright position.*

### Decline Press (N)

*Set weight level. Fasten seat belt. Push with your feet against the large foot pedal to raise handles into position. Grasp both handles, palms in. Keeping head back, smoothly push handles forward as far as possible. With elbows held wide, allow handles to slowly return slightly beyond starting position. Repeat.*

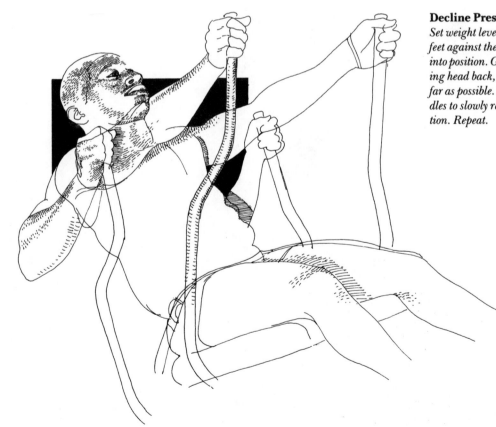

# Shoulders

### Overhead Press

*This exercise can be performed either standing or seated, in front of the body or behind the neck (seated behind-neck is illustrated). Use a wide grip on the barbell, palms out. Raise barbell to chest level. Extend arms straight up overhead. Slowly lower bar to shoulder level (either in front of body or behind neck). Repeat, lifting from shoulder level. Use a spotter if working to failure, and wear a wide leather support belt.*

### Upright Row

*Grip barbell in center, with hands palms down and about six inches apart. With legs shoulder-width apart and knees slightly bent, lift barbell just to point that your arms are hanging down fully extended. (Always lift with your legs, not your back.) Raise barbell to chin. Lower slowly. Wear a wide leather support belt during this exercise, and be careful not to use too much weight.*

### Shrug

*Hold a dumbbell in each hand, arms hanging fully extended. Move your shoulders in a forward circle with a shrugging motion. This exercise also can be done with a backward motion.*

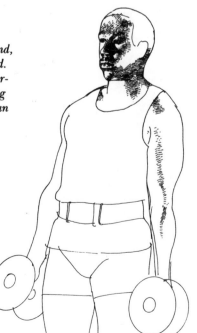
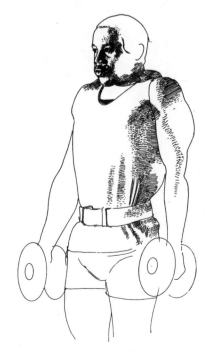

**Bent Lateral Raise**
*Stand with legs shoulder-width apart and torso bent forward. Hold dumbbells together, arms hanging fully extended. Keeping elbows slightly bent and head up, raise dumbbells across front of body to shoulder height. Lower slowly. Wear a wide leather support belt for this exercise.*

**Lateral Raise**
*Same as Bent Lateral Raise (above) without forward lean.*

**Frontal Raise**
*Stand with feet shoulder-width apart, knees slightly bent. Hold a dumbbell in each hand (palms down), with arms hanging fully extended at sides. Raise dumbbell straight up, elbow locked, until arm is parallel to floor. Lower dumbbell slowly. This exercise can be done with both arms simultaneously, alternating reps with each arm, or alternating sets with each arm. Wear a wide leather support belt.*

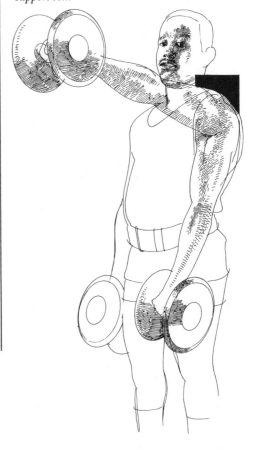

## Overhead Press (N)

*Set weight level. Fasten seat belt. Grip handles of bar. Push bar straight up overhead, keeping elbows wide. Do not arch your back. Slowly lower bar. If you find yourself pushing with your legs, extend them straight in front of you, ankles crossed, during exercise.*

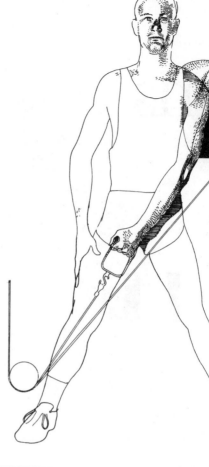

## Lateral Raise (U)

*Set weight level. Stand with legs well apart, right shoulder toward apparatus. Grip cable handle with left hand. Without bending or twisting, draw handle diagonally across body, from waist to shoulder level. Slowly lower handle. Complete set. Reverse position to exercise right arm.*

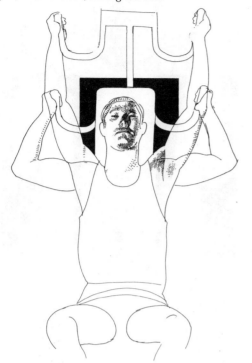

## Lateral Raise (N)

*Set weight level. Fasten seat belt. Grip handles tightly, with tops of wrists against pads. Keeping arms locked in bent position, raise elbows as high as machine allows. Lower slowly. To keep from using legs to push, sit with ankles crossed.*

# Arms

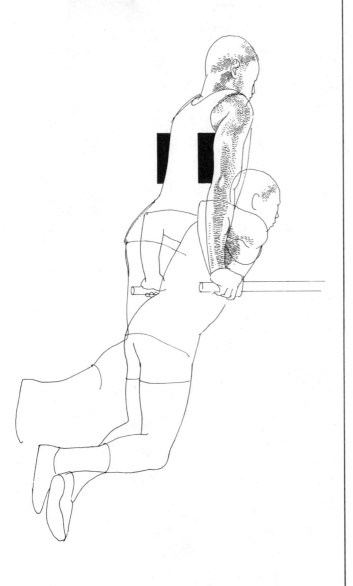

### Dip
*Requires parallel bars or machine such as Nautilus Multi-Exerciser. Stand between bars. Gripping one bar in each hand, raise body until arms are fully extended. Slowly lower body as far as you can, then return to fully extended position.*

### Chin-Up
*Grip bar with hands (palms toward you) about shoulder-width apart. Pull body up so that chin is above level of bar. Slowly lower body to full arm extension. Repeat. For a variation, try a* Narrow-Grip Chin-Up, *which differs only in that your hands are placed side by side on the bar. Narrow-Grip Chin-Ups isolate the biceps better.*

## Triceps Push-Up

*Extend arms behind body, placing hands (knuckles forward) on edge of a bench. Extend legs forward so that you are balanced on heels. Lower body as far as possible, then raise body by fully extending arms. This exercise can be performed between two stable chairs. For a highly effective variation, elevate the feet on another bench.*

## Triceps Extension

*Sit on bench, or a preacher's bench with backrest. Grasp dumbbell between thumbs and forefingers of both hands. Extend arms so that dumbbell is directly overhead. Lower the dumbbell slowly in a backward arc behind the head. Raise the weight by reversing arc. This exercise also can be performed with each arm individually, holding a light dumbbell in each hand.*

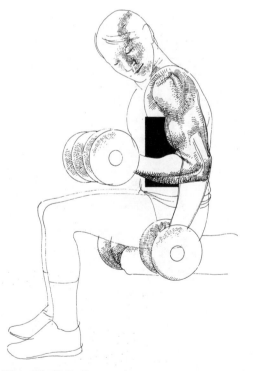

## Seated Dumbbell Curl

*Sitting on a bench (preferably with a backrest), hold a dumbbell in each hand, arms extended at your sides. Raise dumbbells completely with an upward curling motion. Try to lift dumbbells up, not swing them. Lower dumbbells slowly.*

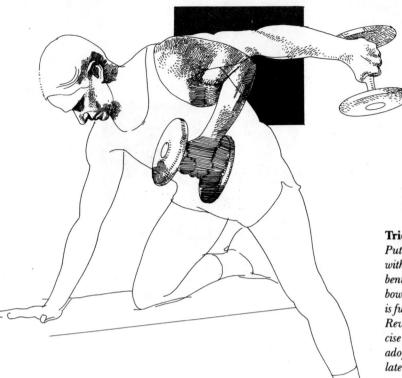

### Triceps Kick-Back
*Put left knee and left hand on bench. Brace body with right leg. Hold a dumbbell in right hand, arm bent with upper arm parallel to floor. Keeping elbow close to body, raise the dumbbell so that your arm is fully extended behind you. Lower weight slowly. Reverse position to repeat with left arm. This exercise also can be performed with both arms at once by adopting a bent standing position (e.g., in a bent lateral raise).*

### Seated Concentration Curl
*Sit on a bench with legs apart. Lean forward and grasp a dumbbell in your right hand (palm up), bracing your right elbow against your right leg just inside the knee. Holding that position, curl the dumbbell upward completely. Reverse position to repeat with left arm.*

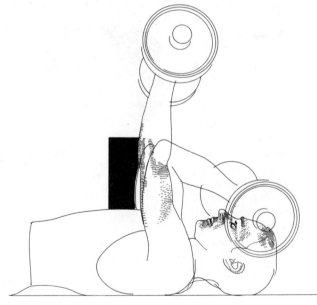

### French Curl
*Lie on your back on a bench. With hands held slightly less than shoulder-width apart, grasp a barbell (palms outward). Extend your arms so that barbell is directly above chest. Keeping elbows in, lower weight slowly by bending elbows until bar approaches forehead. Raise weight slowly back to extended position. If working to failure, have a spotter.*

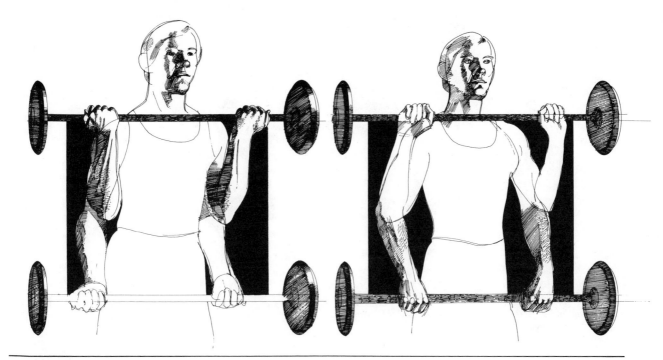

### Standing Curl

*Squat in front of barbell. Grasp the bar with hands (palms up) about shoulder-width apart. Using legs, not back, stand up so that you are holding barbell with arms extended downward in front of you. Keeping elbows close to body, curl barbell upward completely, exhaling as you raise it. Lower barbell slowly. Repeat.*

### Reverse Curl

*Same as Standing Curl, but barbell is grasped with palms down.*

### Preacher Curl

*Using a preacher's bench, sit with arms extended, upper arms against downward-angled pad. Grasp a barbell with your hands (palms up) slightly less than shoulder-width apart. Curl barbell upward completely, exhaling as you raise it. Lower barbell slowly until arms are fully extended. Repeat.*

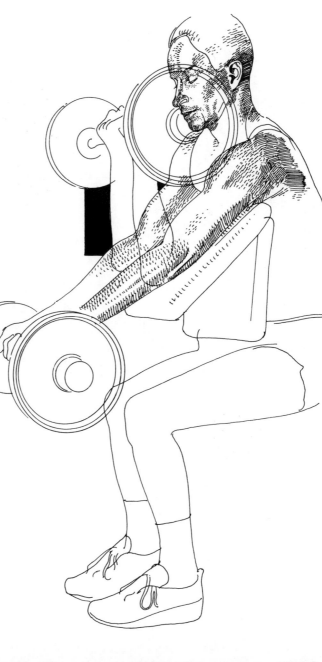

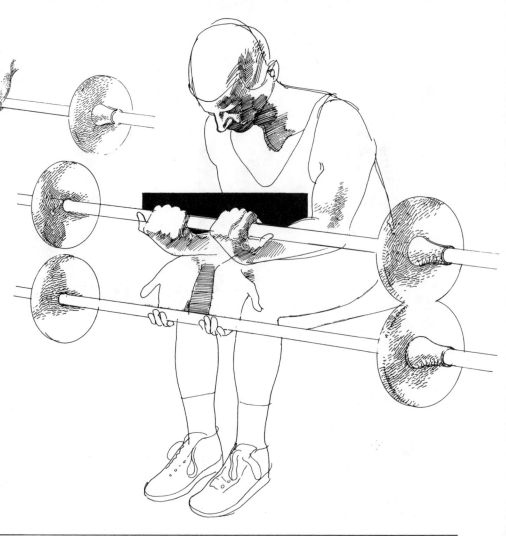

## Wrist Curl

*Sit on a bench, feet close together. Hold a barbell with hands (palms up) about six inches apart. Place your arms on the tops of legs so that your wrists extend just past your knees. Lower barbell slowly, bending wrists completely backward. Curl barbell upward completely using wrists only. Repeat. This exercise can be performed one arm at a time using dumbbells.*

## Reverse Wrist Curl

*Same as standard Wrist Curl except barbell is grasped with palms down.*

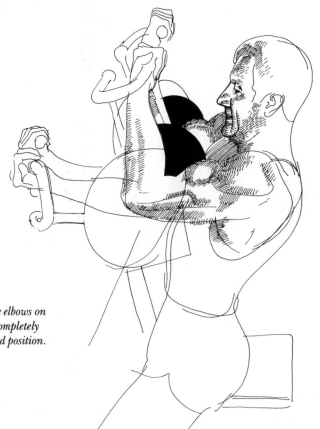

## Multi-Biceps (N)

*Set weight level. Sit straddling bench. Place elbows on pad and grasp handles. Curl both arms to completely contracted position. Lower slowly to extended position. Repeat.*

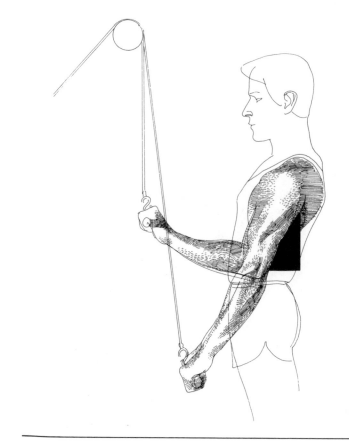

### Cable Push-Down (U)

*Set weight level. Stand facing the apparatus, grasping the bar with both hands, palms down. With elbows bent and held close to body, push bar down to fully extended position. Exhale as you push. Allow bar to rise slowly to starting position. Repeat.*

### Cable Curl (U)

*Set weight level. Stand facing apparatus. Grasp handles in each hand, palms up. Pull handles upward completely with a curling motion. Lower weight slowly. Repeat. This exercise can be performed one arm at a time, both arms at once, or alternating arms.*

# Midsection

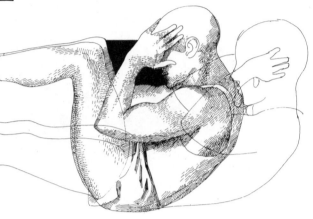

**"V" Sit-Up**
*Lie on your back on the floor.
Put your hands behind your
head, and raise your feet and
shoulders about six inches off
floor. From that position, bring
your knees up as you bring your
upper body up from the waist.
Return to starting position with
feet and shoulders off the floor.
Repeat.*

**Partial Sit-Up With Reach (a)**
*Lie on your back on the floor with your legs
spread slightly and knees bent. Extend your
arms, keeping your palms together. To begin
exercise, raise your shoulders about six inches off floor. Bring your upper body up from
the waist until your wrists are between your
knees. Return to starting position with
shoulders off floor. Repeat.*

**Partial Sit-Up With Reach (b)**
*Same as Partial Sit-Up (a) above, except
that reach is to a point directly above chest.*

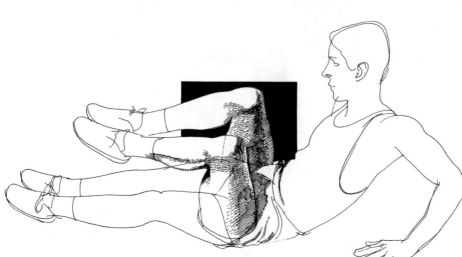

### Side Bend Sit-Up
*Lie on your left side, bracing your upper body by placing your hands beside and slightly behind you. Keeping your feet together and slightly raised off the floor, extend your legs. To begin exercise, bring knees up toward chest. Return to starting position with legs extended and feet off floor. Complete set, then repeat exercise lying on your right side.*

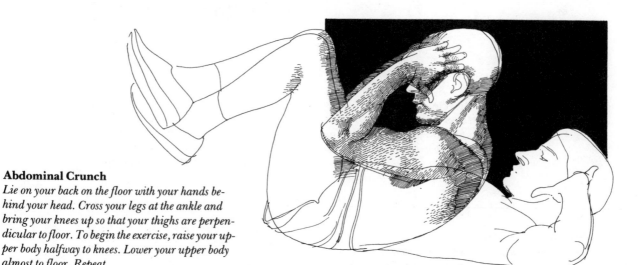

### Abdominal Crunch
*Lie on your back on the floor with your hands behind your head. Cross your legs at the ankle and bring your knees up so that your thighs are perpendicular to floor. To begin the exercise, raise your upper body halfway to knees. Lower your upper body almost to floor. Repeat.*

### Side Crunch
*Lie on your left side with your knees bent and your hands behind your head. Raise your upper body as far up off the floor as possible and twist, bringing your left elbow toward your right hip. Complete the set, then repeat the exercise lying on your right side.*

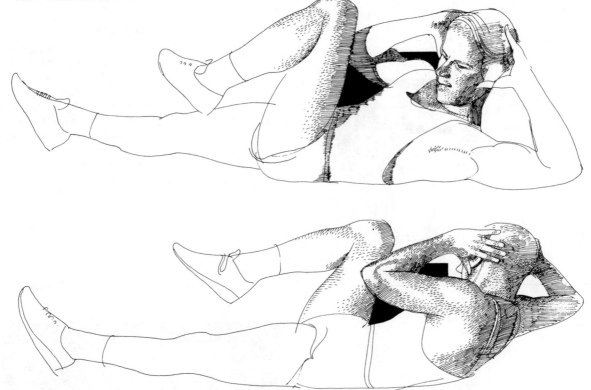

### Bicycle

*Lie on your back, with legs extended and hands behind your head. Bring your left knee up toward your chest. Simultaneously, raise your upper body, twisting to touch your right elbow to your upraised knee. Lower your upper body and re-extend your left leg. Bring your right knee up and touch it with your left elbow. Establish a steady rhythm, alternating elbows touching knees.*

---

### Reverse Abdominal Curl

*Lie on your back, with arms extended along sides, palms down. Raise your knees so that your thighs are perpendicular to the floor. To perform the exercise, bring your knees backward toward your head. Bracing yourself with your arms, raise your head and shoulders toward your knees. Lower upper body and return legs to beginning upraised position. Repeat.*

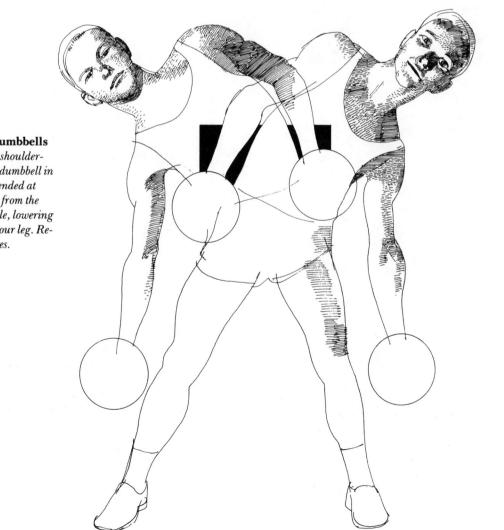

## Trunk Twist

*Stand with legs shoulder-width apart. Drape your arms over a pole (or broomstick or length of PVC pipe) that is placed across the top of your shoulders, behind your neck. Twist from the waist as far as you can to the right, then to the left, keeping your head facing forward. Repeat to complete set. Doing this exercise sitting down on the edge of a bench better isolates the oblique muscles.*

## Side Bend with Dumbbells

*Stand with your feet shoulder-width apart. Hold a dumbbell in each hand, arms extended at sides. Lean sideways from the waist as far as possible, lowering the dumbbell along your leg. Repeat, alternating sides.*

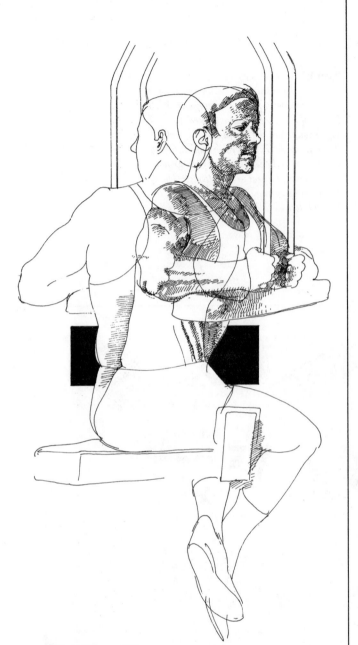

**Forward Torso (N) (U)**
*Set weight level. Sit in apparatus with upper chest and fronts of shoulders against pads. Place fronts of ankles against roller pads. Bend forward from the waist as far as possible. Slowly return to full upright position. Repeat.*

**Abdominal Crunch (N) (U)**
*Set weight level. Sit in apparatus with your knees spread and the fronts of your ankles against roller pads. Grasp the handles above and behind shoulders. Keeping your shoulders against rear pad, bend forward. Use your abdominal muscles only; don't pull with your arms. Slowly return to an upright position. Repeat.*

**Rotary Torso (N)**
*Set weight level. Straddle the seat and cross your legs at the ankles. Place your forearms on the pads, grasping middle bars with hands. Rotate torso from left to right without using the muscles of the arms or legs (note: your head moves with your torso). Pause, then return to starting position. Complete set. Repeat, moving torso to the left.*

# Selected Bibliography

Anderson, Bob. *Stretching*. Bolinas: Shelter Publications, 1980.

Arnot, Dr. Robert, and Gains, Charles. *Sports Selection*. New York: Viking Press, 1984.

Cooper, Dr. Kenneth H. *The Aerobics Program for Total Well-Being*. New York: M. Evans & Co., 1982.

Darden, Ellington. *The Nautilus Bodybuilding Book*. Chicago: Contemporary Books, 1982.

Garfield, Charles A., and Bennett, Hal Zina. *Peak Performance*. Los Angeles: J. P. Tarcher, 1984.

Garrick, Dr. James G., and Radetsky, Peter. *Peak Condition*. New York: Crown Publishers, 1986.

Hagerman, Dr. Fredrick C. *How to Increase Your Speed and Agility*. New York: Putnam Publishing Group, 1986.

Hatfield, Frederick C. *Aerobic Weight Training*. Chicago: Contemporary Books, 1983.

Hyams, Joe. *Zen in the Martial Arts*. Los Angeles: J. P. Tarcher, 1979.

Jerome, John. *The Sweet Spot in Time*. New York: Summit Books, 1980.

Mirkin, Dr. Gabe. *Dr. Gabe Mirkin's Fitness Clinic*. Chicago: Contemporary Books, 1986.

Pearl, Bill, and Moran, Gary T. *Getting Stronger*. Bolinas: Shelter Publications, 1986.

Riley, Daniel P. *Strength Training for Football: The Penn State Way*. West Point: Leisure Press, 1982.

Sheehan, Dr. George. *Dr. Sheehan on Fitness*. New York: Simon & Schuster, 1983.

Tyne, Phillip J., and Mitchell, Matt. *Total Stretching*. Chicago: Contemporary Books, 1983.

# How to Use the Training Schedule

*Here's how to fill in the weekly NFL All-Pro Workout Training Schedule on the following page. The schedule is divided into two sections: a daily activity schedule to help you plan and track your daily workouts; and strength workout specifics charts to list the details of up to three weight workouts.*

*Write in warm-up activity.*

*Check appropriate box(es) to indicate whether you stretched before and/or after day's activity.*

*Write in the day's main exercise or sports activity, along with exercise time, distance, and pulse rate, if applicable. If your main activity was a strength workout, use the Strength Workout Specifics charts (below).*

*Note any specific agility work.*

*Note any specific mental training performed.*

*Use these charts for detailing strength workouts. List the specific exercises performed in your strength workout (by area of body worked), including sets, weights (pounds or machine plates), and reps for each.*

|  | Monday | Tuesday | Wednesday |
|---|---|---|---|
| **Warm-up** | JOG 1 MILE | EXER. BIKE 10 MIN. |  |
| **Stretch** | Before ✓ / After ✓ | Before ✓ / After ✓ | Before ✓ / After |
| **Activity** | RUNNING | STRENGTH | TENNIS (SINGLES) |
| **Time Distance Pulse** | 37  5mi.  130 |  | 2 HR. |
| **Agility** | TENNIS SPRINTS |  |  |
| **Mental Training** |  |  | VISUAL 2 |

**STRENGTH**   Day: TUESDAY

| Exercise | Set 1 wt. | reps | Set 2 wt. | reps | Set 3 wt. | reps |
|---|---|---|---|---|---|---|
| LEG EXTEN. (N) | 7 | 15 | 7 | 15 | 7 | 15 |
| LEG PRESS (N) | 8 | 15 | 8 | 15 | 8 | 12 |
| LEG CURL (N) | 6 | 15 | 6 | 12 | 6 | 7 |
| CALF RAISE (N) | 9 | 20 | 9 | 20 |  |  |
|  |  |  |  |  |  |  |
| PULLOVER | 35 | 15 | 35 | 15 | 35 | 10 |
| BARBELL ROW | 55 | 15 | 55 | 13 | 55 | 9 |
| WIDE-GAP CHIN-UP | 4 |  |  |  |  |  |
|  |  |  |  |  |  |  |
| BENCH PRESS | 110 | 12 | 110 | 10 | 110 | 6 |
| ARM CROSS | 5 | 10 | 5 | 8 | 5 | |

**STRENGTH**

Exercise

# The NFL All-Pro Workout
## Training Schedule

| | Monday | | Tuesday | | Wednesday | | Thursday | | Friday | | Saturday | | Sunday | |
|---|---|---|---|---|---|---|---|---|---|---|---|---|---|---|
| **Warm-up** | | | | | | | | | | | | | | |
| **Stretch** | Before | After | Before | After | Before | After | Before | After | Before | After | Before | After | Before | After |
| **Activity** | | | | | | | | | | | | | | |
| **Time Distance Pulse** | | | | | | | | | | | | | | |
| **Agility** | | | | | | | | | | | | | | |
| **Mental Training** | | | | | | | | | | | | | | |

**STRENGTH**    Day: _____

| | Set 1 | | Set 2 | | Set 3 | |
|---|---|---|---|---|---|---|
| Exercise | wt. | reps | wt. | reps | wt. | reps |

**STRENGTH**    Day: _____

| | Set 1 | | Set 2 | | Set 3 | |
|---|---|---|---|---|---|---|
| Exercise | wt. | reps | wt. | reps | wt. | reps |

**STRENGTH**    Day: _____

| | Set 1 | | Set 2 | | Set 3 | |
|---|---|---|---|---|---|---|
| Exercise | wt. | reps | wt. | reps | wt. | reps |

**LEGS**

**BACK**

**CHEST**

**SHOULDERS**

**ARMS**

**MIDSECTION**